Historicizing Online Politics

Telegraphy, the Internet, and
Political Participation in China

Historicizing Online Politics

Telegraphy, the Internet, and
Political Participation in China

Zhou Yongming

STANFORD UNIVERSITY PRESS

Stanford, California 2006

Stanford University Press
Stanford, California
© 2006 by the Board of Trustees of the
Leland Stanford Junior University

Library of Congress Cataloging-in-Publication Data

Zhou Yongming.
    Historicizing online politics : telegraphy, the Internet, and
political participation in China / Zhou Yongming.
        p.   cm.
    Includes bibliographical references and index.
    ISBN 0-8047-5127-7 (cloth : alk. paper) —
    ISBN 0-8047-5128-5 (pbk. : alk. paper)
    1. Political participation—Technological innovations—China.
2. Telegraph—China—History—19th century.   3. Internet—
Political aspects—China.   4. Internet in public
administration—China.   I. Title.
JQ1516.Z457   2006
320.951'01'4—dc22

                                        2005023283

Original Printing 2006
Last figure below indicates year of this printing:
15   14   13   12   11   10   09   08   07   06

Typeset at Stanford University Press in 10/13 Sabon

To my parents

ZHOU ZHONGQI

and

ZHANG HUILIAN

Contents

Tables

Acknowledgments

In seven years of researching and writing this book, I have received help from so many people and institutions that space does not allow me to name everyone who made it possible. However, I owe special thanks to Professor Gao Hua at Nanjing University, whose friendship and help has been important at every stage of this study. I am also grateful to Richard Fox, Arif Dirlik, Judith Farquhar, Orin Starn, Robert Weller, and R. Bin Wong for their continuous support and encouragement throughout these years.

A major portion of this research took place after 1999, when the University of Wisconsin–Madison became my intellectual home. My deepest thanks go to Edward Friedman, who has been a consistent source of both inspiration and information on the politics of China. I also want to express my appreciation to my colleagues Doug Price, Katherine Bowie, Larry Nesper, A-Xing Zhu, and Leyuan Shi who provided me with useful Internet-related materials. I am grateful as well to Anatoly Khazanov, Ken George, Frank Salomon, Tom Broman, M. Giovanna Merli, Julia Murray, Nan Enstad, and Zhongdan Pan, who took time to read my research plan, listened to my presentations, and provided insightful suggestions. My intellectual neighbor Barrett McCormick at Marquette University in Milwaukee was an early reader of chapters and stalwart enthusiast.

For useful critiques, comments, and advice, I thank Jim Millward, Jie Chen, Takeshi Matsuda, Andrew Meier, Robert Hathaway, Gang Lin, and Lawrence Reardon at the Woodrow Wilson Center; Yongnian Zheng, Tianjian Shi, Guo Yanchun, Gu Xin, and Tong Yanqi in the East

Asian Institute at the National University of Singapore; Caroline Hum-
phrey and Alan McFarland at Cambridge University; Steve Tsang and
Vivienne Shue at Oxford University; Craig Calhoun at New York University; Erik Baark at Hong Kong University of Science and Technology;
James Benn at Arizona State University; Guobin Yang at the University of
Hawaii; and Chin-Chuan Lee of the University of Minnesota. I am also
grateful to the two anonymous Stanford University Press referees for their
constructive comments.

My gratitude goes as well to all the people who provided me with help
during my fieldwork in China. I particularly thank Min Dahong, Guo
Liang, Bu Wei, and Fang Ning at the Chinese Academy of Social Sciences,
Chen Shaofeng at Beijing University, Meng Jian at Fudan University, Guo
Yuehua and Cui Baoguo at Qsinghua University, Zhu Qingbao at Nanjing University, Jiang Yaping and Shan Chengbiao at People's Daily Online, Duan Yibin at the Chinese Academy of Sciences, Wang Yingbai at
the Chinese Post and Telecommunication Museum, and Duan Bingren of
the Beijing municipal government. In addition, Wang Aiyin and Wu
Fengshi provided great assistance in locating fieldwork sites and conducting interviews.

I was fortunate to have the exceptional service of Judy Lu at the Asian
Reading Room of the Library of Congress. Thanks also go to helpful li-
brarians at the Library of the National University of Singapore, Nanjing
University Library, the Library of the Journalism School at Fudan University, the Library of the Beijing Post and Communication University,
the East Asian History of Science Library at the Needham Research Institute, Cambridge University Library, the Library of the Hoover Institution, and the Library of the Woodrow Wilson Center.

⌒

At various stages of this study, I have received financial support from a
number of sources, including a research fellowship from the East Asian
Institute at the National University of Singapore, a fellowship from the
Woodrow Wilson Center, a fellowship of the National Program for Advanced Study and Research in China from the Committee on Scholarly
Communication with China, and a Mellon Fellowship to conduct research at the Needham Research Institute. In addition, the Graduate
School of the University of Wisconsin provided research support for two
summers. I thank all these institutions that have helped make this study
possible.

I would like to thank Patricia Katayama at Stanford University Press for her confidence in my work at its conception stage, and Muriel Bell, who so smoothly took over the editorship after Pat left for a new position. I am also grateful for the assistance I received from Carmen Borbon-Wu. Lastly, I want acknowledge the helpful editorial support provided by Peter Dreyer, Philip Holden, and Geoffrey Owens.

I would never have completed this book without the blessing of my family. My gratitude and love for my parents, Zhou Zhongqi and Zhang Huilian, is boundless. My younger daughter Julia was born in 2002 and the joys of her birth gave me the final inspiration to finish the book, just as the birth of her sister Caroline did with my previous book seven years ago. Last but not least, I want to thank my wife Lan for her unfailing patience, understanding, and support throughout these years.

Historicizing Online Politics

*Telegraphy, the Internet, and
Political Participation in China*

Introduction

THIS BOOK examines the complex relationships connecting information technology and politics in modern China. It has two parts: the first examines the impacts that telegraphy had on national politics in the last decades of the Qing dynasty, and the second focuses on the Internet and its impact on politics in China since the late 1990s. In retrospect, these two technologies fared quite differently in modern China. When Western countries tried to set up telegraph lines in China in the 1860s, they met strong resistance from the Qing court. It was not until two decades later that China finally set up its telegraph services. China's attitude toward the Internet has been startlingly different. By all accounts, the development of the Internet in China has been phenomenal, as shown by the number of Internet users, which had increased from a mere 620,000 in October 1997 to 94 million by the end of 2004.[1] In this volume, I aim to historicize the study of the Internet in China by taking the detour of first examining the introduction of telegraphy, and by so doing, revealing the paradigmatic shifts, to borrow Thomas Kuhn's term, that affect our views on technology and society in China. The first question that needs to be confronted is, why has so much attention been paid to the Internet in China today?

It is safe to say that no other technology has attracted as much attention and been as politicized by observers of contemporary China worldwide as the Internet. The development of the Internet in China is followed closely in Western countries and the increasing number of its users is periodically reported. Government regulations on Internet use are scrutinized and the use of technologies to censor and police the information flow on the Net are protested. Government crackdowns on dissent activities in cyberspace are condemned and details of each case are gathered and made public both online and through traditional media. Hearings on the Internet in China have been held by both the U.S. Congress and human rights groups. In addition to the attention generated by journalists' reports and activist organizations, the development of the Internet in China has given rise to an increasing number of academic studies on the Internet in China, making this new and growing intellectual field as busy and active as the cyberspace it reports on.[2]

In the middle of conducting research for this book, I spent the year 2001 at a major research center in Washington, D.C., where I was not only surrounded by scholars but also had a chance to interact with politicians and journalists. Upon hearing of my research topic and acknowledging that my research was "very interesting," they often proceeded to ask me the same question: "Will the Internet change China?" This was a question that I found difficult to give a clear-cut answer to, because the way it was asked had obvious political implications. The assumptions of those who raised the Internet question with me were clearly grounded in the idea that the Internet may have a democratizing influence on Chinese society. Whether the Internet will change China is a political question as well as a scholarly one, and as we shall see, these two aspects have been increasingly intertwined in the field of Internet study.

Nobody would disagree that the Internet has had and will continue to have profound impacts on Chinese society, and that these impacts are being felt technologically, economically, and politically, as well as socioculturally. Western multinational corporations are helping China build an expanding network infrastructure and moving production facilities and even research and development centers there, and the Internet has created new behavioral patterns in how people communicate with one another, spend leisure time, shop and consume, buy and sell stock, commit crimes, and enjoy music and films, but the attention given to its economic, technological, and sociocultural aspects has certainly been dwarfed by that accorded to its political aspect in China. If we take a closer look at reports on the Internet in China, it becomes even clearer that the issue of the Chinese government's efforts to control it by blocking the free flow of information and suppressing political dissent online has been the focus of the attention.

This attitude toward the Internet in China reflects what I call the "monster complex" shared by many observers of China, who first see the

Internet as a benign monster that will break through the authoritarian Chinese political system with its incessant waves of free flow of information engulfing the legitimacy of the current regime. At the same time, they assume that the Chinese communists will see the Internet as an evil monster that, if not brought under total control, may constitute the biggest danger to their rule. Nonetheless, their control efforts will be in vain, it is thought, because the Internet, with its unique quality of being without a central structure and without hierarchy, is uncontrollable and will change the Chinese society anyway. This prediction has turned out to be just another case of political fortune telling, as is so often encountered by researchers on contemporary Chinese politics. The benign monster is not as powerful or omnipotent as thought, and worse still, unlike the initial response to telegraphy by the Qing rulers, the People's Republic of China (PRC) has adopted a proactive policy toward the Internet. Over the past few years, the PRC has successfully achieved phenomenal Internet growth without losing much control. Correspondingly, some observers have since shifted their attention to how the PRC has tightened its control on the Internet. With news titles such as "China Enacts Sweeping Rules on Internet Firms" from Reuters or the more eye-catching and misleading "Amnesty International: China Orders Death Penalty for Internet Use" from NewsMax.com, the PRC has been depicted as a monster intent on destroying the Internet in China.[3]

The politics of the Internet in China today is a legitimate and important subject. The question is, how to study it? The complex relationships between information technology and politics in modern China should serve to discourage people from making the kinds of simplistic and technologically deterministic statements and predictions that are too often heard in studies of the Internet in China. In believing that the Internet has the intrinsic power to democratize Chinese society, technological determinists base themselves largely on the ideological conviction that democratization is the path China should follow. The idea of the Internet's intrinsic democratizing function was widely accepted or wished for from the outset, and this optimistic belief in Internet technology persists. People have realized, however, that, while this technology can be employed to enhance democracy, it can also be used to maintain undemocratic regimes.[4] So, even though we may all agree that China will change with the Internet, we still have to address the issue of what direction China will take and how the process of change will turn out.

To achieve a more balanced and sophisticated study of the Internet and politics in China, we have to view the focus of current Internet research on China as a historically specific phenomenon. To Westerners, science and technology have been an important measure of human achievement, and they have been employed to establish and legitimize the ideological dominance of the West.[5] In an earlier historical period, people focused on the "civilizing" or "modernizing" effects of science and technology. Today, employing a different intellectual paradigm, we emphasize the "democratizing" function of the Internet, a technology that is perceived as both a very good fit with and even an enhancement of liberal democracies and free market economies modeled on contemporary Western societies. Not surprisingly, when this technology is projected onto other societies, it is often gauged, consciously or unconsciously, by the underlining paradigm most of us have accepted and lived with. Most of us raise questions about the Internet in China using the dominant paradigm of our historical era of globalization, but we should keep in mind that the current paradigm is itself a historical entity and subject to change.

A little reflection will not only help us better understand why we are interested in studying political aspects of the Internet in China but also open up new approaches to study the issue. I believe that in order to get a more in-depth knowledge of the impact of the Internet on Chinese society, especially its potential for being used by Chinese to participate in politics and to promote democracy, we have to historicize our research by looking at how other, similar technologies fared in different historical contexts. After all, the Internet is only the latest development of so-called modern information technology. Since the mid nineteenth century, there have been numerous breakthroughs in the technological arena, starting with telegraphy and going on to the telephone, radio, television, the facsimile machine, and satellite TV, before finally reaching the era of the Internet in the 1990s. The appearance of each technology had impacts on society and politics, yet the earlier technologies have received far less scholarly attention, especially from a political perspective, than the Internet.

This study tries to historicize the impact that telegraphy and the Internet have had on Chinese politics over a span of one and half centuries. I have chosen these two technologies for two reasons. The first is that, even though they constitute two poles of the modern development of information technology, they have many similarities and have both had enormous impacts on human society. Technologically speaking, the appearance of telegraphy meant that for the first time in human history, a single technology overcame the vast distances separating people and potentially connected the whole world online on an instant basis, a characteristic vastly multiplied by the later Internet technology. Socially speaking, in retrospect, the impact that telegraphy had on Western societies was so profound that it cannot be dwarfed by the Internet. As pointed out by the communications scholar James Carey, the use of the telegraph facilitated the development of stock and commodity exchanges, enabled the birth of news agencies, and reshaped Americans' consciousness of time and space.[6] The emergence of telegraphy was a huge event in the nineteenth century.

The second reason I have chosen these two specific technologies to study is simply my own personal interest. Initially, telegraphy and the Internet attracted my attention for very different reasons. The application of the telegraph in national politics first aroused my interest during the mid 1990s, when I was conducting research on anti-drug crusades in modern China. I was made aware that sending publicly circulated telegrams was one of the main weapons of nongovernmental anti-opium organizations in their fight against various schemes for profiting from the opium monopoly by different Chinese regimes in the 1920s and 1930s. These circular telegrams were usually reprinted by newspapers nationwide, and they were therefore very effective in mobilizing public opinion against the government plans.[7] I was fascinated by this new genre of public text but disappointed by the fact that scholarly inquiry concerning the circular telegram was virtually nonexistent. From 1999 to 2003, I laboriously read about 100,000 pages of the *Shen Bao* from 1872 to 1912, in addition to other early Chinese newspapers. What I found was that the circular telegram was an important means of political participation and also was closely related to major events of national politics in the last years of the Qing dynasty. In the meantime, because I have been studying and teaching in American universities, I was exposed to the rapid development of the Internet earlier than most of my contemporaries in China.

After the development of the Internet took off in the late 1990s, optimistic predictions about its democratizing attributes attracted a large following. But the more I looked back at the history of the role played by the telegraph in modern Chinese politics, the less persuaded I was by these rosy predictions. The key was not the technology itself but how it was used by people. As we shall see, both telegraphy and the Internet have been used by different parties for very different purposes. Therefore in order to get a more sophisticated view of the real impacts of these two technologies on Chinese politics, researchers should examine each of these phenomena in its concrete historical context.

To cover the entire scope of Chinese politics or all forms of information technology is a task beyond the scope of this book. In addition to narrowing down my discussion to only the earliest and latest cases of modern information technology, I shall focus my inquiry on their impacts on Chinese politics mainly from two angles: how members of Chinese society employ these technologies to participate in politics and how Chinese governments have tried to regulate and control them. While some political scientists insist that the term "political participation" is only applicable to the study of democratic polities, this study adopts a more recently developed and more encompassing definition that defines political participation as the "efforts of ordinary citizens in any type of political system to influence the actions of their rulers."[8] Even this definition needs some modifications when applied to the study of China, because in the late nineteenth century, most Chinese did not have a fully developed concept of citizenship in a modern state. They took part in national politics based mainly on the Confucian idea that "each individual is responsible for the ups and downs of national fortune," most notably during the turmoil resulting from the disintegration of the Qing empire. So replacing "citizens" with "individuals" in the definition of political participation is more appropriate to this study.

As far as government control is concerned, there is considerable continuity between the history of telegraphy and the Internet. Just as the Qing court sought to regulate and control telegraphy, the PRC is keen to try to regulate and control the Internet—in each case, with an emphasis on trying to prevent the technology from becoming a threat to the government. Over 140 years, then, it seems that little has changed in this respect. Yet if we examine the two technologies in their respective historical contexts, the discontinuities become obvious. As we shall see in the following chapters, the anxieties and motives of the Qing court differed from those of the PRC's leadership. Qing officials' fear of losing actual control and the tangible benefits of telegraphy to foreign hands impeded their acceptance of this technology for two decades. In contrast, in today's China, foreign control of the Internet is out of the question and a more confident Chinese state has quickly accepted this new technology and embraced its enormous technological and commercial potential. In the meantime, the government has been alert to the use of the Internet to access and disseminate undesirable information or to promote political dissent in China.

However, despite the different historical contexts of these two technologies, each of them appeared and evolved in a time of accelerated change in Chinese society, the first from 1894 to 1911, and the second from the mid 1990s to the present. These are the periods on which this book focuses. The former period represented the last phase of the changes and crises that eventually brought down the Qing dynasty. The second period represents the continuation phase of the reforms that commenced near the end of the 1970s, and the Internet arose in the mid 1990s, at a time when China was increasingly immersed in a global market economy. In both periods, state control loosened to a certain degree, thus providing more room for political participation compared to the prior periods. Students of modern Chinese studies, including historians, political scientists, and anthropologists, have pointed out that during the late Qing period, China saw the emergence of a burgeoning civil society. But the development of a civil society in China was subsequently suppressed by the authoritarian nationalist and Maoist regimes. It was not until the reform era of the late twentieth century that China started to see the growth of a civil society again.[9]

So when dealing with the fact that political participation in these two periods expanded through the availability of new information technologies, should we adopt the concept and framework of civil society in our analysis? Although scholars engaged in Internet research have embraced the concept, and some have even imagined the creation of a "cyber civil society," I remain skeptical as to the applicability of the civil society model to the study of modern Chinese society.[10] After all, this is a concept used to analyze the fundamental structural features of modern Western societies. The transformations of Chinese societies in these two periods are complex, and they certainly do not follow the same path as the Western societies where civil society arose and developed.[11] It is one thing to notice some seemingly autonomous societal elements existing in late Qing or contemporary China, but a totally different thing to assume that a "civil society" exists or is bound to appear in China. Instead of examining technological advancement and expanding political participation from the preconceived angle of civil society, I shall therefore take another approach, which relies on concrete historical facts rather than on a preconclusive theoretical framework to reach conclusions.

In dealing with political participation in the two aforementioned time periods in China, one cannot avoid the issue of modern Chinese nationalism. Although this term is also of Western origin, nationalism has spread throughout the world in the form of political movements and ideologies and become a global phenomenon. The deepening political crisis of the last two decades of the Qing dynasty saw the rise of modern Chinese nationalism, and the renewal of nationalism in China in the 1990s has been a staple of the Western media as well as in academia. Both telegraphy and the Internet have been closely connected with modern Chinese nationalism. The research reported in this book demonstrates that in the earlier period, individuals often issued circular telegrams during times of national crisis. Strong nationalist sentiment made these more appealing to their audiences and also legitimized the motives of telegram senders. In the case of the Internet, Chinese citizens used the newly accessible cyberspace tools, such as bulletin board systems (BBS), to vent their nationalist and anti-American sentiment in the wake of the NATO bombing of the Chinese embassy in Belgrade in 1999 and the U.S.-China military plane collision incident in 2001. Chinese nationalism is an issue that will be encountered and dealt with throughout this book, with a focus on its specific characteristics under different historical circumstances.

The anthropologist Benedict Anderson defines the nation as an "imagined community." Nationalism is often emotionally charged because it is built upon the imagining of solidarity and comradeship among very different members within this imagined community. Newspapers, museums, and other forms of public display help to enhance the individual's sense of belonging to a community using forms of psychological persuasion so strong that the individual is often willing to die for this community.[12] Telegraphy and the Internet have undoubtedly made nationalist emotions more publicly visible and widely felt, thanks to their key function in transferring information in a speedier way to a wider audience. With the appearance of modern newspapers, circular telegrams made urgent political news and opinions publicly known to a large audience beyond regional boundaries for the first time in Chinese history, thus helping to form an "imagined community" of the awakening subjects of the Qing emperor. On the other hand, burgeoning nationalist consciousness made political participation more emotionally engaging, therefore influencing others to feel the same way. Looked at from this perspective, nationalistic conversation in BBS forums is the latest development of community imagining, even though the conceived unlimited capacity of the Internet to reach the widest possible audience may in fact have made its audience more scattered than expected and diminished its effects, as discussed in detail later in this book.

This research reveals that the most profound effect of the telegraph and the Internet on modern Chinese politics is that they helped to transform it into a far more public affair than ever before in Chinese history. Their capacity to speedily transfer information makes it more difficult for the government to control the dissemination of political information. With the rise of Chinese nationalism, and the dramatic transformation of Chinese society during these periods, individual Chinese were and are able to employ these two technologies to expand political participation. Nationalism often legitimizes this political participation, and the resulting societal transitions force the state to loosen political control to a certain degree. It is under these historical circumstances that modern information technologies have been able to play their roles in making Chinese politics more public. My focus is always on human agency rather than technologies, however. What I intend to show is that it was human beings who used these technologies in creative ways and under special historical circumstances that have made modern Chinese politics more public, not the technologies alone.

Public politics is certainly something of a rarity in Chinese society. Does the increased degree of participation in national politics by the public, and in a more public way, suggest that a public sphere existed in the late Qing era or is emerging in China today? Realizing the shortcomings of applying the concept of civil society to the study of Chinese society, some scholars have suggested that the concept of the public sphere is more applicable. "By 'public sphere' we mean first of all a domain of our social life in which such a thing as public opinion can be formed," Jürgen Habermas observes. "Access to the public sphere is open in principle to all citizens. . . . Citizens act as a public when they deal with matters of general interest without being subject to coercion; thus with the guarantee that they may assemble and unite freely, and express and publicize their opinions freely."[13]

History tells us that a "public sphere" such as that as defined by Habermas has never existed in Chinese society. At the risk of being too general, it can be said that the late Qing regime was authoritarian, as is that of the PRC, so there has never been a time in which individuals could express their opinions "freely," which is exactly why people were so enthusiastic and optimistic about the Internet when this new technology first appeared. People hoped this seemingly revolutionary and omnipotent technology would provide a way to break the ever-present government control of free expression of political opinions.

Even so the concept of public sphere, given its Western origin, can nevertheless be used as an analytic tool for this study if it is contextualized and modified. Reforms in the late Qing era were crisis-induced, and this is also true of the PRC, leading in both cases to profound social transitions, weakened state control, and increased political participation in an expanded public space, as shown by the circular telegrams reprinted in national newspapers in Qing China and BBS messages circulating in cyberspace today. However, although authoritarian governments realize that they cannot completely restrict public participation in times of political or foreign crisis, especially if the public is mobilized by nationalism, the space for it is both limited and selective. Both the Qing court and the PRC have sought to keep public space as circumscribed as possible and to prevent political participation from touching on issues that they are not willing to deal with, such as political reforms and freedom of the press.

To make a general statement, in both late Qing China and today's PRC, as a result of the historical conditions, a limited public sphere emerged in Chinese society, allowing individuals to express their opinions publicly on certain political topics. Telegraphy and the Internet undoubtedly enlarged the scope and effectiveness of political participation. But the availability of these technologies is not the reason why people are able to participate, why they want to participate, and what the outcomes of their participation are. One can only get answers to the above questions by looking into the complex historical forces in those two periods. It is politics that determines how a technology is used, not the other way around. This is not to say that politics and technology do not have an interactive relationship, but the political needs of a government or an individual are usually more decisive in determining how the technology is used. As this study shows, it would be naïve to conclude that telegraphy changed the course of modern Chinese politics. The same is true of the assumption that the Internet will democratize China. Technology facilitates politics; it does not dictate it. As shown in the latter part of this volume, contemporary Chinese politics has in fact, to a large degree, shaped the contour of online political participation today. By depoliticizing researchers' preconceptions and historicizing concrete technological cases, this study hopes to interpret how historical factors and agents shaped the relationship between information technology and Chinese politics at the turn of both the twentieth and twenty-first centuries.

⌒

This book is the outcome of an intellectual experiment. It covers the telegraph and the Internet, two technologies with a timespan from the early 1860s to the beginning of the twenty-first century, and the two parts are written in very different ways. Although some of my colleagues advised me to publish each part in a separate volume, I decided to keep the book in its present form and leave it to readers to judge the benefits of having both the historical and comparative aspects in one volume. One thing that needs to be noted here is that this volume is not intended to be merely a comparative study of telegraphy and the Internet. As mentioned earlier, my aim in studying telegraphy was to provide a historical perspective to study of the Internet. It would be ideal if the many other media that appeared between the late Qing and today were also covered in the volume. Due to constraints of both time and ability, however, I deliberately limited the scope of my study to telegraphy and the Internet, and I hope that it will encourage broader coverage in the future. Historical study always brings some comparative perspectives when it is linked with contemporary issues; this volume is no exception.[14]

I wrote the first part of this book utilizing a historical perspective. In it, relying mainly on archival materials, I try to reconstruct the historical trajectory of the telegraph and its role in late Qing politics. Because the Internet has had only a very short existence and is continuing to unfold, the second part of the book tries to present a panoramic view (though limited and incomplete) and to cover multiple aspects and forms of online political participation by presenting a number of case studies. In this latter part, the materials derive mainly from the fieldwork I conducted between 1999 and 2002, when I made four trips to China and spent a total of twelve months there. The fieldwork was conducted using a combination of interviews, participant observation, and archival research. While historical and ethnographical methods are the mainstay of this book, it also draws upon methods and concepts from media studies, literary criticism, and political science.

Conducting fieldwork on and about the Internet has been a challenge to anthropologists as well as other researchers.[15] The difficulties arise from the enormous amount of information that the Internet carries and the fact that it is in a constant state of flux, making cyberspace extremely fluid and, sometimes even puzzling. The Internet is thus a field site very different from those an anthropologist typically faces. In earlier times, when the anthropologist entered a community to study culture, he or she usually selected a group of people in a certain locale and stayed and in-

teracted with them for a prolonged period of time. That is how participant observation, the trademark of the profession, has been done. But
since a community in cyberspace has no definite boundary, and its members can easily join and leave, what is the essential characteristic that defines it? The answer is social relations. As pointed out by Raymond
Williams, the sense of community has to do with "the quality of holding
something in common, as in community of interests, community of goods
. . . a sense of common identity and characteristics."[16] From that perspective, this study has focused on those individuals and groups that have
one thing in common—that is, they are all involved in online political
participation, while their actual locales in cyberspace may not always be
in the same spot.

In facing the vast and constantly changing world of the Internet, the
question arises as to whether traditional ethnographic methods are applicable. In fact, many researchers value ethnographic methods in the
study of the Internet. Some find Clifford Geertz's influential view of culture as "webs of significance" to be quite "Internet friendly," because one
can study the Internet just like any other culture. "[O]ne can start anywhere in a culture's repertoire of forms and end up anywhere else. . . .
One has only to learn how to gain access to them," Geertz observes.[17]
Confirming the worth of ethnographic methods in the study of online forums, the sociologist Lori Kendall has commented that "much as my personal biases lead me in that direction, I would never have the audacity to
suggest that all social research projects ought to include participant observation. Yet with regard to research on interactive online forums, I rec-
ommend just that."[18]

Though delighted by these observations, I proceeded with my own
study cautiously, because I was dealing with an area in which I had never
labored before. My primary approach has been to treat cyberspace as an
extension or new dimension of the "real" world created by human beings. In spite of all the hype that hails cyberspace as something of an independent entity, it is always made by individual netizens who are issuers,
transmitters, receivers, and interpreters of the data and information circulating in cyberspace on an interactive basis. As to the topic of my research, the most important questions for studying these online political
participants are who they are, what position they hold, why they have
adapted the Internet to politics, how they try to accomplish their aim,
and what effect their activities have on politics in contemporary China.
For these purposes, I conducted person-to-person interviews. If these
were not enough or not available, I supplemented them with online in-

terviews. I employed traditional participant observation techniques to observe people's behavior in a monitor room and in an Internet café. In the
meantime, I have spent countless hours "observing" online forums that I
have been following. Most of the time, I just "lurk" around in the forum,
but if needed, I also participate in the forums and interact with members.
Both my online and off-line fieldwork experiences have been of help in
producing this study.

To my surprise, the most difficult part of carrying out this Internet-related anthropological research is how to collect, preserve, and analyze the
data. No matter how specific and well defined a topic is, the Internet researcher is always in danger of being overwhelmed by the sheer volume
of information he or she faces. The traditional way of writing up field
notes is not that helpful, because it is certain to leave out most of the
available information. The only option is to observe online forums as
much as possible and continuously archive the important data, although
this is more easily said than done. The difficulty is enormous. First, on
the Internet, activity takes place and information flows continuously, and
no anthropologist can conduct participant observation in cyberspace
around the clock. My method was to observe several online forums relevant to this study at regular intervals, but placing special emphasis on significant historical events (e.g., the Taiwan election in March 2000, the
U.S.-China military plane collision in April 2001, and the events of September 11, 2001). I decided to follow the Chinese online responses intensively for many continuous hours, as long as my body and schedule
permitted. Secondly, since numerous online forums coexist in cyberspace
at any given time, in order to cover multiple aspects of online political
participation in China, I continuously had to move in and out of different online forums, which made the data I encountered more heteroge-
neous and voluminous.

My main method for managing the data was to download them into
computer files and then view them as historical texts. In cyberspace, the
boundary between real-time and archival data is very thin, because the
incessant flow of data makes the real-time data archival in a matter of
seconds. Furthermore, downloading online messages and texts has turned
out to be a very effective way of preserving data in cyberspace because of
the high turnover rate of online forums and their archives, in which
whole volume of texts can be deleted by the touch of a fingertip on the
computer keyboard. Many online forums do not provide file retrieval services; some of them regularly "refresh" out old archives. Even with those
forums that do keep old messages in their archives (such as the Strength-

ening-China Forum at People's Daily Online), the difficulty is compounded by the fact that in Chinese cyberspace these forums are often monitored, and undesirable texts can be removed from the archive by the webmasters anytime. Therefore, the online forum archive is not a fixed entity, in its traditional sense, and the number of texts it includes can be altered significantly. To preserve online texts as closely as possible to their unaltered "real state" online, I have to constantly download important data simultaneously with observing the forum, hoping to keep them before the webmasters step in. For example, I downloaded the voluminous messages that appeared on the Strengthening-China Forum in the first hours after the news broke on September 11, while following the forum responses in real time. The saved files are historical materials in their own right, because they were deleted from the forum shortly afterward. Today, nobody would be able to retrieve them from the existing archive. Although laborious at times, this method works in the context of Chinese cyberspace to turn online texts into historical materials, on which the second part of this book is based.

↬

Chapter 1 confronts the question of why it took two decades for China to adopt telegraphy in the late Qing era. As an alternative to the often-cited explanations that attribute the delay to the elite belief in Confucian cultural superiority or the popular belief in feng shui, I propose that political concerns, rather than cultural ideas, played a more critical role in shaping the thinking of Qing policymakers at the time. The Qing officials' anxiety to keep control of this technology (*quan*) and underestimation of its use (*li*) directly caused the belated adoption of telegraphy. The last part of the chapter gives a brief description of the development of a Chinese-run telegraph network in the 1880s and 1890s.

Chapter 2 discusses the impact of the telegraph on the nascent Chinese press in the late Qing era. As the case of *Shen Bao* shows, it was the appearance of modern newspapers, assisted by the telegraph, that resulted in general changes in ways of disseminating news and made possible the formation of large-scale public opinion. China's deepening crisis after the Sino-Japanese War caused the public to pay more attention to political news and prompted the emergence of the public telegram as a new genre of political text. The eventful years after 1895 provided the public telegram with a more receptive environment in which to flourish.

Chapter 3 analyzes the fact that even though the Qing court was quite successful in employing telegraphy as a new means of political governance early on, the decline of the legitimacy of the court made its control of this technology increasingly ineffective and open to challenge by the end of the nineteenth century. The Chinese elite in metropolitan areas used telegraphy to participate in national politics, as shown in waves of protest telegrams sent to Beijing by imperial loyalists in 1899 and 1900. The skillful maneuvering of the use of telegraph communications in the "mutual protection" scheme in 1900 provided a precedent in discussing and voicing differing opinions on significant policy issues by high-ranking officials. These cases signaled that the telegraph would play a more important role in national politics in the first decade of the twentieth century.

Chapter 4 presents brief historical accounts of the Boycotting American Goods Movement in 1905 and Railway Rights Recovery Movement in 1907–8, with a focus on how the public telegram was used as an effective means of conducting large-scale nationalist mobilizations by the Chinese elite for the first time. Public telegrams were sent by the newly established chambers of commerce and other organizations, and numerous telegrams between policymakers were made public, indicating the unprecedented degree of political participation mobilized by increasing Chinese nationalism.

Chapter 5 explores how the public telegram became such an important means of political communication, maneuvering, and mobilization in late Qing politics. On the one hand, the public telegram went through an "authority-enhancing" process that gave it enormous textual power and helped establish it as an authoritative and effective new genre of political discourse in China. On the other hand, the impact of public telegrams mainly derived from the benign "receiving context" that was the historical context of the New Policies and Constitutionalism. Public telegrams were skillfully aimed at this receptive audience, and their effects were strongly felt.

Chapter 6 starts with a brief review of how the public telegram fared in the politics of the PRC, and moves on to the development of the Internet today. While paying attention to the government's efforts to regulate and control the Internet, this chapter points out that the PRC has been handling the Internet with a proactive policy—not only attempting to control its dissemination and content, but also actively promoting it. The case of the Strengthening-China Forum at People's Daily Online shows that the government is proactively establishing a relatively controlled public space on the Internet by selectively opening up some previously controlled space and trying to channel political discourse in the direction it most desires. In this new practice, the state takes initiatives that should be seen not as merely manipulative but also as innovative and experimental.

Chapter 7 focuses on one unique niche in Chinese cyberspace—intellectual web sites—to demonstrate the unfolding process by which the party state and intellectuals are trying to take their positions in cyberspace, a process that is full of conflict, negotiation, compromises, and sometimes even cooperation between the state and intellectuals. Based on the analysis of the evolution of three representative intellectual web sites, this chapter tries to show that the interactions between state and intellectuals on this new e-front are far more ambiguous and complex than a clear-cut picture of an authoritarian state versus a burgeoning civil society would suggest. So far, the proactive actions taken by both the state and intellectuals have resulted in turning intellectual web sites into an expanded space under more refined control.

Chapter 8 examines the political writings of so-called *minjian* ("private," "nonofficial," "independent," or "marginalized") online writers to illustrate how they have contributed greatly to the enlargement of space for political participation in China. The case of *minjian* online writers has shown that both the Chinese state and Internet users constantly negotiate new boundaries in this new domain. In the process, *minjian* online writers have adopted various strategies to fight against political pressure, mainstream prejudice, and inaccessibility of resources. Nonetheless, the extremely diverse positions taken by these *minjian* writers present a picture more complex than that expected by Internet utopians, reflecting the richness, fluidity, and complexity of Chinese cyberspace.

Chapter 9 focuses on the so-called "military web sites" in Chinese cyberspace to examine the complexity of contemporary Chinese nationalism. Pointing out the fact that the majority of military web site members are well educated and well informed, yet nationalistic and anti-Western, I argue that the key factor in shaping their nationalist thinking is the formation of a new interest-driven, game-playing paradigm in the past two decades that Chinese have used to interpret current national policies and international relations. Equipped with the Internet and this new paradigm, the more informed Chinese are, the more nationalistic they may become.

Finally, the book's Conclusion summarizes the main topics discussed.

PART I

Telegraphy

CHAPTER ONE

Telegraphy, Culture, and Policymaking

IN JUNE 1865, a British businessman, E. A. Reynolds, attempted to erect a telegraph line between Shanghai and Wusong, a distance of ten miles. To his dismay, after two-thirds of the line was completed, a total of 227 poles were pulled down and taken away by the local population. The British vice-consul, J. Markham, complained to local officials about the incident, but received the reply that the treaties did not permit the construction of telegraph lines and that foreign construction of telegraph lines overland would therefore not be allowed. Suspecting that the pulling down of the poles had been instigated by local officials, the British countered by arguing that the treaties did not prohibit telegraph line construction. They not only requested the right to continue construction but also demanded monetary compensation and protection of the line in the future. The district intendant, Ding Richang, declined all the British requests, claiming that the local population had acted out of their fear of the presumably harmful effects the line would have on the feng shui, the Chinese geomancy belief system. He insisted that there was no clear stipulation in the treaties of Chinese responsibility to protect such British undertakings—especially one initiated without Chinese permission. Official correspondence reveals that the British suspicions were well founded. It was indeed Ding Richang who, after discovering that the British had commenced their project, secretly instructed the local population to pull down the poles.[1]

Telegraphy and the railroad were the two most important technological wonders that further accelerated the industrialization of European countries in the nineteenth century and ultimately helped to transform the world into a truly global community. The railroad appeared slightly earlier than telegraphy, yet the two were closely related. Some scholars have attributed the rapid spread of telegraphy to its association with the railroad.[2] Even though knowledge of the railroad was introduced into China by foreign missionaries and Chinese pioneers in Western learning in the 1840s, it had received little attention by the 1860s. To Chinese, the railroad was as unfamiliar as telegraphy in the early 1860s, and the two were sometimes presented to Chinese by the foreigners as a package. But railways did not fare any better than telegraphy in China. In 1865, a British merchant constructed a half-kilometer narrow-gauge railroad outside Xuanwumen in Beijing, hoping in this way to advertise this new technology to the Qing rulers in the capital. It was dismantled by the order of the Office of the Gendarmerie (Bujun tongling yamen) because it had provoked "puzzlement and rumors" among capital residents.[3]

The above incidents show that Chinese attitudes toward the telegraphy and railroad, the two most advanced technologies of transportation and communication of the time, were not only less receptive than attitudes to other modern forces but are also seemingly puzzling to readers today. Why did the local officials pull down telegraph line poles and pull up rails in Shanghai and Beijing in 1865? This was four years after the establishment of the Zongli Yamen, a new government bureau in charge of all foreign-related affairs, which adopted Western diplomatic practices, and five years after the end of the Second Opium War, which resulted in the signing of a series of treaties between China and major Western powers to open up more port cities for trade and grant protection to missionaries. The year 1865 was also important in the so-called "Tongzhi Restoration" (1862–74), when a number of extraordinarily capable officials tried to save the dynasty from a spiral of decline. Simultaneously, the Self-Strengthening Movement (or Western Affairs Movement), aiming to introduce Western technologies and artifacts into China, proceeded with the setting up of arsenals and dockyards in Nanjing, Shanghai, and other cities. To answer the puzzle of why telegraphy was rejected then, a brief history of the Chinese response to telegraphy will be a good starting point.

Foreign Pressures on China to Adopt Telegraphy

By the 1860s, telegraphy had had a short but glorious history in the West. The technology was a result of efforts by multiple inventors in different countries in the first quarter of the nineteenth century. From the 1840s onwards, the technology matured, and its commercial potential was quickly recognized and exploited by Western countries. Thus it experienced explosive development in western Europe and North America. In America, the first telegraph line between Washington and Baltimore was constructed in 1844 and opened to public service the next year. Forty miles of telegraph wire at the beginning of 1846 had grown to more than 2,000 by 1848 and to 12,000 by 1850. By 1852, there were 23,282 miles of telegraph lines in the United States.[4]

In western Europe, the situation was little different. The new technology was adopted at an increasing pace after the mid 1840s. In Great Britain, for example, the Electric Telegraph Company was registered in 1845 and for some years enjoyed a monopoly before it was challenged by other companies.[5] The growth of the company was phenomenal and is readily comparable with the "dot-com" boom in the late 1990s. By 1851, the company owned a total of 10,000 miles of telegraph line; the mileage doubled in two years, and then increased to 30,000 miles by 1857. In 1851, the company handled fewer than 100,000 telegrams annually; by 1859, the number was over 1,000,000.[6]

Since most Chinese were unaware of what was happening outside the boundaries of the Qing empire, it is not surprising that missionaries first introduced them to telegraphy. In 1852, Daniel J. Macgowan, an American missionary based in Ningbo, published *Zhexue Nianjian (Philosophy Annals)* in Chinese, in which he devoted six chapters to explaining the principles of electricity, electromagnets, and the working of a telegraph machine. The publication of the book caught the attention of local gentry-scholars and was reported by the *North China Herald*. Mainly out of a concern for commercial benefits, foreign merchants in Shanghai had long hoped for a telegraph line that would speed up communications between East and West.[7] Meanwhile, submarine cable technology matured; a transatlantic line opened in 1866, and other lines were rapidly extended to many parts of the world. For the first time in human history, a truly global communication system was in the making.

It was in this context that Russians and other foreigners sought permission to construct telegraph lines in China in the early 1860s. In 1861, the Russian minister L. de Balluseck asked the Zongli Yamen for permission to construct a line between Beijing and Tianjin. His request was declined by Prince Gong, the head of the Zongli Yamen, saying that setting up the telegraph line would cause "many inconveniences," including the

difficulty of protection of the line after its completion. Balluseck then requested, in 1862, an assurance that if China were to allow foreigners to
set up lines in the future, the Russians should be granted the right to establish the first line. The Zongli Yamen granted his request but obviously
did not foresee that this concession would put the Qing court in a very
awkward position in its dealings with foreign powers on the telegraphy
issue in the years to come.[8]

The British, American, French, and Danes followed up with similar requests, but these were all refused by the Zongli Yamen. To the surprise of
Qing officials, foreigners were united on this issue and very persistent.
The Chinese used the phrase *zhiyi shenjian, jouchan buyi* (stubbornly determined and constantly nagging) to describe the situation.[9] In 1865, the
Zongli Yamen sent a letter to governors and generals on its policy concerning telegraphy and railroads, asking them to instruct local officials to
uphold and follow the extant policy. Responses from provincial officials
were overwhelmingly in agreement with the current prohibition policy,
with the exception of Li Hongzhang, then governor of Jiangsu, who, after stating his support for the current policy, proposed that if the construction of the lines was inevitable, China should build them itself in order to prevent them from falling into hands of foreigners.[10] His opinion
was not listened to at the time, but his thinking predicted the policies that
eventually guided the setting up of a Chinese telegraph network in the
1880s.

Nevertheless, the persistence of the foreign powers' efforts to set up
telegraph lines paid off. The Atlantic line opened in 1866, and lines were
being extended rapidly to other parts of the world. In 1870, the Qing officials were persuaded by the British minister, Thomas F. Wade, that there
was a difference between setting up telegraph lines on land and at sea.
The Zongli Yamen thus made a concession that allowed foreign companies to lay submarine cables along the Chinese coast, with the condition
that the end of the line could only be on a boat some distance from
China's coastline.[11] After obtaining this concession, the British Eastern
Telegraph and the Danish Great Northern companies reached an agreement to limit British operations south of Shanghai and Danish operations
north of Hong Kong, while the two would share business between Hong
Kong and Shanghai. Since the Great Northern had a plan to extend its
lines from Vladivostok to Nagasaki, Shanghai, and Hong Kong, the
British gave up their plan to construct a separate line at this time.[12]

Although the Chinese attached conditions to their concession, the foreigners did not take them seriously. In 1871, after the completion of the proposed maritime lines, the Great Northern secretly extended its line from Wusong harbor to Shanghai, arranging for its terminus in the American concession without the knowledge of local officials. Frustrated by the frequent line damage caused by fishing junks in the harbor, the Danes went on to erect poles and changed the underwater line to a land-line in 1873. At the beginning of the same year, the Great Northern extended another line to Gulangyu Island in Xiamen (Amoy). The Qing officials eventually found out about these two breaches of the agreement, but their repeated protests against the extension of the lines and requests to stop operations were simply ignored.

In 1874, the Japanese sent troops to Taiwan, ostensibly to retaliate against the killing of Liuqiu (Ryukyu) fishermen and merchants by the aboriginal people on the island. Shen Baozhen, then the director of the Fuzhou Dockyard, was appointed the imperial commissioner to protect Taiwan from the Japanese intrusion. To speed up communication across the Taiwan Strait, and between Fuzhou and Beijing, Shen, along with local officials, proposed to the Qing court to construct telegraph lines in Fujian and Taiwan and connect the two places with a submarine line across the strait. This proposal was approved by Beijing. This was the first time that the Qing policymakers took the initiative and seriously considered constructing telegraph lines, and they chose the Great Northern to do the construction work.

Yet their relationship with the Great Northern turned out to be extremely unpleasant. For the Taiwan lines, Shen Baozhen asked his associate at the Fuzhou Dockyard, the Frenchman Prosper Giquel, to negotiate with the Great Northern to construct two lines, one from the government seat of the Taiwan prefect (then Tainan) north across the strait, extending to Fuzhou and Mawei. The other sea line was to connect Taiwan with the Pescadores. A contract was drawn up in which the total expenses were calculated to be 242,500 taels. However, when the contract reached the company headquarters in Copenhagen, it was disallowed by the board of directors, who demanded a renegotiation because the price was felt to be too low to cover even the costs of materials and labor. Shen was alerted of the intentions of the Great Northern and the new round of negotiations to raise the price was stalled.[13]

In Fuzhou in early May 1874, the American consul, M. M. de Lano, petitioned the Fujian Board of Trade to allow the Great Northern to construct a line between Fuzhou and Mawei. Unaware of Shen Baozhen and the local officials' prior proposal to the court, the foreigners in both Fuzhou and Shanghai were surprised to hear that the petition had been approved in June. Overjoyed, the Great Northern responded in an unusually swift way, requiring only twelve days to complete the ten-mile-long Fuzhou-Mawei line at a cost of a mere 4,000 silver dollars, and encountering no opposition from the local population. Encouraged, and aiming to expand its privileges of telegraph construction, the Great Northern asked the American consul to petition the Chinese again for permission to construct the much longer Fuzhou-Xiamen line.

The Great Northern proposed three options to the Fujian Board of Trade. The first was to permit it to construct a Fuzhou-Xiamen line, in return for which the Great Northern would allow Fujian officials to send official telegrams to Xiamen, Shanghai, and Hong Kong free of charge. The second was to construct two parallel lines at once, one belonging to the Great Northern and the other to the Fujian authorities. The Great Northern would be in charge of the operation of the latter line until the Chinese were ready to take it over. The third option was for the Great Northern to construct and operate the line under a contract from the government covering the costs of materials and labor. Of the three options, the second was the most tempting to the local officials, because it enabled them to obtain a telegraph line without spending a penny. However, the local officials did not realize that it would breach the long-standing policy of the Zongli Yamen that no foreigners were to be allowed to construct and operate telegraph lines on Chinese soil, and this caused problems for the court in the ensuing years.

Negotiations between the Fujian Board of Trade and the Great Northern continued and a six-article contract was drafted in August. In addition to the two-line arrangement proposed by the Danes, another key article gave the Great Northern the exclusive right to run the Fuzhou-Xiamen line for thirty years; the local authorities, however, could buy back the line at any time. Among the policymakers in Fujian, opinions differed on how to proceed with the telegraph project. Shen Baozhen wrote from Taiwan to Li Henian, the governor-general, suggesting that the line be constructed under the auspices of the government, thus retaining total control of it. Although Li considered the article allowing the buyback would have provided enough assurance of eventual Chinese control, Shen's letter made Li more cautious and he decided to postpone the signing of the contract. After further negotiations, the Great Northern was asked to estimate the total expenses incurred in building the line in order to prepare for a Chinese buyback upon its completion. Based on this mutual understanding, the Board of Trade agreed that the company might start erecting poles and lines.

The ongoing negotiations in Fujian had not yet been reported to Beijing when, on August 30, the Russians informed the Zongli Yamen that a foreign telegraph company had completed a line between Fuzhou and Mawei, and that other lines were being constructed. According to the agreement between the Zongli Yamen and Russians in 1862, Russia would have the right to construct the first telegraph line on Chinese land. The Russian claims caught the Zongli Yamen off guard. After making inquiries to local officials, it replied to the Russians claiming that "all lines were managed by Chinese officials and all expenses were covered by government funds. No permission was granted to any foreign country." Two months later, the Russians countered this claim by providing a copy of the contract draft between the Board of Trade of Fujian and the Great Northern. The Zongli Yamen found itself in a very awkward position and felt it imperative to stop the construction of the Fujian telegraph lines under the present terms.

Under pressure, local officials in Fujian started negotiations to buy back the lines from the Great Northern. However, the company refused to sell the Fuzhou-Mawei line and proceeded with the construction of the Fuzhou-Xiamen line. On January 22, 1875, Chinese field workers employed by the Great Northern were attacked by mobs, poles were pulled down, and lines and other materials were taken away. After discovering that the mob had apparently been incited by local officials, the company finally decided to halt the construction work and reported the incident to the Danish minister in Beijing, hoping the issue could be solved through diplomatic pressure. Diplomacy in Beijing settled on two principles for solving the Fujian telegraph lines dispute: the Qing government would compensate the Great Northern for its losses, while the company would sell the completed sections and remaining materials to the Chinese. However, in a subsequent agreement reached between the Great Northern and local Chinese officials in May, it was agreed that the Danes would continue to build the unfinished line after the sale, that the local authorities would provide protection for the materials and the workers, and that the line would be finished by August 15. This agreement apparently exceeded the scope of two agreed-upon principles and in a way that worked in Great Northern's favor, and this angered the Zongli Yamen and further incited sentiment against the Danes in Fujian. Sabotage against the construction team and theft of materials increased after the Great Northern resumed the project, and, after a series of lootings and attacks, the Danes eventually gave up their attempt in the fall of 1875.

The dispute dragged on. It was not until Ding Richang, the official who had ordered the dismantling of the Shanghai-Wusong line ten years earlier, and now an experienced Western Affairs advocate, became the Fujian governor, that a new strategy was proposed. According to Ding, as long as construction of the line proceeded, trouble was sure to follow. The best way to solve the problem once and for all was to buy back the whole Fuzhou-Xiamen line, even though most of the line was not completed. In so doing, the government would obtain total control on issues such as whether or not to continue to construct the line, at what time, and under what conditions. In subsequent negotiations with the Danes, Ding insisted on discarding the agreement made in May of the previous year and successfully concluded a new agreement in March 1876 under which the whole line was purchased for 124,500 silver dollars.

The fiasco finally ended. The Great Northern was fully paid for a mostly uncompleted line—not a bad deal from the Danish perspective. The Qing officials were more than happy that a thorny issue had finally been resolved. This unpleasant experience with the Danes may well have further delayed the establishment of telegraphy in China for several years, and the controversy may also have confirmed a Chinese concern to keep control of this technology in their own hands, which in turn contributed to the setting up of a Chinese-controlled telegraph network in the 1880s and 1890s.

Weighing *Li* and *Quan*: Chinese Reluctance to Accept Telegraphy

It took three decades for the Chinese to accept telegraphy—from 1852, when knowledge of it was introduced into China, to the end of 1881, when the Imperial Telegraph Administration started to provide services. Why did it take so long? If the Qing policymakers were simply preoccupied with suppressing the Taiping uprising in the 1850s, and had little exposure to this technology, then why wasn't telegraphy a top priority in the 1860s, after they had initiated the Self-Strengthening Movement, given the fact that technological expertise was available from foreign companies? Two explanations have frequently been given for the belated adoption of telegraphy. One attributes the failure to insistence on the superiority of Confucian morality by Chinese conservatives, reinforced by scholarship professing negative views of Western technology and science, which was looked down on as "bizarre techniques and excessive tricks." The other blames Chinese feng shui beliefs, which caused public resistance to the erecting of telegraph lines across fields and graveyards, since they would cause a great disturbance to the geomantic composition of these places.

Both explanations focus on the "cultural" aspects of the question, and in this respect, they are well founded. Culture, whether in its elite or popular form, does exert an important influence on people's thinking and actions. However, as the anthropologist Richard Fox points out, there is always the danger of the mighty concept of culture being taken out of context and used to explain too many things. The interpreter risks falling into the fallacy of the organismic conception of culture that conceives of it as "a structure, a system that constrains and constitutes individuals and that persists in doing so over time." According to Fox, "culture only exists in a specific time and place and as a result of a field of differing interests, oppositions, and contradictions."[14] The explanations cited provide insights into the question of Chinese resistance to telegraphy in the 1860s and 1870s, but they do not suffice to solve the whole puzzle. They need to be supplemented by further scrutiny of the historical context. Even though at the time most Qing officials were not open-minded enough to recognize the need to adopt Western knowledge, and even though most Chinese believed in feng shui, these facts do not necessarily mean that the Chinese were constitutionally unable to adopt a particular technology such as telegraphy. Besides talking generally about the feeling of cultural superiority among the Qing rulers, one has to ask who the people making policy decisions about telegraphy were, and why they acted in the ways described above. Similarly, it is insufficient to identify feng shui as the motive for the destruction of telegraph lines without knowing how much it actually influenced Qing policymaking.

Historical facts show that a belief in Chinese culture's superiority and the adoption of Western technology were not always in conflict, because the Qing ruling elite at the time was never monolithic. In fact, in facing the daunting national situation in the late Qing period, there were officials who emphasized acquiring and applying foreign knowledge with practical effects on the governance of the dynasty well before the 1860s. Called the Statecraft School, this element of the ruling elite gained momentum in the years of internal uprisings and external threats. In the

1860s, officials of the Statecraft School were among the first to promote the Self-Strengthening Movement, of which learning Western technology and science was the most important component. Later labeled the "Western Affairs Clique," these were China's first modernizers. Among them were a number of influential governors and governors-general who were very interested in the technologies for manufacturing rifles, artillery cannons, and steamboats. Zeng Guofan set up a machine shop in Anqing as early as 1861; Li Hongzhang set up an arsenal in Suzhou in 1864 and the Jiangnan Arsenal in Shanghai in 1865; and Zuo Zongtang founded the Fuzhou Dockyard in 1866. In Beijing, where Prince Gong was in charge of the Zongli Yamen for over two decades, from its inception in 1861, initiatives by regional officials found a receptive audience in the Qing court. An attempt was even made to create a modern navy by buying gunboats from Britain in 1863.[15] Our question might thus be modified into an inquiry into why the Western Affairs advocates failed to make a quicker decision on adopting telegraphy. What were their concerns when Qing officials ordered the dismantling of telegraph lines in Shanghai and the railroad in Beijing?

As to the second explanation, feng shui, it is certainly true that most Chinese knew little about telegraphy and may have been fearful about its alleged detrimental effects on the balance of geomancy surrounding their graveyards, houses, and villages, or the whole local landscape. The Chinese translation of "telegraph line," which literally means "lightning wires," certainly did not help in this account.[16] Nevertheless, the importance of feng shui ideas should not be exaggerated. First, feng shui belonged to a popular Chinese belief system and was never fully accepted by mainstream Confucianism, which generally shuns discussing the afterlife and metaphysical issues. Officials might either ignore feng shui concerns as "sheer nonsense" (*wuji zhitan*) or, worse, interpret it as "spreading devilish words and inciting the mass" (*yaoyan huozhong*) and suppress it. Furthermore, despite sporadic attacks on engineers and workers, feng shui ideas were not a major obstacle to the construction of telegraph lines in the 1880s and 1890s after the Qing court decided to build them.

When feng shui ideas were mixed with anti-foreign sentiment, however, they gained much greater force. In retrospect, feng shui ideas were often employed by the Qing officials for two purposes: first, as a ready excuse for popular resistance in order to decline foreigners' requests to erect telegraph lines, especially in the earlier years; secondly, as a means to mobilize mobs to drive foreigners away when officials could not achieve their goals at the negotiating table. In many cases, foreigners were suspicious that local officials were orchestrating villagers' actions. Their suspicions were well founded in the case of the Shanghai-Wusong line incident, and local officials were certainly behind the attacks on the Fuzhou-Xiamen line. Feng shui served mainly as an element of negotiation between the Qing mandarins and foreigners on the issue of official protection of telegraph line construction and operation. The so-called Western Affairs Clique and local officials, even though they took popular sentiment into account, do not seem to have felt that the feng shui issue was a main concern in policymaking. Indeed, it has been shown that if the local officials insisted on protecting the line, they were usually successful.

The similarity between the incidents involving the Shanghai-Wusong and Fuzhou-Xiamen lines is that they were both responses to construction by foreigners on Chinese soil without official permission. Looking at Qing policymakers' discussions and debates about telegraphy and, later, the railway, we might note that the concept of *liquan* is often mentioned by different sides as constituting the core of the issue. As historians have pointed out, this is different from *quanli* (rights) in modern Chinese. It had special meanings in the context of the late nineteenth century.[17] An analysis of this key concept will help us better understand the thinking of Qing policymakers at the time.

Like most two-character words in classic Chinese, *liquan* consists of two separate concepts in modern Chinese, with the first, *li*, referring to "interests," "benefits," or "resources" and the second, *quan*, referring to "power," "rights," or "control." In different contexts, however, the two concepts have many extended meanings. *Li* was most often mentioned from the standpoint of usage. As aforementioned, in 1865, the Zongli Yamen asked for opinions on the telegraph from governors and generals, and with the exception of Li Hongzhang, no one expressed interest in or support for setting up telegraph services.[18] These assessments were predominantly against telegraphy because it would not bring China any benefits but would endanger China's rights. Ruilin, governor-general of Liangguang (Guangdong and Guangxi provinces), argued that the foreigners' true intention was only to "squeeze out Chinese interests without any consideration of harmful effects on local areas."[19] Shen Baozhen, then governor of Jiangxi, pointed out that telegraphy would enable the foreigners to gain an advantageous position in transferring military and commercial information, thus posing a threat to the Qing dynasty.[20] Apparently, the focus was on the "usage" aspect by the foreigners, with the word *li* representing the commercial interests of foreign telegraph companies, direct benefits to foreign traders in China, and potential military advantage to the Western powers.

To the Western Affairs advocates, the immediate *li* or usage of the Western technologies was the main reason to adopt them. Zeng Guofan and Li Hongzhang had witnessed the unprecedented firepower of the modern guns used by British and French troops to repel Taiping attacks in Shanghai in the early 1860s, and their own prompt adoption of these guns immediately made their military units the most powerful in the outdated Qing army. When activities of Western Affairs advocates gradually broadened to include commercial navigation, and the mining and textile industries in the 1870s, their appreciation of telegraphy's potential military and commercial applications increased. Zeng Guofan envisioned the construction of a line in 1870. Shen Baozhen also changed his position and proposed:

The foreigners are very persistent in erecting telegraph lines. It would be ideal if we could prohibit them from doing so; the less trouble, the better. If it is too difficult to stop them, we had better build the lines ourselves. By giving foreigners the difficult task and making them responsible for construction and training, we let them share the interests while holding the controlling power in our hands. So doing will not have detrimental effects on public affairs of our ocean frontier. If we allow foreigners to construct lines by themselves, in the case of urgent and secret affairs, they could get news in a couple of days, while we would not be informed in more than a dozen days. This will constrain our ability to make swift and appropriate responses to situations.[21]

By 1874, the crisis in Taiwan made the *li* of telegraphy apparent to most Qing policymakers, but even though the *li* was now recognized, how to handle the *quan* had not yet been settled. Qing officials' anxiety regarding *quan*, indeed, played a crucial role in their decision making. Like the concept of *li*, the meaning of *quan* differs in different contexts. In the responses to the Zongli Yamen's inquiry on telegraphy policy, several governors pointed out the importance of keeping *quan* in the government's own hands. Analytically, in political discourse of the late nineteenth and early twentieth centuries, the concept of *quan* had three different meanings, namely, commercial rights (*shang quan*), political (administrative) power (*zhi quan*), and national sovereignty (*zhu quan*). As far as telegraphy was concerned, *quan* often referred to actual control of the telegraph line, thus falling into the second of these three categories of meaning. In the 1860s and 1870s, the Chinese did not have a clear concept of sovereignty yet.[22] The issue of sovereignty would become a crucial concern in disputes on the construction of railroads at the turn of the twentieth century, as discussed in Chapter 4. Concerns regarding who would have control of telegraph lines show the deep suspicion with which Qing officials viewed foreigners.

The Qing court had several rounds of discussion on strategies for conducting the Self-Strengthening Movement. The first was in the mid 1860s. In 1865 and 1866, Robert Hart and Thomas Wade made suggestions to the Qing court in which they listed steamboats, modern weaponry, modern machinery, modern warfare methods, the minting of coins, mining, metallurgy, telegraphy, and the railroad as "new methods" to keep the dynasty prosperous and strong. Coastal provincial officials were asked by the Zongli Yamen to respond to these suggestions in 1866. Their responses were in general not as enthusiastic about telegraphy and the railroad as about other "new methods," many expressing deep suspicion of these two technologies. Guanwen, governor-general of Huguang (Hunan and Hubei provinces), replied:

Even though there are many opinions on telegraphy and the railroad, the obvious purposes of their advocates are to monopolize these interests, while their hidden purposes are more malicious. My humble opinion is that it is uncertain whether their construction is feasible. Even if it were, they would have the same detrimental effect as steamboats do. Since steamboats navigate only rivers and seas, the railroad will be used [by foreigners] to reach places that have not been reached by steamboats, complemented by the telegraph connecting all places, thus controlling the *li* and *quan* of all under heaven. This is the true purpose of the foreigners, nothing else.[23]

Liu Kunyi, then the governor of Jiangxi, claimed:

It is appropriate to follow foreigners in areas such as establishing mints, building ships, making weaponry, and studying the art of modern warfare. However, the construction of telegraph lines and railroads would make it easier for the foreigners to communicate with each other and also make us lose strategic passes [*aizhu*]. Thus it is absolutely necessary to reject the suggestions by Hart and Wade.[24]

These responses corresponded closely to the opinions of Prince Gong. While generally endorsing the other suggestions, he thought that there were insurmountable obstacles to constructing telegraph and railroad lines in China. In addition, since the foreigners were so enthusiastic and persistent in these issues, he was worried that they would cause diplomatic disputes between the Qing court and foreign powers. It should be emphasized that the idea of telegraphy as a potential troublemaker was deeply rooted in the minds of Qing policymakers. Zuo Zongtang pointed out in 1866 that telegraph lines were difficult to protect all the time and thus impractical and potentially troublesome.[25] In the context of the 1860s, when the Qing dynasty had been defeated militarily and forced to accept the Western treaty system, neither the Zongli Yamen nor local officials wanted to be involved in foreign disputes of any kind. The fear that foreign telegraph lines being damaged by the local people would cause diplomatic disputes accordingly also played a big part in Qing policymakers' decision not to allow telegraphy in the first place.

The ideas of *li* and *quan* thus dominated the thinking of Qing policymakers in the 1860s and 1870s on the issues of telegraphy and the railroad. These ideas were manifested in their evaluation of "usage" and how much "control" they would have over the new technology. Unlike steamboats and modern guns and machinery, the potential "usage" of telegraphy was generally underappreciated by many policymakers. As far as the control aspect was concerned, their anxiety was twofold: first, they feared that by allowing foreigners to set up telegraph services, they would lose control of lines within the empire and thus of communications; second, they were deeply concerned that they could not control the local population and protect the foreign lines from been vandalized and becoming the source of disputes. Along with other factors, underestimation of *li* and concern about *quan* contributed to the delay in the endorsement of telegraphy by the Qing rulers.

The Making of a Chinese Telegraph Network

After the settlement of the Fuzhou-Xiamen line disputes with the Great Northern in 1876, the Qing policymakers reached a consensus about constructing a Chinese-controlled telegraph network. When the policy disputes were put aside, China experienced a period of rapid development of telegraphy under Li Hongzhang and his associate Sheng Xuanhuai. In less than twenty years, a telegraph network was established across the vast territories of the Qing empire. But the credit for establishing China's first telegraph line belongs to another Western Affairs advocate, Ding Richang—the very man implicated in the affair with Reynolds in 1865 mentioned in the beginning of this chapter.

In 1877, Ding Richang, then governor of Fujian, constructed China's first telegraph line from Tainan to Dagou (now Gaoxiong) on Taiwan, using materials left over from the now-defunct Fuzhou-Xiamen line. The previous settlement on the Fuzhou-Xiamen line had featured a clause asking the Great Northern to train Chinese telegraph students for one year. As a result, China's first telegraph school was opened in Nantai, near Fuzhou, in April 1876, with an enrollment of forty. Ding Richang relied on graduates from the school to construct and operate his 42.5-kilometer-long line. These first Chinese telegraph engineers and technicians not only provided the technological know-how for the Taiwan line but also helped carry out the much bigger national telegraph project under Li Hongzhang.

Li constructed a short line between Dagu Fortress and Tianjin in 1879 in order to facilitate military communication. Further convinced of the usefulness of telegraphy, he petitioned the emperor to construct a Tianjin-Shanghai line on September 16, 1880. In the petition, he emphasized the vital role of speedy communication in military and diplomatic affairs. He also provided a well-thought-out plan, using military funds to construct the line at first, and then privatizing the line and transforming it into a commercial enterprise under official supervision. His plan also proposed setting up a telegraph school in Tianjin to train Chinese students, in order for Chinese to be able to operate the line. By so doing, Li noted, "we shall have long term control of the line"; he thus specifically emphasized the control issue in the petition.[26]

This time the Qing court responded swiftly, approving Li's plan in just two days. Li acted with equal speed, establishing the Imperial Telegraph Administration in Tianjin during the next month and at the same time setting up the school and ordering equipment and materials. The 1,537-kilometer-long line was commenced in April 1881 and completed in December the same year, with seven branch telegraph administrations along it. On December 28, the Tianjin-Shanghai line started to send and receive both official and private telegrams. From this time on, China entered a telegraphy boom. Before 1884, China had erected 5,030 kilometers of landline. Between 1884 and 1899, another 27,750 kilometers were added. By 1908, the total length of telegraph lines, including both commercial and official lines, reached 45,448 kilometers. A comprehensive telegraph network had thus been constructed.[27] Key dates in the development of telegraphy in late Qing are as follows:

1881   Construction of the Shanghai-Tianjin line
1882   Lines extended from Tianjin to Tongzhou and also set up in Jiangsu and Shandong provinces
1883   Lines extended from Nanjing to Hankou and set up in Zhejiang, Fujian, and Guangdong provinces

1884   Beijing connected and line extension undertaken in Anhui,
        Jiangxi, Hubei, and Guangdong provinces
1886   Sichuan and Yunnan lines built
1887   Guizhou and Taiwan lines set up
1888   Henan lines set up and Chinese and French lines connected on
        the Vietnam-Yunnan border
1890   Lines extended to Shanxi, Shaanxi, and Gansu provinces
1892   Chinese and Russian lines connected
1893   Line extended to Xinjiang
1894   Chinese and British lines connected on the Burma-Yunnan
        border
1896   Lines extended to Tibet
1897   Lines extended to Mongolia
1899   Rehe lines set up[28]

The rapid development in the 1880s and 1890s was owing to Li
Hongzhang's 1882 policy of privatizing major lines to merchants and
turning the Imperial Telegraph Administration into a commercial business under official supervision. The Shanghai-Tianjin line was constructed with military funds from Li's Huai army, with a total expendi-
ture of 178,700 taels. After only several months' operation of the newly
established Imperial Telegraph Administration, Li promptly placed the
officially owned lines in the hands of private merchants. His experience
convinced him that this was the best way to manage the new lines, in
terms both of enhancing management efficiency and freeing the Qing
court from any further financial burden.

Li realized with considerable acuity that the main incentive for merchants was obtaining li, or business profit, in this case. Since the Imperial
Telegraph Administration was operating in the red, he offered a number
of very generous provisions, including granting monopolies, tax exemp-
tions, and interest-free loans to private investors. The response was very
positive. Jing Yuanshan, who would become the Chief of the Shanghai
Telegraph Administration, bought one-eighth of the total shares and became the biggest individual investor. The investment of the private capital of the Chinese economic elite, including compradors, landlords, and
high-ranking officials, in telegraph services, along with the managerial
expertise they provided, eventually turned the Imperial Telegraph Administration into one of the most profitable modern enterprises in late
nineteenth-century China.[29]

The rapid development of Chinese telegraph lines also had to do with pressure and stimulation from the foreign companies that had been hoping to crack the Chinese domestic market for a long time. Vigilant to protect China's *li* and *quan* at all times, both the Qing policymakers and private merchants viewed the development of an indigenous Chinese telegraph network as the best way to keep the foreigners out. Surprised by the changed Chinese attitude to telegraphy, Great Britain, the United States, France, and Germany proposed at the end of 1882 to set up an International Telegraph Company and to construct submarine cables from Shanghai to Hong Kong. The British were further planning to extend submarine cables from Shanghai to the southeast coastal cities of Ningbo, Wengzhou, Xiamen, and Shantou.

Alarmed, the Chinese responded with a preemptive strategy involving the swift construction of landlines connecting Zhejiang, Fujian, and Guangdong in 1883 and 1884, thus to a great degree diminishing the business potential of the proposed foreign plans. The line was 2,175 kilometers long and cost more than 400,000 taels. The Chinese elite in the coastal areas was mobilized, and the Zongli Yamen noted, "[I]n order to prevent the foreigners' conspiracy and get back our rights (*quan*) and interests (*li*), it is very important for Chinese merchants to construct the coastal landlines. They all hope the lines will start soon and will be united in supporting the project."[30] The Chinese merchants kept their promise and raised the huge amount of funds necessary among themselves. It was a mobilization in the name of protecting *li* and *quan*, a successful forerunner of similar mobilizations to construct railroads two decades later.

The subsequent Sino-Franco conflicts between 1883 and 1885 certainly stimulated the rapid construction of several lines in south and southwest China. The speedy exchange of information was critical to military maneuvers, and the Qing court faced a dismal situation in this regard. Without telegraphy, official correspondence between local areas and Beijing often took weeks. The situation prompted the newly established Imperial Telegraph Administration to construct lines at unprecedented speed. Lines were extended from Zhenjiang along the Yangzi River to Hankou in 1883, Beijing was connected to the telegraph in 1884, and a line between Guangzhou and Longzhou was also constructed. By this time, the dispute among Qing policymakers on the *li* aspect of telegraphy seems to have ended.

Concern about *quan* was assuaged by buying out the existing foreign landlines and contracting out overseas telegraph business with foreign companies. In 1883, after repeated negotiations, the Great Northern dismantled its landline in Xiamen and sold the existing Shanghai-Wusong landline to the Qing government. Even though the latter line would be "rented" back to the Great Northern, the Qing government basically thus obtained control of all landlines in China, while contracting out overseas business to the undersea cables of the Great Northern and the Eastern Telegraph.[31] In 1884, 1888, and 1892, Chinese landlines were connected with the lines of French Vietnam, British Burma, and Russia respectively.[32] The connection with the Vietnamese and Burmese lines was pivotal to communication between China and overseas Chinese in Southeast Asia, as we shall see in Chapter 3. By the end of the nineteenth century, the Qing dynasty had finally set up an independently run, comprehensive telegraph network connecting the vast empire electrically for the first time in its history.

Summary

Knowledge of telegraphy was introduced into China in the early 1850s, quite speedily, considering that the technology had matured only a few years earlier in the West. Yet it took three decades for the Qing rulers to decide to set up telegraph services. In the early to mid 1860s, their rejection of telegraphy was demonstrated by incidents involving the dismantling of established telegraph lines. Retrospectively, these cases seem to have been puzzling to contemporary observers, and they are often used to illustrate how incompetent the Qing rulers were in response to foreign challenges. Yet if we put the issue into its historical context and examine the complex factors behind the policymaking process, a clearer picture surfaces that makes the issue more plausible than puzzling. The discussion so far has shown that in the 1860s and 1870s, multiple factors contributed to the slow adoption of telegraphy in China. As an alternative to the often-cited explanation using the elite belief in Confucian cultural superiority and the popular belief in feng shui, I have proposed that political thinking, especially concerns focusing on *li* and *quan*, played a critical role in Qing policymaking. These concerns were further compounded by pressure from the Western powers and the inconsistency of policy implementation between central and local officials, contributing to further delays in adopting the technology.

It is true that Chinese cultural views, both elite and popular, were not hospitable to this new technology. But no matter how strongly they believed in the superiority of Confucianism, the Qing rulers, especially members of the Western Affairs Clique, nevertheless recognized the necessity of adopting "the superior foreigners' technologies in order to control the foreigners." Feng shui ideas, never a central part in the ruling Confucian culture, had no major effect on the Qing policymakers either. In fact, feng shui ideas were often used by the Qing policymakers as a handy excuse to decline foreign requests for telegraph line construction and protection. More important, feng shui ideas were not strong enough to prevent line construction initiated by the Chinese themselves and could be easily constrained if the government was resolved to implement its policy.

Political concerns, namely, concerns about *li* and *quan*, played a more important role in shaping the thinking of the Qing policymakers at the time. Based on their observations regarding the Qing dynasty's changing relations with the Western powers, they were very conscious of protecting China's *li* and *quan*. The concern for *li* manifested itself in their evaluation of the degree of usefulness of various Western technologies. Compared to steamboats and modern guns, which had direct military applications, telegraphy was definitely underestimated at first. Starting from the early 1870s, some members of the elite started to change their position on the usage of telegraphy, and the Japanese military expedition on Taiwan in 1874 made most of them realize the military usefulness of the telegraph lines.

The attitude of the Qing court toward *li* in its dealings with other countries had also undergone a sea change by the 1860s. Before the nineteenth century, the granting of trade privileges was seen largely as a political means to make foreigners acknowledge the legitimacy of a Chinese-centered tributary system. The severe drain on silver caused by the opium trade made the Chinese realize that foreign trade was damaging Chinese commercial interests. Attempts by the Qing to challenge Western powers were disastrous. Two Opium Wars later, in the 1860s, after they had been forced to accept the treaty system, Qing policymakers no longer focused on granting interests to foreigners but rather on how to protect their own interests (*hu li*); how to take advantage of foreign benefits (*yong li*); and how to compete against foreigners' interests (*zheng li*).

The Qing policymakers thus saw the benefits of telegraphy as very much a zero-sum game. Wade emphasized that even though the "new methods" he suggested "would benefit foreign countries, they would benefit China to a greater degree."[33] The Russians, together with others, argued repeatedly that telegraphy would benefit all parties involved. Yet concern about *quan* came to occupy a more prominent position in the policymaking considerations of modernizers.[34] Concern about *quan* was manifested in Qing officials' anxiety to keep control of this technology, both in terms of keeping it in Chinese hands and of preventing it from becoming a potential source of diplomatic disputes. When the Qing government started to build telegraph lines in Fujian and Taiwan, the lack of consensus among local Fujian provincial officials on how to proceed with the project, the contradiction between local officials' willingness to grant the Great Northern rights to construct the landline and the Zongli Yamen's insistence on keeping the line under government control, and the unscrupulous business practices of foreign telegraph companies all contributed to further delay in the introduction of telegraphy in China.

In retrospect, and to be fair to the Qing modernizers, aside from the early underestimation of telegraphy's applications and the subsequent delay in its introduction, there was no major blunder in their handling of the technology, given the domestic and international conditions. After the policy was finalized in 1880, they proceeded with efficiency and speed to set up a telegraph service, while warding off foreign operation of landlines. The Imperial Telegraph Administration was one of the best managed and most profitable enterprises run by Western Affairs advocates, and it was nationalized in 1909 without stirring up strong resentment. Compared to telegraphy, the handling of the railroad by the Qing dynasty was a disaster. As we shall see later, resistance to railroad nationalization based on the popular appeal of protecting *li* and *quan* eventually become the catalyst that brought down the dynasty.

In sum, the belated adoption of the telegraph in China had multiple causes, including unwelcoming elite and popular cultural views, a zero-sum approach to the issue of *li*, an overriding concern for the control of the technology, distrust of foreigners that was constantly reinforced by the foreigners' own behavior, fear of provoking diplomatic disputes, early underestimation of the technology's commercial and military applications, and the later inconsistency between local and central officials in dealing with the actual construction of telegraph lines. The concern about *li* and *quan* reflected a uniquely Chinese attitude to telegraphy and other foreign technologies in the late Qing era. This attitude was later invigorated by emerging Chinese nationalism at the turn of the twentieth century and would play a much bigger role in modern Chinese politics in the years to come, with help, perhaps surprisingly, from telegraphy and newspapers.

CHAPTER TWO

Telegraphy, Newspapers, and Public Opinion

It is a fact that foreign steamers [carrying mail] are faster than the Chinese horse-relayed postal delivery. [This situation] has already put constraints on our handling of official affairs. If foreigners are allowed to construct telegraph lines, they will be able to exchange news instantly over a distance of a thousand miles. Worse still, it will be more difficult to prevent them from spreading rumors in newspapers to disturb public opinion.

Shen Baozhen, memorial to the Zongli Yamen in 1865

S HEN BAOZHEN'S attitude would change a few years later, but his hostility to telegraphy in 1865, when he was governor of Jiangxi, reflected the common opinion of Qing officials in the mid 1860s.[1] His comment on the possibility of telegraphy being used to spread subversive rumors in newspapers is worth noting, however. This is not the only instance that we shall encounter of concern about a new technology's effects on newspapers and public opinion in the time period that this book covers. But Shen made his remarks well before the telegraph actually came to play an important role in Chinese newspapers, especially in expressing political views and shaping public opinion—in fact, in 1865, there was only one modern newspaper, *Shanghai Xinbao*, published in Chinese. As this chapter will show, Shen's remarks on the possibility of unregulated telegraphy being used by newspapers to influence public opinion proved prophetic.

Newspapers, Telegraphy, and News Transmission

When Shen submitted his memorial to the Zongli Yamen, most Chinese had never seen a modern newspaper. Although modern newspapers appeared in China in the first half of the nineteenth century, most of them were published by missionaries. From 1815 to the First Opium War (1839–42), newspaper publication was concentrated in Southeast Asian

Chinese communities and Hong Kong, Macao, and Canton, and was not conducted on a large scale. After the First Opium War, from 1840 to 1890, missionaries and churches published about 170 newspapers and magazines in China, or about 95 percent of the total number.[2] Except in the case of some comprehensive publications such as *Wanguo Gongbao (Review of the Times),* the focus of these newspapers was, understandably, not on reporting current national and international news but on preaching Christianity to the Chinese, thus limiting their ability to reach out to a general audience and to influence public opinion. In all, from 1815 to the end of the nineteenth century, around 250 newspapers and magazines were published in China, about 200 of which were published by non-Chinese.[3]

Starting in the 1850s, several commercially oriented newspapers in English appeared in Shanghai. In 1850, Henry Shearman, a British merchant, published the *North China Herald,* which had a circulation of between 100 and 200.[4] In 1857, missionaries in Shanghai published the first magazine in Chinese in Shanghai, the *Shanghai Serial.* Five years later, the first newspaper in Chinese, *Shanghai Xinbao (Chinese Shipping List and Advertiser),* was set up by the publisher of the *North China Daily News* in Shanghai. The paper was, as its English title suggests, very commercially oriented, and advertisements, shipping schedules, and commercial price lists made up most of its contents, with only limited coverage of political and social news. It kept a steady circulation of 400 for its decade of publication, and most of its subscribers were foreign trading companies and Chinese business establishments.[5]

Politically speaking, the publication of the English newspaper *North China Herald* and of Chinese-language newspapers and magazines generally was of significance because it broke a long-standing official prohibition on the publishing of newspapers by ordinary people. Under Qing dynastic rules, ordinary people had no right to comment on current affairs and policies, nor were they allowed to spread news in printed form. Before the Opium War, although the Qing authorities were tolerant of foreigners publishing newspapers in foreign languages, they continued to maintain a zero-tolerance policy with respect to publishing books and newspapers in Chinese. The foreigners chose an opportune time to break this prohibition in Shanghai in the late 1850s and early 1860s, when Qing officials had their hands full dealing with the Taiping uprising, and the outcome of the Second Opium War (or Arrow War, 1856–60) had in any case made them reluctant to provoke conflicts with foreigners. Furthermore, the focus of the early publications in Chinese was either religion or commerce, which to a degree lessened the concern of the Qing authorities.[6]

Shanghai Xinbao was the first Chinese newspaper to publish news conveyed by telegraph. The first case I have encountered, a report on the prices of silk and tea in London under the heading "China and Foreign News," was printed in the issue of July 31, 1869. The telegram had been dispatched from London on July 6, transmitted to a Russian station bordering Manchuria, and then carried overland by courier to Tianjin, finally reaching Shanghai by steamer on July 28. The whole trip took twenty-two days to complete.[7] On August 3, another item of market news is said to have reached Shanghai by telegraph in seventeen days.[8] The time it took for telegrams to reach Shanghai was sometimes prolonged by troubles along the way, such as floods or steamer delays. On October 5, 1869, three telegrams sent within a period of fifteen days were printed in the same issue of the paper because floods in Heilongjiang had caused them to reach Shanghai at the same time.[9] Shortly thereafter, *Shanghai Xinbao* stopped printing telegraphed market news on a regular basis, probably owing to the opposition of the association of foreign traders, who had previously insisted that any new telegraphed information only be printed in *Shanghai Xinbao* after a delay of twenty-four hours.[10] On November 6, the market news was reported one more time.[11] The newspaper would not resume printing such news until May 1871. By this time, with the completion of the Hong Kong–Shanghai undersea cable, the time it took for a telegram from London to reach Shanghai had been shortened to three days.[12]

Despite its heavy commercial orientation, *Shanghai Xinbao* carried limited but focused political news from time to time. In the early days, the focus was on the Taiping uprising. In 1870, *Shanghai Xinbao* carried a series of news reports on the Tianjin massacre, an anti-Christian riot in which more than a dozen Catholic missionaries and other foreigners were killed. On August 4, it carried an article praising the speedy transmission of news by means of the telegraph. According to the report, it took eight days for news of the Tianjin massacre to be carried to Heilongjiang, and it then reached London over the Russian telegraph line in two days.[13] Shortly after this, the outbreak of the Franco-Prussian War encouraged *Shanghai Xinbao* to carry extensive war news received by telegraph. There were three ways that the newspaper could get telegraphed news. One was via the old London–Russian Far East–Tianjin–Shanghai route;

the second was from Shanghai-bound steamers from Hong Kong or London; and the last was to reprint telegraphed news from Hong Kong newspapers, especially from *Zhongwai Xinbao* (*China and Foreign Daily*). In the course of the war, Singapore was connected by undersea cable to India and thus to Britain. Telegrams could be sent to Singapore and then carried by steamer to Hong Kong, substantially shortening the time taken for communication.[14]

At the peak of the Franco-Prussian War, *Shanghai Xinbao* published telegraphed news in almost every issue. After the war ended in 1871, however, telegraphed news decreased dramatically, even after the completion of the Hong Kong and Shanghai line in early 1871. Obviously, the newspaper's focus was on Western-related news, not on political news of Chinese concern. Therefore, even though it was published in Chinese, its coverage of political news had a limited effect on the majority of Shanghai residents at the time. A newspaper with a more social and political orientation that would attract most attention from Chinese on a broad scale would not appear until the publication of *Shen Bao* (*Shanghai News*) in 1872.

Telegraphy and the Change of Political News Dissemination

Long before the arrival of modern newspapers, the Chinese had had a unique way of disseminating political information. This was *Di Bao*, a semi-official publication that can be traced back to the Tang Dynasty (618–907 A.D.). The character *di* literally means "lodgings for officials on a business trip," and *bao* means "report." The contents of *Di Bao* included imperial edicts, records of royal activities, notices of official appointments, promotions and demotions, and copies of official memorials. It was sent to local government officials through *di* along main thoroughfares and usually circulated solely among the powerful elite. By the Northern Song dynasty (960–1127 A.D.), a new kind of report appeared. These reports were called *Xiao Bao*, which literally means "trivial report," and were published by people who made a living out of collecting various pieces of political information in the capital, compiling them into *Xiao Bao* and selling it to interested people, usually officials, scholars, and influential merchants. Because the information sources were highly arbitrary and the publication was illegal and therefore surreptitious, the content of *Xiao Bao* was often unreliable.[15]

Under the Ming (1368–1644 A.D.) and Qing (1644–1911 A.D.) dynasties, *Jing Bao* (literally "Capital Report") was the main publication containing political information. Although granted publication permission by the government, *Jing Bao* was not an official publication, and its main aim was profit. The compilers of *Jing Bao* lived in the capital and made every effort to collect as many as edicts, announcements, and memorials as were available, putting these together in the report and selling it to readers. Obviously, the information that *Jing Bao* could collect was general government information that was not kept secret, and most of it was quite outdated. However, during the Ming and Qing dynasties, there was little transparency to court politics, and any wrong move by an official could have resulted in catastrophe. It was exactly for this reason that *Jing Bao* was highly valued by officials and members of the gentry class who needed to make political judgment calls from time to time. By the late Qing, *Jing Bao* was published daily, with a circulation of more than 10,000 copies.[16]

Thus, when modern newspapers such as *Shanghai Xinbao* and *Shen Bao* appeared in Shanghai, *Jing Bao* was still the main source of political information. The modern newspapers would publish selective excerpts from *Jing Bao* periodically, and *Shen Bao*, with its Chinese readership, gave more space and attention to *Jing Bao*. Indeed, *Jing Bao* was published as an integral part of *Shen Bao* on a daily basis for a long period of time. In its first years of publication, *Shen Bao* was a newspaper of eight pages, of which one to two pages were usually devoted to reprinting *Jing Bao*. Later, *Shen Bao* increased its number of pages per issue, and *Jing Bao* was sometimes published as an appendix and distributed with the newspaper free of charge. The status of *Jing Bao* was largely unthreatened by the newly appearing newspapers; rather, it became incorporated into the latter as an attraction to politically conscious readers. The arrival of the telegraph, however, resulted in a more general change in ways of disseminating political information.

This impact came from changes in official communication as a result of the telegraph. Even though managers of the Imperial Telegraph Administration (ITA) thought that telegraph lines should put commercial interests first, Li Hongzhang and most Qing officials felt that priority should be given to the speedy transmission of military, diplomatic, and administrative telegrams. After the opening of the Tianjin-Shanghai line, telegrams were classified into two major types, official and private, with the former enjoying priority over the latter. Official telegrams were further divided into different classes, first class official telegrams being given top priority. Such telegrams were sent by the members of the Zongli Yamen and the Junji Chu (Grand Council), as well as by Qing diplomatic representatives overseas, governors-general, governors, and Manchu generals. A first class official telegram required no payment, but merely the filling out of a record. The waived cost of such telegrams, usually listed as a part of the "contributions" to the government from the ITA, totaled $2.42 million from 1884 to 1908, before the ITA was nationalized by the Qing court.[17]

After 1882, urgent edicts, government notices, and directives were sent out by the court by telegraph, and officials with access to the telegraph service also sent memorials to Beijing by this method. In 1884, after the line was extended to Beijing, official communication between the court, local officials, and overseas diplomats by telegraph rapidly increased. All official telegrams going in and out were received, translated, and processed by an office in the Zongli Yamen, thus making it the nexus of political information in the capital.[18] In 1884, the Zongli Yamen set up two government archives, the *dianji dang*, containing imperial edicts sent out by telegraph, and the *dianhui dang*, containing memorials from local officials.[19] Modern transportation and communication techniques greatly shortened the time needed for correspondence between central and provincial bureaucrats. After the completion of a comprehensive national telegraph network around the turn of the twentieth century, all edicts and memorials started to be sent from or to Beijing by telegraph.

Using the telegraph speeded up the dissemination of political information by modern newspapers. Before the telegraph, it took a half dozen days for political news to reach Shanghai from Beijing. After the Tianjin-Shanghai telegraph line opened at the end of 1881, the time was shortened to two to three days. Newspapers were keen to take advantage of this new technology. On January 16, 1882, less than three weeks after the opening of the line, *Shen Bao* carried an edict issued on January 14, which was delivered to Tianjin and then forwarded to Shanghai by telegraph. The content of the edict was of no special importance, mainly concerning the demotion of a delinquent official, but it was the first item of Chinese telegraph news to appear in a major Chinese newspaper, and signaled a revolution in the dissemination of political information in Chinese history. *Shen Bao*'s action was bold in terms of business practice, because at that time sending telegrams was very expensive. It was also politically sensitive. *Shen Bao* was immediately attacked by a rival newspaper as not showing respect to the emperor, since errors were often made in decoding telegraphs at the time. *Shen Bao* countered the accusation by emphasizing the value of the speedy delivery of political news from Beijing.[20]

From the very beginning, *Shen Bao* used the telegraph to disseminate political information speedily yet selectively, two characteristics that we shall see in later Chinese newspapers. After 1882, political news transmitted by telegraph steadily gained prominence in Chinese newspapers. With their speedy methods of publishing political news and attracting wide audiences, modern newspapers such as *Shen Bao* gradually made the traditional *Jing Bao* obsolete and eventually caused it to cease publication shortly before the fall of the Qing dynasty in 1911. It is safe to say that by the turn of the twentieth century, with an established telegraph network and a new wave of newspapers being published, modern newspapers had become the most important means of disseminating and receiving political information in China. In order to better understand the process of how newspapers were transformed after the arrival of the telegraph, let us first take a detour to look at a brief history of *Shen Bao*, a publication that will be cited extensively in the first part of this book.

Telegraphy and *Shen Bao*

Shen Bao was established by a British businessman named Ernest Major in 1872. Major differentiated himself from other foreign newspaper publishers in two areas. First, from the outset, he made it clear that the new newspaper would be for Chinese readers, and thus that it would emphasize news and issues of interest to Chinese, not foreigners. Secondly, he put Chinese compradors in charge of running the business and let Chinese editors pick news items and write editorials. These two methods proved to be very effective. While the Chinese compradors used their knowledge of and connections with the local community to raise circulation and attract advertisements, they kept the price of the paper lower than that of its competitor. Simultaneously, Chinese editors did a better job of making *Shen Bao* appeal to Chinese readers' taste. Within one year, *Shen Bao* had put *Shanghai Xinbao* out of business and became the only Chinese newspaper in Shanghai until the appearance of *Xin Bao* in 1876 and *Hu Bao* in 1882.

The aforementioned news dispatch of 1882 was not the first time *Shen Bao* had published news obtained from telegraphic sources. As we have seen, news had been telegraphed to China much earlier, following the extension of telegraph lines throughout the world. In the West, the telegraph prompted the birth of modern news agencies such as Reuters and Havas (subsequently Agence France-Presse). As early as 1867, Reuter's Telegram Co. Ltd. set up an agency in Shanghai, collecting news mainly on China for its London headquarters, as well as providing news to the *North China Daily News*. After the Great Northern's submarine line reached Shanghai in 1871, Reuters formally set up a branch in Shanghai, issuing news dispatches both outside China and exclusively to the *North China Daily News* within China.[21] Even though *Shen Bao* started to publish telegraph dispatches in January 1874, it had to rely mainly on copies of telegrams from foreign trading companies or reprints from foreign newspapers.[22] Before 1882, *Shen Bao* was thus in no position to compete against foreign-language newspapers in Shanghai in terms of the telegraph dispatches.

After the appearance of *Hu Bao*, *Shen Bao* found itself in an even worse competitive position as far as telegraph news was concerned. Since *Hu Bao* was published by the same company that also published the *North China Daily News*, it shared the same source of telegraph news with the English newspaper. To the relief of the editors of *Shen Bao*, its inferior position with regard to telegraph news did not cause much harm, because the majority of telegraph dispatches provided by foreign sources were items of international news, which the local residents did not pay much attention to. The opening of the Tianjin-Shanghai line, and the subsequent extension of the Chinese domestic network, made it possible for *Shen Bao* to collect and transmit China-centered news more rapidly. In fact, the swift, extensive, and shrewd usage of telegraph news contributed to the further consolidation of *Shen Bao*'s position as the premier newspaper in Shanghai in the 1880s.

This success can be illustrated in *Shen Bao*'s political, social, and military news reports at the time. From its inception, *Shen Bao* distinguished itself from other newspapers by its attention to current political and social issues. For more than three decades, from 1872 to 1905, when an editorial overhaul occurred, *Shen Bao* devoted an enormous amount of space to commentaries and editorials on a variety of issues. These commentaries and editorials, usually written by editors, were on the first page or at the beginning of the second page after the first page became an advertisement page in the late 1880s. Imperial edicts and other important political news immediately followed these commentaries. After Beijing was connected by telegraph line in 1884, edicts could be published in *Shen Bao* the day after they were promulgated. This section of court news received by telegraph was a fixed feature of the newspaper from 1882 to 1905, with only a short hiatus from August 1883 to March 1884. In addition, other kinds of political news sent by telegraph appeared in subsequent years. For example, the emperor's summoning of particular officials was reported, especially in times of political upheaval. On other occasions, an important official's whereabouts and activities were followed by the newspaper through a series of telegrams.[23]

Inasmuch as urban Chinese were *Shen Bao*'s main targets, social news was used to attract more readers. The prompt reporting of events that captured public attention was crucial to outdo the paper's rivals. *Shen Bao* scored a big victory in 1882, when it first published the results of that year's civil service exams, the focus of attention for many Chinese. On October 24, after the results were made public in Beijing, a reporter forwarded the names of the successful candidates from Jiangsu, Zhejiang, and Anhui provinces to Tianjin, whence they were wired to Shanghai and published in *Shen Bao* the next day.[24] This farsighted strategy was a great success. From then on, until the demise of China's civil service exams in 1905, the results were extensively reported by telegraph. Examination topics and the names of the supervising officials, the top three scorers, and the full list of successful candidates were all relayed by wire.

Besides focusing on the Chinese elite through news items such as the results of civil service exams, *Shen Bao* also published other social news received by telegraph. For example, on April 5, 1883, a reporter sent a dispatch from Suzhou about a criminal who had committed suicide. This is the first dispatch on a topic of social news that I have been able to find in *Shen Bao*. Another example of social news arises from the fact that in the 1880s and 1890s, lotteries became popular in coastal China. The winning numbers were announced by telegram, because foreign companies in Southeast Asia issued most of the tickets (commonly called Lusong [Philippine] tickets). Telegraphed lottery results thus became common in *Shen Bao*'s advertising section, and these "happiness-reporting" telegrams certainly expanded the paper's readership to the middle and lower strata of society.

Right after China started its own telegraph services, the country faced a series of international events that became the focus of public attention. In 1882, Korea, then under Chinese suzerainty, suffered a military coup, and *Shen Bao* was able to use the Tianjin-Shanghai line to report on it quickly. Telegraphed military reports on the Sino-Franco War gave *Shen Bao*'s circulation its biggest boost, however. Starting in 1882, with French advances in Vietnam, another country under China's suzerainty, the relationship between China and France became tense, and a series of military conflicts ultimately occurred between 1883 and 1885. As previously mentioned, this prompted the Qing government to construct telegraph lines in southern and southwestern regions, thus facilitating the transfer of news concerning the ongoing conflicts.

The Sino-Franco War lasted more than two years and it was the focus of the Chinese elite at the time. The French attacked Taiwan, destroyed the Chinese southern navy fleet in Fuzhou in 1884, and engaged in a number of battles with the Chinese militia troops (the Black Flag Army) in Vietnam during 1883 and 1885. No decisive victory was scored by either side, which made news about the conflict even more unpredictable and attention-grabbing. *Shen Bao* was determined to use this opportunity to outdo its rival and took a couple of key measures to enhance its reporting of the war.

First, *Shen Bao* hired a number of special correspondents to cover the war in different places, including Haiphong, Hong Kong, Guangzhou, Ningbo, Fuzhou, Xiamen, and Danshui (Taipei). They were among the first field correspondents in Chinese journalism's history. When the war was waged in Vietnam, Ernest Major, the newspaper's owner, hired a Russian to report on it from the battlefront. Although facing obstacles from the French, the Russian was able to spend several days at the front lines and send reports from Haiphong to Hong Kong. These dispatches were then relayed to Shanghai via Xiamen. The same Russian correspondent also covered fighting in Zhenhai in Zhejiang province in March 1883.[25] *Shen Bao* specifically publicized this undertaking to the public in the newspaper, trying to head off furious competition from *Hu Bao*, which enjoyed news dispatches from Reuters, and thus to make itself the most authoritative source of news about the war.[26]

Secondly, *Shen Bao* used telegraphy extensively to transmit war reports. On this front, it enjoyed the advantage of being able to use the newly completed Chinese telegraph lines from Guangzhou to Longzhou in Guangxi province, which is close to the Sino-Vietnamese border. Chinese reporters could use this line to forward news from northern Vietnam to Shanghai, and this subsequently shortened the time needed to transmit news from more than forty days to a matter of a couple of days.[27] By 1884, China had regained control of all landlines. After the war broke out, the Imperial Telegraph Administration stopped the French from issuing and receiving coded telegrams, and intercepted all open-code telegrams related to the war. In the fighting in eastern Zhejiang, the French had to bribe the Great Northern to send telegrams from the mouth of the Yangzi River.[28] This changed situation made the *Shen Bao*'s telegraph dispatches very competitive with other sources.

The availability of telegraphy also helped the appearance of newspaper extras during the Sino-Franco War. Newspaper extras were used to cover urgent news received after the newspaper had already been published on a given day. At seven o'clock on August 6, 1884, *Shen Bao* published its first extra, a telegram informing the public that French warships in Fuzhou had not seen any action. On August 23, *Shen Bao* published an extra predicting the imminent outbreak of a large-scale battle. Indeed, on the afternoon of that day, the battle of Mawei broke out, in which the southern fleet of the Qing empire was destroyed. In 1884 and 1885, *Shen Bao* issued a number of extras on the ongoing war between China and France, which collectively constitute the first extras published by Chinese newspapers.[29]

All these measures made *Shen Bao*'s coverage of the war both extensive and timely, thus greatly enhancing its popularity among Chinese readers and consolidating its position as the leading Chinese newspaper in Shanghai. In summary, the telegraph's impact on Chinese newspapers such as *Shen Bao* was profound and comprehensive. It was not merely limited to providing political information, but also disseminated social, cultural, economic, and military news. Telegraphed reports shortened the time lag between an event and the news of it reaching the public and provided timely follow-ups on both unfolding developments and public responses, enhancing the impact of news on the public. Telegraphed news traveling vast distances also condensed the sense of space among people sharing concerns regarding the same event, making them identify themselves more in terms of their attention to an issue than through their physical location. It was the appearance of modern newspapers, assisted by the telegraph, that made the formation of large-scale public opinion possible. I shall come back to and substantiate this claim in the last part of this chapter.

Newspapers, Social News, and Public Opinion

The formation of public opinion depends on several conditions: common access to information, the availability of channels for expressing individual opinion, and the ability to disseminate individual opinion.[30] In

China, traditional ways of spreading political and social news consisted of word of mouth, private correspondence, official communications, public notices, publications, and papers such as *Di Bao*. The shortcomings of these methods were obvious. It took a long time for the information transmitted to reach a large number of people and, correspondingly, to get feedback. It was also extremely difficult to spread information simultaneously over a vast area by such methods. In other words, the old means of information dissemination were limited both temporally and spatially. The appearance of modern newspapers removed these obstacles and a vibrant, expansive sphere of public opinion could thus be formed.

Social issues seem to have elicited strong reactions from *Shen Bao*'s Shanghai readership in the paper's early days, and extensive follow-up coverage of a single issue could sustain public attention for a significant period of time, as illustrated by its reports on opium den waitresses. In 1872–74, the issue of opium dens using waitresses became a matter of great public concern. Although Shanghai had had brothels and opium dens long before, it had become popular for opium dens to employ young females as waitresses to enhance their attractiveness to their exclusively male clientele in the 1870s. This practice stirred up public uproar, because of the perceived effects of degrading social morals and customs. To the defenders of public morality, this practice blurred the demarcation line between acceptable and unacceptable practices by putting waitresses in the ambiguous position of implicitly providing sex services in the opium dens. Worse still, the opium dens embracing this practice were mostly located in the French Concession, connecting the issue to the presence of foreigners in Shanghai.

Certainly, nothing would have been more eye-catching than drugs, sex, and foreign devils all put together for the consumption of newspaper readers. *Shen Bao* made this matter a focus of public attention at the time and issued several commentaries and editorials appealing for the suppression of the practice of hiring opium den waitresses. Under pressure, the local officials took action, banning the practice in Shanghai proper. Negotiations were also initiated with the French to ban this practice in the Concession too. An opium den operator tried to continue the practice after the public uproar had waned a bit, but was caught. After the French turned the man over to the local authorities, he was severely beaten in the process of interrogation by a local magistrate, prompting a protest from the French, who accused the Chinese of torture. The dramatic yet prolonged unfolding of this issue gave *Shen Bao* plenty of ammunition in cranking out news to feed the public appetite. The editorials and reports in the paper show that public opposition to this practice was so strong that it prompted the local authorities to take serious prohibition measures, at least temporarily. However, according to later *Shen Bao* reports, this practice was never totally eradicated and it eventually made a comeback a few years later.[31]

Shen Bao's reports on the case of Yang Yuelou are another example of public opinion formation. Yang was a famous Peking Opera actor in Shanghai. A Cantonese woman fell in love with Yang after watching his performance and wrote to him asking to be his wife. In the late Qing era, the social status of an opera actor was equivalent to that of a prostitute, and actors were excluded from privileges such as taking the civil service exams. Yang was thus hesitant to accept the woman's proposal. Seeing her daughter falling sick out of love, the woman's mother asked a matchmaker to propose to Yang formally, and this time she was accepted by Yang. However, this arrangement angered the woman's uncle, who thought this marriage would bring dishonor to the extended family, and he asked Yang to break the engagement, to which the latter did not agree. After Yang married the Cantonese woman, he was subsequently accused by the bride's relatives of "seducing a virtuous woman from a good family" and jailed by the magistrate of Shanghai county. Since the case involved a famous actor and a touching love story, it became widely discussed news in Shanghai in the summer of 1873.

Many expected that the local magistrate would nullify the marriage and release the actor after sentencing him to 100 strokes of the cane, as had been done in similar cases before. However, the local magistrate punished Yang by exiling him to a nearby county. This was thought too harsh by *Shen Bao*, because the woman had voluntarily married Yang and there had thus been no "seduction" involved. *Shen Bao* expatiated on the arbitrariness of the magistrate's decision and published readers' letters in support of the newspaper's position. It also revealed that the current magistrate had used torture to interrogate suspects and thus turned public opinion against the magistrate's handling of the case. In the meantime, the woman's family found itself an object of public opprobrium, and the woman was ridiculed as representing the "looseness" of Cantonese women from Xiangshan county, which happened to be the magistrate's home county.[32]

Reactions to *Shen Bao*'s reports on the case came from two sources. On the one hand, the enraged magistrate issued a public notice accusing

Shen Bao of taking a bribe from Yang Yuelou and threatened reprisals against the newspaper. On the other hand, after the attack against the woman's family spread to an attack on people from that region in general, a number of wealthy and influential compradors and officials from Xiangshan county, including Tang Jingxing (manager of the China Merchants Company), Zheng Guanying (later manager of the Imperial Telegraph Administration), and Ye Tingjuan (the Shanghai magistrate) also raised their voices in protest of the newspaper's actions. Furious about *Shen Bao*'s alleged prejudice against the people of their region, and realizing their disadvantaged position without a supporting newspaper, they set up a newspaper called *Hui Bao* (*News Collector*) to compete against *Shen Bao*, although it was only published for one and a half years.[33] This episode shows that the Shanghai elite had realized the important role a newspaper could play in making their voice heard and influencing public opinion.

Shortly after the case of Yang Yuelou, the case of Yang Naiwu and Xiaobaicai also helped raise the profile of *Shen Bao*. As one of the most complex and publicized trials in the late Qing era, the whole story need not concern us here, but the following is a brief outline. Yang Naiwu was a *xiucai* (a candidate who had passed the first level of the civil service exams) in Yuhang (now Hangzhou) and thus a member of the local gentry class. He was accused of having had an adulterous relationship with his neighbor, Xiaobaicai, and of having murdered her husband. The local magistrate, who had had previous conflicts with Yang, tried to use this opportunity to settle personal scores. By falsifying evidence, engaging in perjury, and applying extreme torture, the magistrate coerced Yang into admitting the accusation and sentenced him to death. Yang's relatives went to Beijing and appealed to the imperial court, and Beijing ordered provincial officials to retry the case twice. The original sentence was twice upheld. Under tremendous public pressure, Empress Cixi ordered another trial in Beijing, which finally exonerated Yang and resulted in the revocation of the titles of more than twenty local officials.[34]

Shen Bao's coverage of the case was extensive and protracted. In more than three years, *Shen Bao* printed more than sixty reports and commentaries on the case.[35] At first, they were presented as ordinary social news. However, the fact that Yang's confession was only made after unbearable torture alerted *Shen Bao*'s editors to a possible official cover-up. When *Jing Bao* printed the Censorate's (Ducha Yuan, entrusted with the duty of censuring officials for their neglect or incompetence in official affairs) memorials to the emperor, a crucial part of Yang's petition was abridged. *Shen Bao* obtained the full text from Yang's family and printed it in its entirety in the newspaper, an action that made the case an issue of everyday discussion in Shanghai.[36] After the two retrials that upheld the original sentence, public opinion, aroused by repeated reports in *Shen Bao* on the unfairness and inappropriateness of the local officials' handling of the case, strongly demanded that the higher authorities hold a thorough investigation and conduct a fair retrial of the case. In 1877, eighteen influential figures from Zhejiang province handed a joint petition to the Xing Bu (Justice Department), along with memorials from other high-ranking officials, finally pressing Empress Cixi to act on the case; this resulted in the retrial that vindicated Yang's innocence.

What interests us most here is that in the above three cases, *Shen Bao*'s reporting of social news went far beyond the purpose of promoting its circulation, even though this might well still have been in the editors' minds. These cases signaled the first time in Chinese history that an institution relatively independent of the government (*Shen Bao*) had spoken out on issues of local administration (opium den waitresses) and judicial issues (the cases of Yang Yuelou and Yang Naiwu) that were traditionally in the sole discretion of government. *Shen Bao* not only discussed incidents that attracted widespread attention but also used them to advocate reforms in Chinese society, especially reform of the traditional ways of interrogation and trial that relied heavily on the use of torture and an official's individual judgment.[37] *Shen Bao* was not afraid of expressing its opinions and did not back down even under the local authorities' pressure and threats.[38] In this regard, *Shen Bao* may have been protected by the fact that it was foreign-owned, which in turn made *Shen Bao*'s reporting on social news sometimes a very political act. The demarcation line between social and political would, indeed, become still more blurred in the years to come. Social news could turn very political, and political news could become very social from time to time in the last years of the Qing dynasty.

The appearance of a newspaper like *Shen Bao* enlarged the space for some Chinese to participate in politics by allowing them to express their opinions on certain matters in public and to a large audience. *Shen Bao*'s editors, most of them low-ranking members of the gentry class, used the newspaper to express their opinions on various issues and exerted a greater influence on the public than they might previously have dreamed of before the newspaper era. The newspaper not only spoke on its own behalf but also often on behalf of the general public. In addition, the newspaper provided an outlet for individual opinion by printing it, promoted particular opinions by endorsing them, and spread public opinion by reporting it, thus pressuring the authorities to take public opinion into account in making decisions. As we shall see, modern newspapers' ability to open up an enlarged space for disseminating news and forging public opinion would be further enhanced by the arrival of the telegraph and the speeding up of the dissemination of news.

Political News and Public Telegraphs

In the late nineteenth century, Shanghai did not yet enjoy the political status it has had since the beginning of the twentieth century. With regional political centers still located in Nanjing (the seat of the governor-general of Liangjiang, who has jurisdiction over Jiangsu, Jiangxi, and Anhui provinces) and Suzhou (the seat of the governor of Jiangsu), local political news rarely attracted as much attention as social news. Yet, paradoxically, as Shanghai increasingly became the commercial and financial center of China in the later years of the nineteenth century, it was an indisputable nexus of various kinds of information of national and international importance. In this sense, Shanghai was an important center for disseminating national and international political news.

Telegraphy came to play a crucial role in helping *Shen Bao* report both national and international political news to a Chinese audience. As early as the mid 1870s, *Shen Bao* reported discrimination against Chinese laborers in the United States. This issue was repeatedly reported throughout the rest of the nineteenth century and finally became explosive in 1905, as discussed in detail in Chapter 4. As mentioned above, telegraph news reporting on the Sino-Franco conflict undoubtedly helped *Shen Bao* become an authoritative source of war news in the mid 1880s. Its extensive and timely news reports kept the Chinese informed of the war's progress and enabled them to respond to it, discuss issues, and forge different opinions on an informed basis. The telegraph provided *Shen Bao's* political news of the war and other events in the years that followed, coverage that transcended local, regional, and even national boundaries.

The Sino-Japanese War in 1894 was a watershed in modern Chinese history in many ways. First, China's defeat by an island country that had been deeply influenced by Chinese culture shattered the residual feeling of cultural superiority among many Chinese intellectuals. Secondly, the fact that Japan had become strong after its adoption of Western technologies and institutions provoked the Chinese to pursue reforms. The subsequent sixteen years before the Qing dynasty fell to the revolution witnessed the most active and widespread political participation in modern Chinese history, leading the public to pay more attention to political news and information. It was in this context that the public or circular telegram emerged.

The term "public telegram" refers to telegrams intended for a broad audience and usually sent to multiple recipients; they are also called "circular telegrams." They were "public" either because they were sent as open-coded telegrams or because they were made public by being reprinted in newspapers. In Chinese, they were called either *gongdian* or *tongdian*, the latter word being both a noun and a verb. They were sent to publicize specific positions, opinions, or statements on a particular issue by individuals, groups of people, organizations, or government organs.[39]

Being aware of the extensive use of public telegrams in the 1920s and 1930s, I tried to trace their origin by reading *Shen Bao* and other early Shanghai newspapers. To my surprise, it was not until 1895 that the first public telegrams appeared in *Shen Bao*. After the signing of the Treaty of Shimonoseki, in which China agreed to cede Taiwan to Japan, Chinese in Taiwan decided not to accept their fate without a fight. On May 25, 1895, *Shen Bao* published the whole text of a telegram reading:

We the people of Taiwan will not obey the decision to cede our land to Japan and have asked Governor Tang repeatedly to convey our opinions to the court. While realizing that it is difficult to change the situation, we feel as much misery as a child who lost his or her parents. Since Taiwan has been abandoned by the court and has nobody to rely on, our only option is to defend her with our lives and establish an island country, a country that will revere the emperor from afar and be a protective shield in the South Sea. Leaders are urgently needed under such circumstances. So we strongly urge Governor Tang to stay in office and General Liu Yongfu to defend south Taiwan. In the meanwhile, we shall plead with countries in the international community to intervene impartially, making decisions on how to handle Taiwan's status according to international law concerning the unwillingness of local people to give up ceded territory. We shall let Governor Tang return to Beijing and General Liu return to his official duties afterward. The reason we take these actions is nothing else but our devotion to the Qing dynasty. By holding firm in defending Taiwan, we hope a favorable change will occur. The situation is so urgent that we appeal you to forward our petition by telegraph to the court.

The sender of the telegram was identified as the "whole people of Taiwan." The designated recipients were the Zongli Yamen, the superintendent of trade for the southern ports, the governor-general of Minzhe (Fujian and Zhejiang provinces), the governor of Fujian, and all officials in Taiwan. The telegram was sent on May 13, so it was not published by *Shen Bao* for twelve days. An editorial note reveals that *Shen Bao* obtained the text from a letter sent to the newspaper from Fuzhou, which was signed "gu zhong du bao ren" (a lonely loyal man), suggesting that the sender was probably involved in the fight to keep Taiwan part of the Qing empire. Clearly, the sender wanted the text to be read by as broad an audience as possible. And from the editor's perspective, although the wording of the text was at times "too extreme," it was a reflection of the loyalty of people on Taiwan, and so he decided to reprint it in its entirety.[40]

The next day, *Shen Bao* issued a commentary on the telegraph petition by the people of Taiwan. "Alas, why cannot the Qing keep Taiwan?" the author lamented. He then gave a brief history of Taiwan, stressing the changes achieved since the island had become a province in 1885, and went on to attack the negotiator of the Treaty of Shimonoseki for ceding Taiwan to Japan, although he did not specifically mention Li Hongzhang's name. In concluding, he expressed doubts about the latest telegraphic news received by Shanghai foreign newspapers, which reported that the people of Taiwan had established a republic with Governor Tang as the president. The paper carried telegraphic news from the *Shanghai Mercury* (*Wenhui Xibao*) and the *North China Daily News* (*Zhilin Xibao*) on the establishment of the Republic of Taiwan on the same page as the commentary.

The news turned out to be true. On June 3, *Shen Bao* printed another public telegram sent in the name of the whole people of Taiwan on its first page. The telegram consisted of only sixteen characters in Chinese: "The Taiwan people will never be servants of the Japanese! We would rather become an island country that will always be loyal to the Qing!" The following entry was the full text of a telegram sent by Governor Tang to provincial governors all over China. In the telegram, he explained to his peers that when he was preparing to return to the mainland under the emperor's instructions, he had been presented with the flag and seal of the Republic of Taiwan, established by the people, who were unwilling to surrender to Japan. He had reluctantly accepted the position of president and had telegraphed the court and informed other countries, but he was not sure how long the republic could last. Tang appealed to the officials for help at the end of the telegram.

An editorial that appeared on the same page the same day, entitled "On Adopting a Protracted Strategy to Defend Taiwan," offered a series of suggestions to the Republic of Taiwan on how to defend itself from attacks by Japan. On the next page, the text of the Treaty of Shimonoseki was printed.[41] Using telegrams, editorials, commentaries, and related news reports, *Shen Bao* was thus able to present a comprehensive picture of events to its readers. What is especially of interest here is the appearance of public telegrams in *Shen Bao*. Although the above two public telegrams were not sent directly to newspapers but were forwarded to *Shen Bao* later by third parties, it is obvious that the latter sent their texts to *Shen Bao* in order to publicize them further. Notwithstanding that it might have multiple recipients, a public telegram could not really become "public" if it was not reprinted or reported by newspapers. The rapid development of newspaper publishing and a series of dramatic political events in the years after 1895 provided the public telegram with a more receptive environment in which to flourish.

According to statistics for the years from 1815 to 1890, a total of seventy-six newspapers and magazines were published in Chinese during that period. Of these, thirty-three, or about 43 percent, were published in Shanghai. Although the statistics are incomplete, they nonetheless give us a sense of the dominant position Shanghai held in newspaper and magazine publishing in China.[42] Starting in 1895, stimulated by the defeat in the Sino-Japanese War and prompted by the need to promote reforms, reformers actively joined the newspaper-publishing fray. The most influential reform-oriented newspaper was *Shiwu Bao* (The Chinese Progress, 1896–98), edited by the famous reformer Liang Qichao, which was published three times a month. Starting with a circulation of 4,000, it reached 7,000 within six months and 13,000 after a year. Its peak circulation was 17,000, a record for any Chinese newspaper at the time.[43]

From 1896 to 1898, reformers set up more than forty societies advocating reforms nationwide and published scores of newspapers. During the One Hundred Days Reform in 1898, Emperor Guangxu issued a declaration allowing the publication of official and private newspapers, which further encouraged the publication of reform-oriented newspapers. By 1898, the total number of newspapers published in China was four times that in 1895, and Shanghai was the undisputed center of reform-oriented newspapers and magazines.[44] From 1896 to the eve of the One

Hundred Days Reform, more newspapers were published in Shanghai than in all of the rest of the country. By 1900, there were five daily Chinese newspapers in Shanghai, including *Shen Bao, Hu Bao,* and the more commercially oriented *Xinwen Bao,* which appeared in 1893. Even though after the failure of the One Hundred Days Reform, Empress Cixi issued an edict prohibiting newspapers, Shanghai's newspapers were not severely affected because of the presence of the foreign concessions; newspapers simply listed foreigners as their publishers and thus circumvented the Qing order.[45]

It is safe to say that by 1900, Shanghai had become the news center of China, or even perhaps of the whole Far East. Ironically, most major pieces of political news originated in Beijing, which was under tighter control by the Qing court, and then were disseminated from Shanghai through its vast newspaper network. By that time, China had constructed a nationwide telegraph network, which made the transmission of urgent news more feasible. The upheaval in political circumstances and the precipitous foreign crises China faced at the turn of twentieth century made telegraph news abundant in newspapers. In addition, the telegraph was not only used to convey urgent news but also employed by the Chinese elite as a means of political mobilization and maneuvering at the national and international levels. The years 1899 and 1900 witnessed large-scale use of circular telegrams for the first time in Chinese history.

CHAPTER THREE

Telegraphy, Political Participation, and State Control

O N JANUARY 24, 1900, Empress Dowager Cixi issued an edict designating a member of the imperial family, Fujun, as foster son of Emperor Tongzhi, who had died without issue. While this kind of practice was not unheard of in dynastic history, it was obvious to the public that her true intention was to replace Emperor Guangxu, who had been deprived of all power after the failed One Hundred Days Reform and placed under house arrest on an island in the imperial compound in Beijing since September 1898. When the news of the edict reached Shanghai next day, it stunned the local elite. Among them was Jing Yuanshan, who happened to be the chief (*zongban*) of the Shanghai Telegraph Administration (henceforth STA). Jing telegraphed a minister in Beijing the same night asking him to appeal to Empress Cixi, along with other high-ranking officials, but the reply was that nothing could be done. Determined to speak out, Jing went to the telegraph administration the next day and met a number of other people who were there to appeal to Beijing. After discussing the matter, Jing and the others promptly agreed to send a joint telegram. Because of Jing's position, he was asked to lead the appeal in this public telegram to the Zongli Yamen, which was signed by 1,231 influential figures in Shanghai. The text of the telegram in its entirety was:

To your Excellencies, Princes and Ministers: My telegraph administration has received the edict of the 24th, which caused an uproar in people's minds in Shanghai. It is said that foreign countries are considering military intervention. We appeal to you, for the sake of the country, to exercise your justice and loyalty, and to petition the Emperor to stay on the throne and not to consider stepping down. By doing so, we could allay the concerns of the Empress, on the one hand, and mitigate the shock both in China and abroad, on the other. This will be fortunate for the imperial family, as well as for all under heaven! Prefect Jing Yuanshan and one thousand two hundred and thirty-one members of the gentry, merchants, officials, and common people residing in Shanghai from various provinces send this joint telegraphic petition.[1]

This telegram was widely circulated in newspapers nationwide. Empress Cixi, under the pressure of extremely unfavorable public opinion, did not go ahead and formally dethrone Emperor Guangxu. However, she was very angry about Jing's telegraph. Two days later, Jing was alerted by Sheng Xuanhuai that he should leave Shanghai immediately. Jing left for Hong Kong the next day and eventually arrived at Macao on February 7. On February 25, he was arrested by the Portuguese authorities acting on a request from the Qing court on a charge of embezzlement and was detained in a fortress on Macao. Jing was well treated by the Portuguese, and, most important, the Macao authorities refused the Qing government's extradition request, but it was not until one and a half years later that he was finally released.[2]

Jing Yuanshan, Telegraphy, and National Politics

The above episode illustrates the increasing role played by the telegraph in Chinese politics at the turn of the twentieth century and the government's efforts to strengthen its control of it. The appointing of an heir to the Emperor Tongzhi was an important event in 1900, but attention to it in history has been obscured by emphasis on the Boxer Rebellion, which broke out later in the same year.[3] Empress Cixi's action arose directly from the One Hundred Days Reform a year and a half earlier. The details of this need not concern us here, but a brief look at the background will facilitate understanding of subsequent events.

China's defeat in the Sino-Japanese War prompted a strong appeal for reforms among the Chinese elite, represented by Kang Youwei, Liang Qichao, and Tan Sitong. These reform-minded intellectuals had the support of the young emperor, but the real power rested in the hands of Empress Cixi and the conservative officials surrounding her. In 1898, when reformers successfully persuaded the emperor to take the initiative, their actions were mostly confined to issuing imperial edicts calling for reforms, of which some were very bold and were seen as threatening the fundamentals of the Qing dynasty. When it became obvious that Empress Cixi's intervention was imminent, Kang and Tan tried unsuccessfully to mount a military coup to get rid of her, which resulted in complete suppression of the reforms, the subsequent execution of Tan and five other prominent reformers, and the house arrest of Emperor Guangxu in Beijing. Kang Youwei and Liang Qichao escaped from Beijing with the help of foreigners and continued to agitate for reform from overseas.

Immediately after the failure of the short-lived reform movement, the fate of Emperor Guangxu became a key concern of the reformers, or according to contemporary classifications at that time, members of the "emperor's party" or "new party," in opposition to the "empress's party" or "old party." These two groups were the primary political players before the "revolutionary party" led by Sun Yat-sen gained increasing influence in the coming years. Away from China and outside the center of power, the reformers continued to rely mainly on public opinion to exert political influence within China and overseas. At the end of 1898, Liang Qichao began publishing a periodical called *Qingyi Bao* (The China Discussion) in Japan, in which the issue of protecting Emperor Guangxu and opposing the crowning of a new emperor was emphasized from the first issue.[4] In July 1899, Kang Youwei established the Society for Protecting the Emperor in Canada and set up more than 170 branches in Chinese communities all over the world. The reformers still enjoyed a great deal of popularity, and the 1,231 senders of the joint telegram were certainly among their supporters or sympathizers.

Jing Yuanshan, the protagonist of the episode, does not readily fit into the dichotomies of empress's party versus emperor's party or conservatives versus reformers, which have been the focus of mainstream scholarly works. Jing had a unique career compared with the Western Affairs Clique and most reform advocates. Jing was born into a wealthy business family in 1840, and after his father died, he was asked at an early age to take over the family-run money-lending business in Shanghai, so he did not follow the normal path of advancement in Chinese society by taking the civil service exams. A shrewd businessman, he made a fortune and became well established in money-lending circles in Shanghai. Jing acquired his social reputation through philanthropic activities in the late 1870s, when China was confronted by a series of natural calamities. Jing organized the Public Association of Relief Funds (Xiezhen gongsuo) to coordinate fund-raising activities in Shanghai and nearby Jiangsu and Zhejiang provinces. He turned out to be a very effective fund-raiser and was praised by the Qing court a number of times. His influence in Shanghai financial circles and his ability to raise a huge amount of relief funds resulted in his being befriended by a number of key figures in the Western Affairs faction, including Sheng Xuanhuai and Zheng Guanying, and also made him known to powerful officials such as Li Hongzhang and Liu Kunyi. Jing was appointed by Li as deputy chief of the STA in the summer of 1881, and the following year, he was promoted to the post of chief, which he held until his exile in 1900.

Jing became head of the STA mainly because of his investments in telegraphy rather than because of political affiliations. In 1882, when the Imperial Telegraph Administration was converted into a commercial enterprise, Sheng Xuanhuai asked Jing to invest 10,000 taels, or one-eighth of the original value of the stock. In Jing's own words, "at the time nobody was sure that the telegraph services would ever be profitable. I did my best, wishing to work together with others and to support the whole plan."[5] As mentioned in Chapter 1, Jing also helped to raise funds to construct a line along the coast connecting Shanghai and Guangzhou. As a businessman, Jing paid less attention to how to keep telegraphy under official control and more to running the STA as a profitable commercial operation. For example, under Jing, the STA extended its service hours and lowered the price of telegrams, thus broadening the accessibility of telegraph service. Under his management, the revenue of the STA and its profits increased steadily. From 1894 to 1898, revenue increased from 139,959 silver dollars to 386,728 silver dollars, while profits increased from 5,723 to 26,085 silver dollars.[6]

The episode described earlier in this chapter was not the first time Jing had tried to use the telegraph for national political ends. At the end of 1894, after China's defeat in the Sino-Japanese War, Jing responded enthusiastically to a ten-article public appeal by Zhong Tianwei, a reformer, for a public fund-raising campaign nationwide to organize a volunteer army to fight the Japanese.[7] In a public letter to fund-raisers nationwide, Jing proposed to compile a special telegraph codebook to keep their correspondence speedy and secret. In addition, using his position at the STA, he would instruct local branches to treat all fund-raising-related telegrams as official telegrams and thus forward them promptly.[8] However, in reality, Jing's enthusiasm met little response, because many felt that the ten-article public appeal was too politically sensitive and beyond their capacities. Soon afterward, the Qing court sent Li Hongzhang to Japan to negotiate a peace treaty, and the fund-raising initiative died before it really even got started.

Jing was also involved in other social activities. He was the founder of the first women's school in Shanghai. He believed that since every individual's education started with his or her mother, it was crucial for women to be educated. When he sought to use surplus telegraph administration funds to finance the women's school, however, Sheng Xuanhuai and other board members did not support him. Not discouraged, Jing raised the funds himself and opened the women's school in 1898.[9] He was also enthusiastic in funding and organizing newspaper-reading clubs in Shanghai in 1898 to educate the general public.[10]

Although he evidently leaned strongly toward reform, Jing was not a clear-cut follower of Kang Youwei, because he sometimes saw Kang's reforms as too radical.[11] In the heyday of the 1898 reform, Jing initiated a fund-raising campaign to renovate the memorial hall for Chen Huacheng, the general who resisted the British in the Wusong fortress during the First Opium War and who has been considered a martyr by the Chinese ever since. He advocated regular gatherings in the spring and autumn by supporters in the memorial hall, in order to "uphold Confucianism and correct people's hearts" (the gatherings were called *jingzhen*, which literarily means "everlasting righteousness"), showing that he insisted that Confucian ideas be the basis for China's rejuvenation. His relationship with the reformers can best be described, using his own words, as "conforming but not identical; a friend but not a clique member" (*he er bu tong, qun er bu dang*).[12] His actions in January 1900 thus went beyond the expectations of most reformers.

As to his relationship with members of the Western Affairs Clique, Jing was more a businessman than a government bureaucrat. He was critical of the system of "commercial management under official supervision" through which most modern business enterprises at the time were run by the Western Affairs Clique. Jing pointed out that "official supervision" was one of the major obstacles that impeded the development of business in China. "It would be nice if the officials could protect business," Jing said, "but today's official supervision is in fact encroaching on private business affairs and results instead in the running of business by officials." The result, Jing lamented, was a vicious cycle "using government to dominate business, and using business to mislead government."[13] He concluded that even though Li Hongzhang and Zhang Zhidong were regarded as leaders in the Qing dynasty's quest for revitalization, given what he had seen and heard personally, it would be a difficult task for the court to achieve its goal under such mediocre stewardship.[14]

In summary, Jing Yuanshan was a complex figure. First and foremost, he was a successful businessman, and this enabled him to participate in social and political activities. He was open-minded on reforms, but only to serve the purpose of preserving the fundamentals of Confucian ideas. He was a true patriot, as shown by his reverence for Chen Huacheng and his proposed fund-raising plan after the Sino-Japanese War. Jing could be called a businessman, a philanthropist, and a pioneer of women's education, but he was definitely not a politician. His actions in January 1900 were not the result of historical contingency, as Jing admitted to a Japanese correspondent, "if I had not been in the Telegraph Administration, I might not have taken such an action," but rather derived from his conviction that the public should be allowed to participate in national policymaking.[15]

Yet Jing's multiple identities and complex sociopolitical positions illustrate the broadened spectrum of political participation in China by the turn of the twentieth century. In fact, like Jing, numerous participants in late Qing politics often had multiple, fluid political identities. They might agree on one issue but disagree on another, and this often made political discussion and participation parochial. However, the succession to the throne was an issue that aroused attention all over the country, and the advantage of being able to use the telegraph as a means of speedy communication was highly appreciated. In fact, through the telegraph and newspapers, the emperor protection movement operated not only within China but also far beyond the borders of the Qing empire.

Circular Telegrams and the Emperor Protection Movement

The telegram sent by Jing Yuanshan and his fellow signers to the Zongli Yamen struck concerned Chinese all over the world like a political bombshell. When the news spread, it stirred up a furious reaction from Emperor Guangxu's supporters and sympathizers. In Shanghai, led by Ye Zhifang and Bao Shiteng, a total of 785 Chinese Christians and merchants also sent protest telegrams to Beijing. The emperor's supporters printed more than 10,000 leaflets to be distributed in the Yangzi River area and planned to print an additional two million copies to be distributed nationwide.[16] In Sichuan, members of the gentry and merchants gathered in front of the governor-general's office compound to ask him to telegraph Beijing to oppose the attempt to dethrone Emperor Guangxu. It was reported that in Sichuan the emperor's supporters were even considering proclaiming autonomy and allying with Shaanxi province in support of the emperor's legitimacy. In Guangdong, concerned people held gatherings to discuss the situation. In Guangxi, a total of 383 members of the gentry sent a joint telegram to the Zongli Yamen asking Empress Cixi to hand over power to the emperor. In Hangzhou, hundreds gathered to discuss the issue and decided to send a protest telegram to Beijing, which was signed by thousands of people.[17]

A more dramatic episode occurred in Hubei when Judicial Commissioner Cen Chunming and fifty-two other officials drafted a petition and went to meet Governor-General Zhang Zhidong and Governor Yinlin, asking them to forward it to Beijing. While the governor agreed to second their petition, Zhang Zhidong declined the request and admonished Cen not to be reckless. Angered by Zhang's attitude, Cen placed his official hat on Zhang's table and asked Zhang to find a replacement for him, because he and others would go to Beijing to protest the edict in person, regardless of whether this endangered their lives. Zhang tried to prevent them from doing so, but to no avail.[18]

Protest telegrams also came from overseas Chinese communities. The telegraph certainly shortened the spatial and temporal distance between Beijing and Chinese subjects overseas. On February 9, *Thien Nan Shin Pao*, the mouthpiece of the Society for Protecting the Emperor in Singapore, published its first issue after the Chinese New Year, in which it printed a compilation of special telegrams on the attempted dethronement. According to reports published in the paper, the newspaper received the news in a telegram from Shanghai at one o'clock on January 26. The sender asked overseas Chinese to telegraph Beijing opposing the dethronement. Chinese all over the world, from Singapore, Kuala Lumpur, and Hong Kong to San Francisco, New York, and Honolulu and Yokohama, Nagasaki, and Kobe, responded strongly.[19] Protest telegrams were often signed by large numbers of people or sent on behalf of all local Chinese. For example, Chinese in Thailand sent a telegram of protest to the Zongli Yamen on January 31. On February 20, a telegram from Beijing spread the news that the emperor had been poisoned and was near to death, and this prompted the Chinese in Thailand to send a strongly worded telegram to Beijing signed by 80,000 people. A similar telegram was sent to Beijing by a group of merchants on behalf of 47,000 Chinese in Burma.[20]

Empress Cixi was apparently caught off guard by the strength of public opinion against her decision to designate an heir to Emperor Tongzhi, and on this issue, she found she could not even get support from her most trusted man in court, Ronglu. It was also widely reported that foreign delegations in Beijing were not supportive of the move. Discouraged, she backed down slightly, giving Fujun only the title of "eldest prince" (da a-ge). Her reported plan to dethrone Emperor Guangxu did not material-ize. The wave of circular telegrams from Chinese all over the world demonstrated the telegraph's ability to speedly disseminate information and showed how effectively it could be used to mobilize public opinion on issues of broad concern. In fact, the telegraphic protest of 1900 was the culmination of an ongoing struggle between Cixi and diehard Guangxu supporters after the One Hundred Days Reform. It was not the first time that the telegraph had been used for political purposes by over-seas Chinese. Indeed, it is instructive to take a retrospective look at the unfolding of the whole series of events from their start after the failure of the One Hundred Days Reform.

There is evidence that Empress Cixi was considering deposing Em-peror Guangxu as soon as she took back power in 1898. In an apparent attempt to prepare for the next step in her scheme, well-known doctors were publicly summoned by edict to offer service to the emperor, who was allegedly "in poor health" in 1898. On September 4, 1899, the em-peror issued an edict declaring that he saw no significant improvement after taking medicine for so long. The emperor's supporters were alarmed by the underlying symbolic political meanings this news carried and saw it as the prelude to Empress Cixi's plot to depose the emperor.[21] Given the fact that reform advocates were under severe suppression in China and that the remaining major figures were in exile and active in promoting their cause in overseas Chinese communities, it is not surprising that it was the overseas Chinese who first used the telegraph to express their loyalty to the emperor.

These overseas Chinese adopted the very politically savvy strategy of sending public telegrams to Beijing to wish the emperor a speedy recov-ery. On September 26, 1899, led by Qiu Shuyuan, a rich merchant with the rank of *juren* (a candidate who had passed the provincial level of civil service exams), several scores of Chinese merchants gathered in Singa-pore, drafted a telegram and prepared leaflets to be distributed in Singa-pore and to nearby islands. When they met again six days later, about eighty more people had signed the telegram, and it was decided to send it ten days later to allow extra time for additional people to sign. The telegram was duly sent on October 12 to the Zongli Yamen and read as follows:

As merchants and common people, we have heard that since the empress started to supervise the court and the emperor had to summon doctors in September last year, the emperor has stopped receiving officials and performing ceremonies. All the emperor's subjects under heaven are deeply worried by this. We have also read the edict of July 30 [September 4 in the solar calendar] saying that the emperor's health has not seen significant improvement [even] after taking medicine for a long period of time, and this makes us extremely concerned and has also caused many rumors to circulate. Although we are in foreign lands, we love our emperor with all our hearts. Please forgive our impudence and allow us to wish his majesty well. We urge our emperor to take better care of his health, for the sake of the dynasty and because of the best wishes from his subjects all over the world. The emperor's good health would bring good fortune to the dynasty, as well as to all under heaven! This petition is jointly signed by all the merchants and people [in Singapore and surrounding areas]. Please forward it to his majesty on our behalf! [22]

The tone of such telegrams was very mild, because at that time, even though most overseas Chinese wished Emperor Guangxu to be restored to power, they still acknowledged the political legitimacy of the Qing dynasty. The initiator of this circular telegram, Qiu Shuyuan, had at one time been a follower of Kang Youwei and shared the latter's primary concern for protecting and restoring the emperor. Kang had a broad following for this cause among overseas Chinese at the end of the nineteenth century.

Those who wanted to send a stronger signal to Empress Cixi chose an appropriate occasion shortly afterward to deliver their message, once again by means of circular telegrams. This time, in the name of celebrating Empress Cixi's birthday, senders of congratulatory telegrams asked her to step down and hand over power to Emperor Guangxu. Cixi's birthday was October 10, 1835, in the lunar calendar (November 29, 1835 in the solar calendar; November 12 in 1899). When news reached Kuala Lumpur that Chinese in Singapore had decided to send such a telegram to Beijing on her birthday, a total of 700 merchants promptly decided to follow suit and sent a telegram of more than 170 characters.[23] On the same day, several hundred Chinese merchants in Batavia (Jakarta in Indonesia) also sent a birthday celebration telegram to Empress Cixi. In addition, a lengthier petition letter was also sent through the Dutch postal service to the Zongli Yamen in Beijing.[24] Although all of them were purportedly sent to celebrate Empress Cixi's birthday, the essence of these messages was the same, requesting her to step down, in the name of "kind wishes" to her, for the sake of her health and a happy old age.

The global scale of the telegraph campaign had much to do with the strong influence of the Society for Protecting the Emperor on the Chinese in general and overseas Chinese in particular at this time. In fact, Kang Youwei and his followers would continue to employ birthday-celebrating telegrams to pressure Empress Cixi to restore Emperor Guangxu. When Guangxu's birthday came in 1900 (June 28 in lunar calendar, July 24, 1900 in solar calendar), the Society for Protecting the Emperor sent a new wave of telegrams to Beijing.[25] By that time, however, the Boxer Rebellion was a more salient issue, and the influence of these telegrams was in no way comparable to that of Jing Yuanshan's telegram of January 26, 1900.

Although the telegraph had come to be more frequently used to convey political messages, it remained a technology that transferred information between two points, namely, the sender and the recipient. Political telegrams might, of course, have multiple senders and recipients, but their effect would have been severely diminished if they had not been widely publicized to focus public attention on them. The best way to achieve this at the time was to reprint them in newspapers. Thanks to the increased number of newspapers in China, political telegrams were reprinted with increasing frequency, but it was the editors who decided which telegrams to publish, and newspapers with different political positions differed in their choices.

Getting protest telegrams into Shanghai newspapers turned out to be relatively easy in January 1900. In fact, a number of influential figures in Shanghai press circles also signed Jing Yuanshan's telegram on January 26.[26] The newspapers they edited, *Su Bao, Zhongwai Ribao, Tongwen Hubao, Yadong Shishi Huibao,* and *Zhongwai Dashi Bao*, all printed editorials and commentaries opposing Empress Cixi's move. It is interesting to note that even Shanghai tabloids (*xiaobao*) were very active in covering this episode, relying heavily on foreign-language newspapers such as the *North China Daily News* for information about the unfolding of the events.[27]

In contrast, *Shen Bao* was one of few Shanghai newspapers, Chinese or foreign, that took Empress Cixi's side. *Shen Bao* had maintained a pro-Cixi, pro-government position ever since Huang Xiexun had taken over the editorship in 1898. *Shen Bao*'s reports on the protest telegram of January 26 thus showed little sympathy for Jing Yuanshan. On February 4, the paper first reported that Jing had been relieved of his position at the STA because he had become mentally disturbed. In ensuing reports,

Shen Bao designated Jing as a "fugitive official" and reported his arrest in Macao with apparent approval.[28]

However, Jing was hailed by Liang Qichao as a hero destined to be remembered in history for his brave action, which had launched a wave of protest all over the world. Liang was editing *Qingyi Bao* in Japan at the time, where it was published three times a month. Although it was not until February 20, 1900, that the newspaper responded in its issue no. 36 to the appointment of an heir to the throne, its coverage was comprehensive, detailed, and spanning several consecutive issues. In no. 36, the paper reprinted the full text of the January 26 telegram initiated by Jing Yuanshan, provided background analysis on the origins of and intentions behind Cixi's move, described the unfolding of the whole event from different news sources, reported the protests all over the world, and compiled reports and comments by a number of Chinese and foreign newspapers.[29] Considering that *Qingyi Bao* had many distribution outlets in Beijing, Shanghai, Tokyo, Yokohama, Sydney, Honolulu, Singapore, San Francisco, Lima, and other places with large Chinese communities, the replacement of Emperor Guangxu not only caught national attention but became a hotly contested issue beyond the borders of China.

In the whole process, Shanghai had demonstrated its role as China's press center at the turn of the twentieth century. Political news from Beijing was telegraphed to Shanghai and reprinted by newspapers there. Because Shanghai was also China's telecommunications center, it was also easy to get news from overseas, especially from overseas Chinese communities. Moreover, the foreign-language newspapers in Shanghai constituted additional news sources for their Chinese-language counterparts. Reports carried in Shanghai newspapers were reprinted in Chinese newspapers around the world and further mobilized overseas Chinese. The predominantly pro-Guangxu position of the Shanghai press had a substantial influence on domestic public opinion, which was a blow to Empress Cixi. Political information was thus disseminated and political participation occurred globally for the first time in Chinese history owing to the role of the telegraph and modern newspapers in communicating across national borders and connecting Chinese worldwide.

Telegraphy, Politics, and State Control

The role of the Chinese press worldwide thirty-five years later shows that Shen Baozhen's fear in 1865 of the potential danger of the telegraph spreading "rumors" by way of newspapers was not baseless. Trying to regain control of the monopoly of political information after the coup of 1898, Empress Cixi attempted to rectify the "wrongdoings" of the reformers by issuing edicts prohibiting newspaper publishing. But Cixi's order met strong resistance. Because many Shanghai newspapers were either registered in the names of foreigners or switched to foreign control on paper after the edicts, the actual effect of newspaper prohibition on Shanghai was not severe. In fact, in August and September 1898, two pro-reform newspapers, *Zhongwai Dashi Bao* (China and Foreign Necessary News) and *Wuzhou Shishi Huibao* started to publish in Shanghai and continued to voice pro-reform opinions after the coup on September 21.[30] The appearance of these newspapers demonstrates that by 1900, the Qing court had virtually lost its grasp on the press in Shanghai.

Attempts by the Qing court to control the telegraph followed the same trajectory and met with similar results. As mentioned in Chapter 1, a concern for control was overwhelming for Qing policymakers from the very beginning. Although the goal of keeping the telegraph under Chinese control was achieved, the Qing court was always concerned with keeping this technology under tight government control as well. In a process with clear parallels more than a hundred years later in current Chinese government efforts to control the Internet, measures were taken to regulate the telegraph at three levels: infrastructure, service, and content.

In the area of infrastructure, the Qing government either took the initiative to construct telegraph lines itself or allowed private entrepreneurs to carry out the task. Two telegraph administrations thus coexisted in China, one called Shangdian Ju (the commercial telegraph administration) and one called Guandian Ju (the official telegraph administration). The former was in charge of commercially constructed and managed lines in China under the auspices of the Imperial Telegraph Administration (ITA), providing both official and private telegraph services, while the latter was in charge of those lines constructed by the government mainly for the purpose of official communications, especially between the center and frontier areas. In most cases, these latter lines had little commercial application, and they were often poorly managed. Thus, unsurprisingly, in the late Qing period, none of the eleven official telegraph administrations was profitable.[31]

The Qing authorities were very keen to control telegraph service providers after 1881. In addition to the Guandian Ju under direct government control, the government also had significant control of the ITA.

Even after the ITA was converted to a shareholder company, it was still a uniquely joint operation between business and government, and its regime of control was described as "commercial management under official supervision." In emergencies, the Qing government could instruct the ITA to stop providing services to specific parties. For example, during the Sino-Franco War, the ITA stopped issuing and receiving coded telegrams for the French, thus substantially decreasing the efficiency of communication between Paris and Beijing. In a complementary fashion, during the war, local telegraph branches were instructed to concentrate on official telegrams concerning the war. Serving the government's needs was thus always the priority of the ITA.[32]

However, it was very difficult for the Qing authorities to control all possible providers of telegraph services. In fact, ten years before the ITA started to operate, a telegraph service was made available to Chinese in Shanghai, of whom the majority were merchants, after the Shanghai–Hong Kong submarine telegraph line was completed by the Great Northern in 1871. Starting on April 22, 1871, *Shanghai Xinbao* ran an advertisement, placed by a *dianbao hang* (telegraph service company) located on Nangxun Road, specifically asking Shanghai merchants who wanted to receive telegrams from Hong Kong to provide their personal and company names. One month later, the same telegraph service company ran another advertisement asking local merchants to go to the company's service office to send telegrams in person in order to facilitate double-checking between Chinese characters and the telegraph codes. The advertisement also proclaimed the availability of a codebook. Buying the book would enable Chinese merchants to code their telegrams themselves, so that they would therefore not have to go to the telegraph office in person.[33] After the establishment of the ITA, all telegrams should theoretically have been sent via the Chinese-controlled landlines, but it was actually easy for well-connected compradors to send telegrams via foreign-controlled undersea cables from Shanghai. The connectivity of the telegraph worldwide, its availability overseas, and the existence of foreign telegraph service in Shanghai were all factors that further complicated government efforts to control telegraphic traffic. The rich and powerful in major port cities and overseas Chinese could always access telegraph services that were beyond the control of the Qing dynasty.

The Qing government also took measures to control the content of telegrams. First of all, as has been noted, telegrams were classified into two major categories, official and private, with the former always enjoying priority over the latter. Official telegrams not only had to relate to official business, but the sender had to be a governor or of higher rank. In 1896, Wang Lian, the Zhili financial commissioner, used an official telegram to plead for leniency on behalf of a person who had been impeached before the emperor. Wang was subsequently accused of using an official telegram to intervene in an official matter that lay beyond his official responsibility. Even though Wang asked Wang Wenshao, one of the most influential officials in the court, to plead on his behalf, he was deprived of his rank by the emperor.[34] Since he was an official only one rank below the governor, Wang's punishment for "misusing" a telegram was unusually harsh and shows how the unauthorized sending of a telegram could trigger a power struggle among Qing officials.

Blocking transmission was another method used to control the contents of telegrams. It was reported that after receiving the first wave of telegrams protesting Empress Cixi's attempt to dethrone the Emperor Guangxu, Beijing instructed the STA to stop sending and receiving any telegrams protesting Cixi's decision. After this order, several dozen protest telegrams were put on hold by the STA. In fact, overseas Chinese sent telegrams not only to the Zongli Yamen but also to foreigners asking them to intervene. The Chinese in Burma put a public fund-raising notice in *Thien Nan Shin Pao* in order to send telegrams to the British minister in Beijing and the emperor of Japan, appealing to them to help protect Emperor Guangxu.[35] In addition to sending telegrams to the Zongli Yamen, the Chinese in Kuala Lumpur also tried to send telegrams to the British minister in Beijing. However, the ITA refused to carry these telegrams when they reached China. Even though foreigners and foreign telegraph companies protested, the Chinese insisted that they had the right to decide which telegrams were or were not admissible.[36] This was reported in newspapers, however, showing that attempts by the court to control the spread of political information were having little success.

This was not the first time that the court had tried to block unwelcome telegrams. When overseas Chinese initiated a wave of telegrams to Beijing supporting Emperor Guangxu and pressuring Empress Cixi to step down in 1899, the ITA refused to accept them. Until the fall of the Qing dynasty, the ITA periodically instructed its local branches to block certain kinds of telegrams from being sent or received. But the Qing officials' ability to control content was also limited by the telegraph technology itself. Telegrams could be sent and received in code, and it was very difficult for the ITA to screen coded telegrams and block inadmissible ones.

To make the things worse, a great number of codebooks were available to telegraph users, and a special set of codes could easily be established for correspondence among a small number of users.[37] It was simply impossible for the ITA to control the content of telegrams completely.

Yet certain features of telegraph technology at the same time also helped ease the task of control for the Qing government. The scope of telegraph services was severely limited by their availability, accessibility, and affordability. Telegraph services were mostly available in urban centers and were highly concentrated in coastal areas where commercial demand was high. They were thus not available in the greater part by far of the empire's territory. In addition, because of the high cost of sending a telegram, only a small portion of the population could afford to use the service. When the Tianjin-Shanghai line opened, the cost of sending an open code telegram to Shanghai was fifteen cents a character from Tianjin, fourteen cents from Jining, and ten cents from the nearest station, Suzhou. When more lines were completed, the highest price reached 23 cents a character, based on the distance between sender and receiver.[38] Only rich and powerful people residing in metropolitan areas were thus likely users, and the task the authorities faced was mostly to control telegraph use by the Chinese elite.

Retrospectively, the Qing government's attempts to control telegraph services fell into three distinct phases. In the first, from 1881 to 1894, the Qing court was a main beneficiary of the telegraph, which it used to help administer its vast empire. The telegraph was also widely used by commercial undertakings, and to a lesser degree, for reporting news, with little explicit expression of political opinions or policy preferences. In the second phase, from 1895 to 1904, the public telegram appeared and was increasingly used as a tool of political expression and participation. In the third phase, from 1905 to 1911, telegrams were instrumental in mobilizing the nation and conducting debates on national policies.

Trying desperately to hold on to its diminishing control at the turn of the twentieth century, the Qing court lashed out by punishing offenders. Its prosecution of Jing Yuanshan is a good example. Nonetheless, the news of Jing's arrest in Macao was featured in many newspapers and was generally reported sympathetically, and the development of his case was closely followed by the press. In addition to many Chinese appealing for his release, it was also reported that the British governor of Hong Kong had intervened personally, asking the Portuguese not to hand Jing back to the Qing authorities. In the meantime, the Portuguese treated Jing more like a political dissident than a criminal fugitive. They put him in a fortress with a number of rooms, allowed members of his family to stay with him, and provided him with various daily comforts. It turned out to be very difficult for the Qing officials to substantiate their embezzlement charges against Jing. After a long trial, Jing was eventually released by the Portuguese in the summer of 1901.[39]

Telegraphy, Political Maneuver, and "Mutual Protection of the Southeast"

With the decline of the political legitimacy of Empress Cixi's rule, divisions among the ruling elite of the Qing dynasty became increasingly visible. As mentioned earlier, important Qing figures were strongly against Empress Cixi's appointing a new heir, although they did not voice their disagreement publicly. Only five months later, in the midst of the Boxer Rebellion, a group of governors-general and governors found themselves in a position totally opposing Empress Cixi's xenophobic policies and had to take swift action to avoid further disaster. This time, it was Sheng Xuanhuai, Jing Yuanshan's superior, who played a critical role in the whole process of promoting consensus among these provincial officials, and the Imperial Telegraph Administration under his direction was instrumental in manipulating political information by selectively blocking or speeding up communications through coded telegrams, in sharp contrast to the use of circular telegrams.

In modern Chinese history, this historical episode in 1900 is referred to as the "mutual protection of the Southeast." In the 1890s, the Boxers (Righteous and Harmonious Fists), who originally belonged to a branch of a secret society named the Eight-Trigram Sect, turned from being anti-Manchu to being anti-foreigner. They claimed that they possessed magic ability that made them immune to bullets. Encouraged first by conservative provincial officials and then by the court, in early 1900, a large number of Boxers entered Bejing and its port city, Tianjin, as well as surrounding areas. Anything foreign or showing foreign influence was their target, including not only Christian churches, missionaries, and Chinese converts but also railroad and telegraph lines.[40]

From mid-June to mid-August, the Boxers besieged the foreign legation compound, until a joint force consisting of troops from eight countries entered Beijing on August 14. Frustrated by the foreigners who had prevented her from carrying out many actions, including appointing a

new heir, Empress Cixi supported the Boxers' attacks on the foreign legation compound, and on June 21, 1900, declared war on all foreign powers. Her action shocked many Qing officials, including Sheng Xuanhuai,
then the director of the imperial railway and telegraph systems. Sheng
was not a supporter of the Boxers at first. On May 29, Sheng issued two
telegraph memorials to Beijing from Hankou, reporting damage inflicted
on the Beijing-Baoding railway by the Boxers and asking the court to order provincial officials to protect the railways and telegraph lines. On
June 5, Sheng issued another memorial by telegraph asking the court to
order local officials to adopt severe measures to suppress the Boxers. He
warned that "internal upheavals and external aggressions would follow"
if action was not taken.[41] Sheng used the telegraph to keep in close contact with government officials—especially with provincial officials in the
Yangzi Valley and coastal areas, whom Sheng kept informed on developments in Beijing and asked them to come up with plans to solve the crisis. In a telegram sent to Liu Kunyi, governor-general of Liangjiang, and
Zhang Zhidong, governor-general of Huguang, on June 14, Sheng
warned that if the two governors-general "did not come up with a strategy, the situation will be one of imminent danger."[42]

Realizing the disastrous consequences of Empress Cixi's declaration of
war and responding to the threat of foreign military intervention, on June
22, an urgent memorial from the governors-general and governors of five
provinces was sent to Beijing asking Empress Cixi to suppress the Boxers
and negotiate a settlement with the Western powers.[43] Sheng Xuanhuai,
along with other provincial officials, sent another telegram to Ronglu
and Prince Qing, suggesting that Li Hongzhang, then governor-general of
Liangguang, be given full powers to negotiate with foreign powers. On
June 25, Li Hongzhang telegraphed Sheng Xuanhuai, calling the June 21
war declaration a "false edict" (luanming) and refusing to acknowledge
its validity.[44] A consensus was thus reached by provincial officials in the
Yangzi Valley and coastal areas that Empress Cixi's declaration of war
should not be followed.

Sheng Xuanhuai was very prominent in advocating actions to protect
Southeast China from the rampages both of the Boxers and subsequently
of foreign troops, as occurred in Tianjin and Beijing. Before war was officially declared, Sheng had already asked Liu Kunyi to inform foreign
consuls in Shanghai that he would protect foreigners along the Yangzi
River and that there was therefore no reason for the latter to intervene,
which Liu agreed was a good way to keep the foreigners calm and pre-

serve stability in the Yangzi River area.[45] On June 24, Sheng telegraphed Li Hongzhang, Liu Kunyi, and Zhang Zhidong and further elaborated on his scheme for the "mutual protection of the Southeast." His main points were that Liu Kunyi and Zhang Zhidong should make an informal pact with the foreign consuls in Shanghai in which they promised to protect foreign lives and property in areas under their jurisdiction and to allow foreigners to protect their concessions in Shanghai. In return, the foreigners would not send troops into Southeast China. Realizing that this was not in accordance with court policy, Sheng emphasized that the governors-general should act on the plan "as an expedient measure to save the dynasty and people." Liu and Zhang both replied the next day and asked Sheng and the Shanghai prefect, Yu Lianyuan, to proceed with the plan.[46] On June 26, Yu met with foreign consuls to discuss a detailed plan of "mutual protection," and on July 3, a formal agreement was reached.

What concerns us here is not the detailed history of the whole episode, but the intensive exchange of political information between high-ranking officials on policymaking issues by telegraph. By historical coincidence, Sheng Xuanhuai, with his control of the ITA, had the unique advantage of timely acquisition and dissemination of vital political information in a period of turmoil. Sheng became a nexus of information from whom local governors sought news during the Boxer Rebellion. Below is an excerpt from a telegram sent to Sheng by Lu Chuanlin, governor of Jiangsu on June 25, 1900:

Was Minister Ketteler [Baron Clemens von Ketteler, the German minister, killed in Beijing on June 20] killed by bandits? Has Governor Yuan Shikai been able to verify the news? Has he informed you secretly? It is said that Governor-General Li Hongzhang will leave Guangdong on June 27, and the news is believed to be reliable. Would you please keep me informed by telegraph whenever you receive news from today on? Would you also please instruct the Baoding Telegraph Administration specifically to transmit telegrams to and from Beijing for me whenever necessary? In addition, please allow me to present two telegrams. One is a note to the British consul; the other is the reply to Governor-General Liu Kunyi, asking him to work out a scheme to remedy the situation.[47]

Telegraphic access to and control of information became vital in surviving the complex historical drama involving court politics, the xenophobic Boxers, important provincial governors, and agitated foreigners. While the ruling elite made elaborate efforts to keep one another informed and in contact, they also realized the importance of keeping the public from knowing the full truth. In this regard, Sheng Xuanhuai, Liu

Kunyi, and Zhang Zhidong skillfully manipulated political information to their advantage. When the declaration of war was issued on June 21, the first action Sheng took was to order local telegraph branches to hand the edict only to the respective governors-general and governors, thus preventing the news from leaking out to the public. Sheng also telegraphed the governors-general and governors telling them not to remit the edict to their subordinates.[48] Since the "mutual protection of the Southeast" in fact meant that provincial officials openly rejected the edict from the court and declared de facto independence, Sheng, Liu, and Zhang all consciously tried to keep their scheme secret at this early stage. On June 24 and 25, Sheng sent Li, Liu, and Zhang two telegrams discussing "mutual protection," each beginning with the words "greatest care should be taken to keep this secret." In a telegram sent to Sheng on June 25, Zhang supported the suggestion of Yuan Shikai (then governor of Shandong) that the plan be kept from the public.[49]

Once again Sheng Xuanhuai played a crucial role in making sure that the "mutual protection" plan was not leaked out. In response to Liu Kunyi's request, on June 27, he instructed local telegraph administrations to keep the correspondence secret and asked Liu to order all provincial officials to do so as well.[50] After finding out that the Baoding Telegraph Administration had transmitted the hawkish June 22 and 25 court edicts to local telegraph branches on June 28, Sheng telegraphed Li, Liu, and Zhang, as well as the governors of Jiangsu, Zhejiang, and Anhui, warning them that if the contents of edicts were to spread among the public, the scheme of "mutual protection" would immediately collapse. Sheng asked them to order local telegraph administrations not to disseminate the news. On June 29, Sheng sent another telegram to Liu, Zhang, and the governors of Jiangsu and Anhui, reporting that "the edicts have been kept secret here [Shanghai] and have not been put in the newspapers. When asked, I always reply that I have no knowledge. I hope officials will not circulate the news in the provinces."[51]

Obviously, the promoters of "mutual protection" also monitored newspaper reports on the subject. After the agreements were reached on July 3, *Shen Bao* reported next day that they included an article stipulating that foreign powers should send troops north to suppress the Boxers, which shocked Zhang Zhidong. He realized that the report was tantamount to claiming that provincial governors had asked foreigners to attack Beijing. Zhang also noted that the report by *Zhongwai Ribao* including a statement that the governors-general and governors of the

Southeast had reached a consensus to resist the court decision, which to him was absolutely inadmissible. He telegraphed Sheng Xuanhuai on July 9, asking him to instruct the two newspapers to make corrections.[52] Their actions were in open defiance of the court decisions from Beijing and would have been surely seen as rebellious or disloyal if they had not happened against such an extraordinary historical background. Understandably, Zhang Zhidong, Liu Kunyi, and Sheng Xuanhuai did not want to provide ammunition to their political adversaries in the days to come.

Thus, throughout the whole process, provincial officials made a great effort to manipulate public reactions by selectively controlling the circulation of political information to their advantage. First, they tried to block the June 21 declaration of war and subsequent hawkish edicts from Beijing. While they discussed the "mutual protection" scheme intensively by telegram, the contents of their communications were mostly kept secret. It was only after they had reached agreement with the foreign consuls in Shanghai that they revealed the whole scheme to the public and tried to make it known to the whole region. Even though they were not able to gain the total control they wished for, because Shanghai had already become an important media center by that time and many foreign newspapers were beyond the control of Chinese officials, in retrospect, Sheng and his co-conspirators did a good job of controlling sensitive political information by controlling the telegraph. It is not surprising that Sheng Xuanhuai twice asked the court to praise and reward the workers of the ITA in 1902 and 1906 for keeping telegraph lines open and telegraph contents secret during and after the Boxer Rebellion.[53]

In summary, as a new communication technology, the telegraph provided a new means both of governance and of political participation. The key was by whom it was used and how. It could be used by the Qing government to facilitate its rule, as shown in the adoption of the telegraph to issue edicts and receive memorials, or to enhance national defense capability, as shown during the Sino-Franco War. This technology could also be used by the Chinese elite in metropolitan areas such as Shanghai, Singapore, San Francisco, and Yokohama to participate in national politics, as shown by the waves of protest telegrams sent to Beijing by the emperor's loyalists in 1899 and 1900. The skillful management of the telegraph by Sheng Xuanhuai, Liu Kunyi, and Zhang Zhidong provided a precedent in discussing and voicing differing opinions on significant policy issues by provincial governors.

It is both ironic and revealing that it was Sheng Xuanhuai and Jing

Yuanshan, heads of Chinese telegraph services, who employed the telegraph against court policies in 1900, signaling to the Qing government that it was starting to lose control over this technology. While there were multiple contributing factors, the declining legitimacy of the Qing dynasty made it ineffective and increasingly open to challenge by the end of the nineteenth century. Jing Yuanshan and other people used the telegraph to protest Empress Cixi's attempt to dethrone the emperor because they did not believe in the legitimacy of her decision, as did Sheng Xuanhui and Liu Kunyi in their "mutual protection" scheme. When the legitimacy of the court declined, it became more difficult to align public opinion with court policy and to prevent people from voicing their dissent in telegrams. The use of the telegraph to participate in national politics would flourish in the years to come, enlarging the space of political participation for various actors on a broader scale, as we shall see, in the first decade of the twentieth century.

CHAPTER FOUR

Public Telegrams and Nationalist Mobilizations

O N MAY 10, 1905, the one-year-old Shanghai General Chamber of Commerce (SGCC) called a special meeting asking the Qing government not to sign a new treaty with the United States in view of the latter country's 1882 Chinese Exclusion Act. The meeting was emotionally charged, and Zeng Shaoqing, a well-respected merchant from Fujian province, delivered a strongly worded speech denouncing the United States for its discrimination against and mistreatment of Chinese. Zeng also proposed that Chinese protest by boycotting American goods if the United States did not revise the Chinese Exclusion Act within two months, and more than one hundred participants enthusiastically endorsed this plan. Led by Zeng, Shanghai merchants decided to send three public telegrams, one to the Foreign and Commerce ministries in Beijing, one to the superintendents of trade for the Southern and Northern Ports, and one to the chambers of commerce in twenty-one cities nationwide.[1] The three telegrams varied slightly in content; that sent to the chambers of commerce read:

The United States has unfairly prohibited [the entry of] Chinese laborers for a long time, and subsequently extended this mistreatment to Chinese officials, merchants, and travelers as well. Since Ambassador Liang [Liang Cheng] refused to sign the [new] treaty, we have heard that the United States intends to negotiate the new treaty directly with the Foreign Ministry. The Shanghai General Chamber of Commerce has appealed collectively to the Foreign Ministry for the postponement of the signing of the treaty and also proposed a boycott of American goods by merchants to give covert resistance to the Americans. It is our hope that you might make this news known to your fellow merchants.[2]

Meanwhile, thousands of miles away, concerned Chinese businessmen in San Francisco also sent telegrams to the Foreign Ministry urging Beijing to stand firm and not bend to U.S. pressure to sign the draft treaty. At the time, the telegraph was the quickest way for these Chinese to contact the Qing court in Beijing. Between May 9 and May 13, a total of twenty-one "frantic telegrams" were sent to the Chinese Foreign Ministry in Beijing.[3] According to *Shen Bao*, on May 14 alone, Chinese in America sent four joint telegrams to the Foreign Ministry.[4] One of the first telegrams sent to Beijing read: "If exclusion treaty is renewed for term of another ten years Chinese in the United States will be extinct. Minister Leong [Liang] refused to sign the treaty. United States sends new Minister to Peking and is to compel the Foreign Secretary to sign. Please protest against it for the rescue of us merchants" (in original translation).[5]

In 1905, the telegraph served as an effective way of transmitting news and mobilizing resistance among the Chinese to oppose the exclusion treaty. Within days, the SGCC received numerous enthusiastic responses to its call, some in the form of public letters, but more coming in by telegraph. Similar meetings were held by local organizations all over the country. *Shen Bao* and other Chinese newspapers in Shanghai provided comprehensive coverage of the development of the movement by issuing detailed follow-up reports and reprinting many public telegrams. The telegraph's role in the boycott campaign of 1905 differed in several ways from its role in the campaign to protect Emperor Guangxu, discussed in the previous chapter. As we shall see, in addition to the dramatic increase in the quantity of telegrams sent and received, the most significant difference was that the telegraph was more widely and skillfully used by newly emergent civil organizations not only to express their opinions but also as an indispensable means of coordinating the campaign nationwide, thus enhancing the effects of such public telegrams to an unprecedented degree.

The Chinese Exclusion Treaty
and the Rise of Anti-American Sentiment

The direct catalyst of the Shanghai businessmen's action was the Chinese Exclusion Act passed by the U.S. Congress in 1882. When the first wave of Chinese laborers came to America, especially to the West Coast, in the late 1850s and 1860s, they engaged in a variety of work in agriculture, mining, and railroad construction, as well as being employed as laundry-men and servants. Because cheap labor was needed in large quantities at the time, Chinese laborers were generally welcomed. In 1868, the United States and China signed the Burlingame Treaty, which recognized "the inherent and inalienable right of man to change his home and allegiance, and also the mutual advantage" of the movement of people "from one country to the other, for purpose of curiosity, of trade, or as permanent residents." More Chinese came to America under this treaty's stipulations in the following years, and the Chinese population in California reached 123,201 in the 1870s.[6]

With the completion of the Pacific railroads in 1869 and the depression of the 1870s however, Chinese laborers became competitors of white workers in a shrunken job market, provoking anti-Chinese sentiment among the latter, motivated by both racial prejudice and economic hardship. After Chinese immigration became an issue of domestic politics, the United States negotiated a modified treaty with China in 1880 stipulating that it could "regulate, limit, or suspend" immigration but "not absolutely prohibit" Chinese laborers coming to the United States.[7] Led by labor unions, the anti-Chinese forces then succeeded in getting the Chinese Exclusion Act passed in 1882, which suspended the immigration of Chinese laborers for ten years. In the following years, a series of more restrictive laws were passed to prevent Chinese immigration to America, and these would last for more than sixty years, only being repealed in 1943 after China became a U.S. ally in World War II.

In 1894, a third immigration treaty was negotiated between the two countries extending the ban on Chinese laborers for ten more years. Under this treaty, all Chinese were excluded except "officials, teachers, students, merchants or travelers for curiosity or pleasure." After 1898, a policy aimed at the total exclusion of Chinese was actively pursued. By deliberately interpreting the term "laborer" in its broadest sense, the immigration authorities severely limited travel by those Chinese who were exempted from the prohibition. Worse still, Chinese entering and reentering the United States were subject to immigration inspections that often resulted in their being confined in detention sheds for many days, weeks, or even months. The Chinese complained about and protested against the exclusion, but to no avail. California's white vote counted for more than Chinese grievances as far as President Theodore Roosevelt was concerned.[8]

Under these circumstances, when the treaty of 1894 was set to expire at the end of 1904, the angered Chinese informed the Americans that they would terminate the treaty and demanded to negotiate a new one. When a telegram conveyed this news to Washington on January 25, 1904, the Americans were caught off guard, because they had expected the Chinese to be "cooperative" and simply let the treaty automatically receive a ten-year extension.[9] On August 12, China's Ambassador Liang submitted a draft of a new treaty in which he requested better treatment of Chinese Americans and of Chinese visiting the United States, laborers aside. The Americans countered with a draft that not only upheld the old restrictions but also added new ones. Obviously angered, Liang submitted a second draft emphasizing reciprocity in the treatment of the nationals of each country. Not surprisingly, his second draft was flatly rejected by the U.S. government. "The Department of Commerce and Labor seemed strong enough to dictate the terms of any new treaty. China could only accept defeat gracefully," the historian Delber McKee writes.[10] The two countries had not been able to agree on a new treaty when the old one expired at the end of 1904. While the negotiations stalled, news spread that the Qing court was about to sign the new treaty on the American terms, and this caused a public outcry in China, as shown by the meeting in Shanghai on May 10, 1905.

Strong anti-American sentiment originating from American mistreatment of Chinese was nothing new. In fact, the Chinese press had carried reports on this issue for a long time, since the beginning of the exclusion movement in the 1870s. On July 12, 1872, *Shanghai Xinbao* reprinted a report from a Hong Kong newspaper on the maltreatment of Chinese in America, focusing on the fact that Chinese were denied the right to be witnesses in American courts.[11] *Shen Bao* covered the issue more frequently. As early as 1872, two months after the newspaper's first publication, *Shen Bao* issued an editorial calling on the Qing court to set up consulates in places with large Chinese populations in order to offer its subjects protection. In 1873, *Shen Bao* reported that the Americans in San Francisco had tried to prohibit Chinese from entering the United States.[12] In the 1880s, after the passing of the Chinese Exclusion Act in 1882, *Shen Bao* carried more reports on anti-Chinese incidents in America. From January to June 1886, for example, *Shen Bao* published five editorials on American mistreatment of Chinese laborers, merchants, and officials, and called on the U.S. government to provide appropriate protection to Chinese in accordance with international law.[13] In addition, *Shen Bao* translated several anti-exclusion articles from New York newspapers and reprinted them in Chinese.[14]

Shen Bao's editorial of April 20, 1886, started by stating that since the United States was a democracy and the laws were made based on the people's will, the U.S. government should protect Chinese personal safety and well being through the law. Using democracy and people's rights to justify discrimination against Chinese was indefensible. The editor commented that "the mistreatment of Chinese was not only an insult to China, but also an insult to the United States itself" and went on to say that the fundamental reason for the passing of the Chinese Exclusion Act was Americans' desire to take advantage of others and their unwillingness to share the benefits of work done with others. In the 1890s, the issue of protecting Chinese laborers overseas continued to attract public attention. On June 24, 1898, *Shen Bao* printed another editorial on the need to protect overseas Chinese laborers.[15]

Shen Bao's coverage of the boycott campaign in 1905 dwarfed previous coverage both in quantity and speed of response. Even though public telegrams figured increasingly in national politics, they had rarely been published in *Shen Bao* since 1895, but thanks to an editorial overhaul early in 1905, the paper started to reprint large numbers of them that year. As has been noted, a telegram could only become public after it had been reprinted and distributed to a large audience by newspapers. From 1898 to 1900, owing to the conservative stance of its editor at the time, *Shen Bao* did not reprint either the telegrams from overseas Chinese wishing Emperor Guangxu good health and congratulating Empress Cixi on her birthday or Jing Yuanshan's telegram protesting the latter's attempt to dethrone the emperor.

This did not change until February 1905, when *Shen Bao* underwent an overhaul. During the Chinese New Year recess of 1905, *Shen Bao* held a staff meeting to discuss the status of the newspaper. By any account, it was not in good shape. Ever since Huang Xiexun had taken over the editorship-in-chief in 1898, the newspaper had taken a conservative stance that was not popular among its readers. Huang's pro-Cixi stance after the coup of 1898 and in the heir appointment episode in 1900 was especially damaging to the reputation of the newspaper. At the same time, *Xinwen Bao*, the main rival of *Shen Bao*, increased its circulation, which reached 12,000 in 1900, far ahead of *Shen Bao's* 6,000–7,000. *Shen Bao* had to play catch-up in the years to come.[16]

Nobody could have anticipated that the staff meeting would last for two days and two nights. By the end of this marathon session, Huang Xiexun had resigned from his position and a sweeping reform plan had been adopted.[17] On February 7, 1905, in its first issue after the Chinese New Year, a different *Shen Bao* in both content and appearance was unveiled to its readers. The newspaper added new pages, changed its layout, adopted news titles, and used better-quality paper. It also promised to add more correspondents nationwide, to publish more commercial and local news and more articles about current affairs, such as the Russo-Japanese War being fought in northeastern China, and to reprint more news from foreign newspapers.[18]

Three of the points in the paper's twelve-point reorganization plan are especially relevant to the discussion here. First, *Shen Bao* made itself more receptive to change. Signaling this shift in its political stance, it published an editorial the next day in which it cited Liang Qichao early on and no longer treated Kang Youwei and Liang Qichao as traitors and usurpers.[19] Second, in addition to the added pages, it launched a column specifically devoted to printing telegraph dispatches, aiming to deliver urgent news in the fastest possible way. Third, the paper proposed to give more space to important memorials, petitions, and official documents, which would help increase the transparency of national policymaking in the last years of the Qing dynasty. Politically reoriented, and with increased coverage of telegrams and political news, *Shen Bao* was thus well equipped to become the leading newspaper in reporting the movement to boycott American goods, which was increasingly supported by the Chinese elite.

The Shanghai General Chamber of Commerce, Telegraphy, and the Anti-American Mobilization

The Shanghai General Chamber of Commerce (SGCC) was the leading organization in the 1905 boycott. As one of its New Policies initiatives, the Qing court established the Ministry of Commerce in August 1903 and issued the Concise Regulations of Chambers of Commerce in early 1904, encouraging the establishment of chambers of commerce in business centers. Following the regulations, Shanghai established China's first chamber of commerce the same year, based on the Shanghai Association of Commerce, which had been in existence since 1902. It is not surprising that the well-organized, resource-rich SGCC was the most important and influential of the various new organizations that appeared in Shanghai during the New Policies period.

On May 5, 1905, *Shen Bao* carried a two-line report on its front page titled "America Forcing China to Sign the Chinese Exclusion Draft Treaty," saying that the U.S. government had ordered its minister in Beijing to force the Chinese Foreign Ministry to instruct Ambassador Liang to sign the treaty.[20] Five days later, *Shen Bao* printed an editorial and a public notice calling on all Chinese to oppose the Chinese exclusion treaty, and these articles occupied almost the entire front page. The public notice pointed out four areas in which the proposed American treaty would harm China: damaging China's national integrity, insulting Chinese dignity, doing away with reciprocal rights between two sovereign nations, and endangering Chinese business interests. In conclusion, it appealed to the public to act together to come up with resistance plans. The public notice was issued in the name of *tongren*, which literally means a group of people with the same opinions and positions, but more likely it was issued by concerned members of the Shanghai elite. The editorial elaborated on why Chinese should oppose the discriminatory treaty and should not passively put up with mistreatment any more. It proposed two methods of resistance. One was to send a jointly signed telegram and representatives to Beijing to petition the Qing court not to bend to U.S. pressure. The other was to send a joint public telegram to provincial governors nationwide requesting them to send similar telegrams to Beijing asking for the abrogation of the old treaty. Issuing public circular telegrams thus seems to have become the most important way of expressing public opinion at this time.[21]

These appeals obviously not only reflected the opinion of newspaper editors but also had a clear effect on the general public in Shanghai. The same afternoon, May 10, the SGCC met, as described at the beginning of this chapter, and resolved to send telegrams of protest to the government in Beijing and chambers of commerce nationwide, the texts of which were reprinted in *Shen Bao* the following day. On May 13, *Shen Bao* reported that Fujian merchants and Guangdong merchants residing in Shanghai had held meetings on May 11 and 12 respectively to discuss ways of resisting the Chinese exclusion treaty, and telegraphing the government, governors, and even American newspapers was again a strategy adopted. It was reported that more than one thousand people had attended the meeting of Guangdong merchants, and that the majority of the attendees had supported the boycott of American goods.[22] Meanwhile, the Gongzhong (Public and Fidelity) Oratory Association and the Ren Jing (Human Mirror) Study Society also held similar gatherings on May 11 and May 13. With more than forty speakers and an audience of several hundred, the Gongzhong meeting featured a proposal to telegraph the U.S. Department of Commerce in protest, in addition to boycotting American goods and schools. It was also proposed to mobilize American merchants and missionaries in China to send telegrams back to America to persuade the U.S. government to change its position.[23]

The responses to the Shanghai merchants' initial telegrams of May 10 were swift. *Shen Bao* reported on May 16 that the governor-general of Liangjiang had replied that he had notified the Foreign Ministry in Beijing by telegraph of the Shanghai businessmen's concerns, urging that Chinese commercial interests be protected. Meanwhile, the chambers of commerce in Tianjin, Hankou, and Yantai also acknowledged that they had forwarded the May 10 telegraph to fellow merchants. The Ministry of Commerce also forwarded a reply from the Foreign Ministry to the Shanghai merchants by telegraph, saying that the Foreign Ministry had telegraphed their resistance plan to Ambassador Liang and instructed him to conduct further negotiations with the U.S. government. In America, on behalf of 100,000 "compatriots," Chinese merchants in San Francisco telegraphed Shanghai on May 19 asking their counterparts to take a firm and persistent position on the boycott. Chinese in Hong Kong held a meeting discussing the treaty issue on May 14. *Shen Bao* also reprinted the telegram from Ambassador Liang in which he proclaimed that he would not compromise on the treaty issue.[24]

Obviously concerned, and only one day after reaching Shanghai, the new American minister, William W. Rockhill, went straight to meet the Shanghai business leaders on the morning of May 21, trying to calm the rising anti-American sentiment. Even though he denied "categorically and emphatically" that the United States was trying to exclude Chinese and argued that the ongoing negotiations were based on a Chinese version of the new treaty, the Chinese merchants were not convinced, and his request for six months to revise the treaty was turned down.[25] Right after the discussion with Rockhill, the SGCC convened a public meeting that afternoon, with 200 in attendance. In his speech, Zeng Shaoqing acknowledged that Rockhill had been very diplomatic, but he cautioned the audience that they should be prepared to take action to prevent the signing of the Chinese exclusion treaty. Finally, a proposal to telegraph Ambassador Liang to find out the status of the ongoing negotiations was unanimously adopted.[26]

From early June to mid July, *Shen Bao* covered the issue regularly, mainly concentrating on the increasing response to the boycott proposal by Shanghai merchants both in China and overseas. Many of these responses came in the form of telegrams and letters. Responses came from Suzhou, Wuhu, Changsha, Xiamen, Hangzhou, Tianjin, Zhenjiang, Yingkou, Shantou, Nanchang, Wuyang, Shashi, Yangzhou, Shaoxing, Beijing, Jiaxing, and Ningbo, as well as from Nagasaki, Yokohama, Penang, Singapore, Honolulu, and Chinese students in the United States.[27] Before the deadline for the Americans to revise the treaty was reached on July 20, things had calmed down somewhat. Even though preparations for the boycott were made, most people were hoping that the Americans would take action before the deadline.

From the very beginning, Zeng Shaoqing's bold and uncompromising stance had made him the leader of the boycott. Though a board member and well respected, he was not among the key figures in the SGCC before the boycott, because the organization was dominated by merchants from Zhejiang and Jiangsu.[28] As he revealed later, when the first SGCC meeting decided to send telegrams to Beijing on May 10, the question of who should lead the action was raised. Aware of political sensitivities, most SGCC board members were hesitant about having their names listed first on the telegrams, but Zeng volunteered, saying, "This action is for the public good and thus risk free. Even if there is a risk involved, the risk is to anger the Americans or get killed by the Americans. If I were to die for the public interest, I would have died for a just cause."[29] The telegrams were accordingly signed, not by the SGCC, but by "Zeng Shaoqing and merchants residing in Shanghai."[30] After they were made public in the Chinese press, Zeng thus emerged as the symbolic leader of the whole boycott movement.

Zeng's leadership status is shown by the fact that many public telegrams and letters on the boycott were often sent directly to him by other chambers of commerce, organizations, and supporters. Boycott-supporting telegrams and letters usually had two destinations: some were sent to the Foreign Ministry in Beijing, but many more were sent to the Shanghai merchants to show solidarity. In the latter case, the designated receiver was listed either as the SGCC, or Zeng Shaoqing, or both. With the July deadline approaching, more telegrams and letters reached Shanghai. Starting on July 15, *Shen Bao* regularly compiled these telegrams and letters and printed them together under titles such as "Collection of Boycott Letters to Zeng Shaoqing" or "Collections of Telegrams and Letters to the SGCC and Zeng Shaoqing on the Treaty Boycott." In many cases, the names "Zeng Shaoqing" and "SGCC" were used interchangeably.[31]

There was no lack of dramatic developments surrounding Zeng. On July 6, *Shen Bao* reported the "abnormal news" (*yiwen*) that the SGCC's board proposed to extend the deadline by another four months, and that Zeng Shaoqing had agreed to this. On the following day, the newspaper printed a letter from Zeng Shaoqing denying there was any truth in the previous report. While claiming that he had not changed his stand, Zeng acknowledged that he had encountered resistance and publicly appealed for help.[32] On the morning of July 20, Zeng met with the U.S. consul in Shanghai, James L. Rodgers, who made a last effort to avert the boycott. After many exchanges between Zeng and Rodgers, the talks ended without any progress. In the late afternoon, the SGCC held a prearranged meeting and approved the formal start of the boycott. The decision was to be made known to thirty-five cities nationwide by telegraph.[33]

From mid-July to mid-September, *Shen Bao* gave extensive coverage to the boycott, focusing public attention on it by means of editorials, reports on boycott activities, reprinting public telegrams and correspondence between Zeng Shaoqing and his supporters, publishing news about developments in the treaty negotiations, reporting on American responses to the boycott, and revealing Chinese government positions on the matter. Over two months, *Shen Bao* carried hundreds of reports related to the boycott and treaty negotiations. This intensity of coverage surpassed that of any other issue in the same period, including the Russo-Japanese War and the subsequent peace negotiations. However, coverage decreased gradually from mid-September on, reflecting the fact that by that time, the boycott movement had lost its momentum.

Many factors contributed to the gradual decline in anti-American zeal. First of all, Shanghai merchants disagreed on how to implement the boycott. There was genuine solidarity among them before the boycott started, but when it was imminent, differences surfaced, especially among merchants whose main business was with American companies or selling American goods. Because of the strong anti-American rhetoric and highly charged emotions, it was impossible not to follow Zeng Shaoqing's boycott initiative in May. With the July 20 deadline approaching, however, some merchants proposed reinterpreting the boycott deadline as the starting date from which no American goods would be ordered, a reworking of Zeng's initial proposal. At the SGCC meeting on July 20, the first speaker in fact suggested setting July 20 as the starting date to stop ordering American goods, while postponing the boycott of American goods for another four months. Though the latter part of his suggestion received little support, his suggested compromise was endorsed by most of those present. American goods in warehouses or ordered before July 20 would thus be registered and labeled and allowed on the market until sold.[34]

Though there were abundant examples of personal sacrifices by Chinese merchants in the boycott, some sought to minimize their losses. On August 6, the Shanghai Educational Society held another meeting, in which the cut-off date for the admission of American goods was again postponed, this time to August 10.[35] These developments exerted huge pressure on the boycott leader, Zeng Shaoqing, who had always kept up an uncompromising stance. On August 11, twenty days into the boycott, Zeng issued a "farewell letter to all compatriots under heaven" in which he revealed that he had received several death threats. Defiant as ever, Zeng made public his daily schedule in the letter to show his contempt for potential assassins, saying:

If I die at the hands of Americans or at the hands of merchants selling American goods, it will be the right way to end my life. I shall still live in the hearts of the people and I shall have no regrets. The only thing that would make me regretful is if, after I die, my compatriots disband the organization and succumb to the threats of foreigners and the repression of the government. If this happens, our two hundred million square miles will be divided and my four hundred million compatriots will be bullied by others. There will be no opportunity for us to regain moral dignity and to restore national strength. I hope that after my death tens of millions of Zeng Shaoqings appear who will stand up to restore national strength and to regain individual integrity, thus protecting us from being despised, bullied, enslaved, and abused by foreigners. If eventually China can coexist with the Western powers on an equal footing, the date of my death might then be seen as the year of my rebirth.[36]

Zeng Shaoqing was right in saying that both the U.S. government and the Qing court were seeking to stop the boycott. The United States initially tried to use diplomatic efforts to prevent the boycott from starting. In late June, President Roosevelt took several initiatives trying to solve the issue, including instructing immigration officials to extend the "widest and heartiest courtesy" to Chinese entering America, other than laborers, and held a number of meetings with Kang Youwei, the exiled

Chinese reform leader. In the meantime, negotiations on a new treaty began in June. With no revision on the Chinese exclusion principle possible, the negotiations reached a dead end, and the United States finally suspended them on August 14. The American position on the boycott then became more hard-line, and the United States exerted more pressure on the Qing court to prohibit it. In mid-September, the U.S. consul in Guangzhou requested that a gunboat be sent, which was promptly done.[37]

Under American pressure, on July 1 and August 31, the Qing court issued edicts instructing provincial officials to protect "normal trade" and discourage the boycott. In August, too, the U.S. minister in Beijing, Rockhill, presented notes to the Chinese Foreign Ministry three times asking the Qing government to deprive Zeng Shaoqing of his official title. The court did telegraph Zhou Fu, governor-general of Liangjiang, twice, on August 22 and 23, to mete out this punishment to Zeng, but Zhou advised against any precipitate action against Zeng and suggested taking a wait-and-see approach.[38] Generally speaking, after the August 31 edict, the boycott lost momentum in Shanghai, and the whole movement gradually came to a slow end, even though it lingered on well into 1906 in Guangdong and in areas along the Yangzi River.

Opinions differ on the actual effect the boycott had on American business interests in China.[39] In any case, its influence reached far beyond commercial concerns. The movement to boycott American goods of 1905 was a campaign propelled by the rise of modern Chinese nationalism. The boycott was one of the first national mass mobilizations that witnessed the leadership of the new Chinese business elite. Using the chambers of commerce as a platform for organization, the Chinese business elite employed the public telegraph widely as a vital means of communicating with one another, coordinating activities, and fostering favorable public opinion. Through the frequent telegraphic traffic between Shanghai and local chambers of commerce, between various organizations and government organs, between Chinese within the country and abroad, between central government and local officials, more and more telegrams were circulated and reprinted in newspapers, thus making the boycott known to the general public. In addition to circular telegrams that were intended to be as public as possible, considerable telegraph correspondence between different parties was also reprinted—even "secret" official telegrams—signaling a new trend in late Qing politics and public life, inasmuch as discussion, deliberation, and the subsequent decision-making process on an issue of great public interest was made increasingly transparent. While the boycott itself was soon over, the trend toward public debate developed further, reaching its full extent in two issues that occupied much of the Chinese elite's attention between 1904 and 1911, namely, the railway-rights recovery movement and the campaign for constitutionalism.

The Telegraph and the Railway-Rights Recovery Movement

With the rise of nationalism, America's Chinese Exclusion Act was not the only thorny issue that attracted a great deal of attention from the Chinese elite. Almost concurrently, the Chinese elite in the Yangzi Delta, namely, in Jiangsu (Shanghai included) and Zhejiang provinces, was engaged in another nationalist campaign, which aimed to regain the right to construct a Suzhou-Hangzhou-Ningbo railway from the British. Once again, at the peak of the campaign in late 1907 and early 1908, the telegraph was indispensable in bringing the movement to public attention.

The attention *Shen Bao* paid to the Suzhou-Hangzhou-Ningbo railway issue was no accident. From its inception, *Shen Bao* had been an enthusiastic champion of the railway in China. According to my rough statistics on its *lunshuo* (editorials and commentaries) section between 1872 and its reorientation in 1905, the number of railway-related commentaries, editorials, and reports exceeded those on any other subject. Coinciding with the changes of 1905 in which the newspaper gave more space and emphasis to telegraph dispatches and took a more pro-reform stance, *Shen Bao*'s coverage of railway-related issues increased further. The focus here will be on some of the significant new features in *Shen Bao* compared with its coverage of the boycotting American goods movement.

However, let us first take a short detour to the historical context of railway development in late Qing China. As a major technological innovation during the industrial revolution, railroads and locomotives appeared slightly earlier than telegraphy. The railway age began in 1825, when the first railroad opened to public service in England. Knowledge of the railroad was introduced into China around 1840. From the early 1860s on, Westerners started to advocate establishing a railroad in China, but were turned down repeatedly by the Qing court out of concerns similar to the early discourse opposing the adoption of telegraphy. As in the case of telegraphy, a change of attitude toward the railroad came after the Sino-Japanese conflict over Taiwan in the early 1870s. After a court-sponsored policy debate on the railway in 1880, officials of the Self-Strengthening Movement finally came out on top. In 1881, China constructed a 10-kilometer railroad in Hebei, the first in its history. In May 1889, the Qing court proclaimed that the railroad was one of the important strategies that should be adopted to achieve self-strengthening.[40] However, it was very slow to carry out its plans. From 1881 to 1894, China built only about 250 miles of railroad nationwide.[41]

It was not until China's defeat in the Sino-Japanese War that the court decided to speed up the construction of railroads. Since the government treasury lacked adequate funds for this, Zhang Zhidong (governor-general of Huguang) and Wang Wenshao (governor-general of Zhili) proposed a policy of "the government borrows the loans, constructs the railroads, and thus owns all benefits [*li*] of the railroads." In January 1897, the officially sponsored Imperial Chinese Railroad Administration was formed and Sheng Xuanhuai, who had established China's telegraph services, was put in charge.[42] Sheng was very much involved in negotiating foreign loans to construct Chinese railways, although in reality the final loan terms often put foreign creditors in charge of the construction, operation, and management of the railroads, differing sharply from the initial Chinese plan of simply borrowing the money while keeping all the rights (*quan*) in their own hands.

Attracted by the enormous Chinese railway construction projects and propelled by a desire to secure their "spheres of influence," Western powers started a furious competition to acquire rights to construct China's railway lines, often backed by gunboat diplomacy. Belgium, backed by the Russians and French, got the contract for the Beijing-Hankou line in 1898. The other Western powers followed. The Guangzhou-Hankou line fell to the Americans, while the Germans secured the right to construct railways in Shandong province. The British, who were the largest foreign investors at the time, were angered that they had lost the Beijing-Hankou line to the French, Russians, and Belgians and been awarded only preliminary contracts for the Tianjin-Niuzhuang and Shanghai-Nanjing lines. The British government accordingly ordered its minister in China, Claude M. MacDonald, to protest to the Qing court and demand a "compensatory" agreement comprising five railway concessions, including the disputed Suzhou-Hangzhou-Ningbo line. Requested to reply to the British "within a time limit," the Qing court submitted and granted the British all their requests.[43]

Compared with the Qing administration's policies concerning telegraphy, its policy on the railways was ineffective, inconsistent, and eventually disastrous. At the end of 1903, the court made a major policy shift regarding railroad construction. In the name of carrying out the New Policies, on December 2, the court issued the Concise Railroad Regulations, in which railroad construction was opened to both Chinese and foreign-owned companies. The Chinese responded enthusiastically to this policy change. From 1903 to 1907, a total of eighteen railroad companies were established in fifteen provinces; of these, the majority were privately owned. These companies were started and managed by Qing officials, overseas Chinese merchants, local gentry, and leaders of chambers of commerce.[44] Thus the Chinese elite was very much involved in this new endeavor.

It was in this context that local elites in Zhejiang and Jiangsu started to advocate that the Chinese themselves construct the Suzhou-Hangzhou-Ningbo line. Since the major part of the proposed line would go through Zhejiang, the Zhejiang elite took the lead. In July 1905, meetings were held in Shanghai and Hangzhou in which members of the elite decided to establish a railroad company. More than 160 prominent Zhejiang natives then jointly telegraphed the Foreign Ministry requesting that the government refuse any foreign railway investment in the province.[45] Lobbied by Zhejiang-born officials in Beijing, the Ministry of Commerce approved the establishment of the Zhejiang Railway Company in August 1905. In May 1906, the Jiangsu Railway Company was approved, led by the Suzhou Chamber of Commerce and supported by Jiangsu-born officials in Beijing. The Zhejiang and Jiangsu companies acted swiftly to raise private funds for the line. The actual construction of the Zhejiang and Jiangsu sections commenced in October 1906 and March 1907 respectively.[46]

There was, however, a preliminary 1898 contract between the Imperial Chinese Railway Administration and the British company Jardine, Matheson & Co. to build the proposed Suzhou-Hangzhou-Ningbo line, which would have to be annulled to grant the Chinese companies the right of construction. On September 23, 1905, an edit was accordingly issued that granted the newly established railway company monopoly construction privileges in Zhejiang and instructed Sheng Xuanhuai, the original signatory of the contract, to negotiate with the British on this matter. Mobilized by nationalistic emotion, the Zhejiang and Jiangsu elites took an uncompromising stand on the Suzhou-Hangzhou-Ningbo line, insisting on nothing short of the abrogation of the existing preliminary agreement.[47] They were certainly encouraged by the precedent of the successful redemption of the Guangzhou-Hankou line from the Americans in 1905.[48] But the British were in no mood to give up their rights and exerted pressure on the Qing government, which thus found itself confronted with the demands of both local elites and the British, backed up respectively by an imperial edict and a signed preliminary agreement. The Foreign Ministry adopted a strategy of deliberately procrastinating, hoping the matter would become less emotionally charged with time. Finally, in the fall of 1907, the Qing court, led by Wang Daxie, vice-minister of foreign affairs, reached a settlement with the British. In an attempt to placate both sides, the court decided to separate the railroad loan and railroad construction. While keeping Chinese companies as the constructors of the railroad, the court instructed the companies to accept a loan of £1,500,000 from the British to supplement the fund they had already raised. The new agreement secured Chinese control of administrative and financial matters but gave considerable financial benefit to the British.[49]

In retrospect, this settlement might have been a compromise acceptable to the British, the Qing court, and the Zhejiang and Jiangsu elites. However, to the local elites, accepting the British loan was totally contrary to their ultimate aim of building the railway using Chinese money and engineering skills. When the new agreement was promulgated by an imperial edict on October 20, 1907, they felt that their interests had been sold out and reacted explosively in a manner that caught the court off guard. Hundreds of telegrams of protest were sent to Beijing, numerous meetings and gatherings were held, and branches of the Society for People's Resistance to Railway Loans (guomin jukuan hui) were set up all across Zhejiang and Jiangsu. Emotions ran high. A Chinese railway school student and a Chinese railway engineer who died as a result of "excessive worry" and a hunger strike respectively became the movement's martyrs. Threats were also made to destroy the ancestral burial ground of Wang Daxie, the negotiator of the loan agreement, who happened to be a native of Zhejiang.[50]

The court decision also prompted increased buying of shares in Chinese railway companies. Because the Qing court used the insufficient fund-raising capacity of the Jiangsu and Zhejiang railroad companies as the reason for taking a foreign loan, opponents of the move sought to raise construction funds, and buying railway shares was acclaimed as a patriotic action. On October 31, at the meeting of the Zhejiang Railway

Company's board of directors, shares worth three million yuan were purchased.[51] On November 13, at a special shareholders' meeting of the
Jiangsu Railway Company, representatives from six prefectures under-
took to purchase shares worth 13,400,000 yuan.[52] Students, despite having limited financial resources, were the most active supporters of the initiative. Reports of students buying shares are too numerous to be listed
here. According to the retired grand councilor and former railway construction commissioner Wang Wenshao, within one month, more than 15
million yuan was raised in Jiangsu and 27 million in Zhejiang.[53]

Facing strong resistance from the local elite, the local governor-general
and governors jointly telegraphed a memorial to the Grand Council asking the court to instruct the Foreign Ministry to handle the matter "following public opinion and to prevent the overall situation from deteriorating."[54] The Foreign Ministry asked the local merchants and gentry to
send representatives to Beijing to discuss the issue. After intense debates,
the two provincial companies overcame resistance from more radical
members and sent representatives to Beijing. The thorny issue was finally
resolved by a modified agreement. In March 1908, the court and the
British reached a final agreement that changed the debtor of the previous
loan from the railroad companies to the Ministry of Posts and Communication and let the ministry reissue the loan to the two provincial railroad companies. Therefore, the railroad would be constructed by the private Jiangsu and Zhejiang railway companies, at least nominally, using
the British loan to supplement their own funds.[55]

A New Phase in the Use of the Public Telegraph

As in the movement to boycott American goods, the telegraph was the
most important means of mobilization and communication for the railway rights recovery movement. For example, when the Zhejiang Society
for People's Resistance to Railway Loans held its inaugural meeting on
October 22, 1907, items on the agenda to be discussed included ways of
resisting British loans; motions; sending telegrams to provinces that had
built railways with their own funds; sending telegrams to provinces im-
pacted by foreign loans; methods of establishing branch societies in all
eleven prefectures; sending a letter to citizens encouraging them to send
protest telegrams to the Grand Council; telegraphing Tang Shouqian (the
director-general of the Zhejiang Railway Company) asking him not to go
to Beijing; and setting up a temporary office. Of these eight issues, four

were telegraph-related. Not only did the society use the telegraph itself to communicate with other provinces, but it also encouraged ordinary people to use it to express their opposition to the loans to Beijing.[56]

There is no need to explore in detail the hundreds of protest telegrams that were sent and reported by or reprinted in newspapers, magazines, booklets, and special volumes. The Chinese press followed the railway dispute extensively from the beginning, and the Shanghai press naturally took the lead because of Shanghai's geographical location. *Shen Bao* was no exception. In general, telegrams that appeared in *Shen Bao* and other publications can be categorized into four types: (1) telegrams sent to Qing government bodies and high-ranking policymakers by individuals, including gentry-merchants, railway company shareholders, overseas Chinese, native-born officials, and students; (2) telegrams sent to the above recipients by organizations, including Chinese railway companies, chambers of commerce, educational associations, schools, and branches of the Society for People's Resistance to Railway Loans; (3) telegrams between various Qing government organs and governors-general, governors, and other officials; and (4) telegrams between railway companies and loan resistance organizations and individuals, as well as government agencies and officials.

The majority of telegrams of the first two types petitioned the Qing government, protested against its decision, and showed support for the anti-loan efforts of the local railway companies. The situation was thus somewhat different from the use of telegrams in the movement to boycott U.S. goods, when Americans were the main target because of the exclusion treaty. Now, along with the foreigners (in this case mainly the British), the Qing government increasingly found itself the target of protest. The following is the text of a telegraph sent to the Foreign Ministry by members of the Ningbo gentry, business, and educational elites after a joint meeting at the Chamber of Commerce on October 21, 1907:

To ministers of the Foreign Ministry: the Zhejiang railway is being constructed with domestic funds following the imperial edict and has achieved significant progress. By changing our policy to accept foreign loans, we lose the railway rights. Since there are a great number of shareholders among the Ningbo people, we shall never give in to foreigners. Everyone has been roused to anger. We petition you to take swift action to refuse the loans.[57]

The implications of this telegram are subtly yet clearly conveyed. First, the Ningbo elites used a previous imperial edict to legitimize their position. Secondly, they attacked the current policy of accepting foreign loans as "losing railway rights," a charge of considerable significance. And, finally, they proclaimed an absolutely uncompromising stand on the loan issue, backed by an implicit warning about the possible consequences of the current policy. This tone is more obvious in a telegraph sent to the Grand Council and several ministries by members of the Jiangsu gentry:

News has been circulated on loans for the construction of the Suzhou-Hangzhou-Ningbo railway and has caused an extreme degree of anxiety for the people. It was long ago proposed by the throne that the Jiangsu-Zhejiang railway be constructed by a domestically funded company, without foreign shareholders. And furthermore, the appointments of director-general and deputy director-general of the company were memorialized to and approved by the emperor. The record is so clear that it is inconceivable the decision could ever be changed later. But we note from the newspapers that an imperial decree has not only instructed the Foreign Ministry to sign the loan agreement swiftly but also instructed the ministry to order local gentry and merchants not to persist in their request. Railway policy and the sovereignty it represents are lifelines to these two provinces. But let us leave this argument aside for the moment. If such an established policy [using domestic funds] put in place by edicts can be changed, how will the court command its subjects thereafter? Popular support for the court will collapse far beyond Jiangsu and Zhejiang [if such an action is taken]! We beg you sincerely to memorialize and ask the emperor to rescind the previous decision, and we anxiously await your reply.[58]

The tone of this is certainly more forceful than that of the telegram sent to the court by Jing Yuanshan and others in 1900, yet the senders were not subject to the prosecution that befell Jing. The court could not afford to resort to such heavy-handed tactics regarding a policy that did not merely concern imperial succession but affected the vested interests of a large number of the local elite. Besides, the court found itself immersed in a problem of its own making owing to its inconsistent policies on railway construction. Unlike the American goods boycott, when the court could make gestures toward petitions from the Chinese opposing the treaty, while reserving the power to make decisions itself, this time, the court had to negotiate, not only with the British, but also with the local elites in making its final decision, thus allowing a larger space to the latter for political participation.

Seen from this perspective, the last three types of telegrams mentioned above constituted significant developments in political participation during the period in question. Let us first examine the telegrams sent and received by railway companies. In addition to the telegrams the two provincial railway companies sent to and received from other individuals and organizations, the sending of telegrams between railway companies, government ministries, and high-ranking officials represented a big step forward in terms of the political power of local elites. Representing shareholders' interests, both the Zhejiang and Jiangsu railway companies rode the high tide of local resistance to the British loans in order to pressure the court to change its decision. The following two telegrams are good examples of this. The first was sent to several "elder statesmen" in Beijing by the Zhejiang Railway Company after the loan decision was proclaimed:

The Zhejiang governor was informed of the loan decision only after [the Foreign Ministry] had granted the request of the British minister, showing that the government has never taken the opinions of Zhejiang people seriously. Right now rumors of an uprising are circulating in Hangzhou, spread by the ministry, and propelled by the edict to which you, distinguished elder statesmen, tacitly consented. Tang Shouqian [the director-general of the company] and Liu Jinzao [the deputy director-general] are trying to stabilize the situation. We shall do our best but can give no guarantee. It is our intention to make this statement to you so that we should not be mistaken for ringleaders [if the situation gets out of control].[59]

Another telegraph was sent to a grand councilor jointly by the Jiangsu and Zhejiang Railway Companies:

The telegraph memorials by Grand Councilor Wang and the governor of Zhejiang in the previous two days show that public emotion has been stirred up. When the government negotiated the agreements on the Tianjin-Zhenjiang railway and the Shanxi mines, it discussed the cases with gentry and merchants and permitted the public to express opinions. How, then, could it single out the Suzhou-Hangzhou-Ningbo railway and make strenuous efforts to conceal the loan agreement from the railway companies? Without consent from local people, the government took out loans on their behalf, and this has angered many people who are not shareholders. Since court edicts, ministerial approval, and commercial law all cannot be counted on, we are afraid that plans to adopt constitutionalism and establish an assembly might remain only on paper.[60]

In contrast, faced with strong local popular resistance to the new loan agreement, Qing officials were pressured to adopt a more conciliatory attitude in dealing with the two provincial companies. In reply to the two railway companies' telegrams of protest, the Ministry of Agriculture, Industry, and Commerce claimed that "it was not only the Zhejiang gentry and governor who are trying to protect the railway, but this ministry is also deeply concerned regarding the public interest." Therefore, if the case fell "within the discretion of the ministry," the ministry noted, it would "do everything to satisfy your high expectations."[61] When asked by the Jiangsu Railway Company to use a telegraph memorial to petition the court, Duanfang, the governor-general of Liangjiang, replied by telegraph and suggested that since the two companies knew more about the whole issue than he did, the companies should issue a joint public telegram with himself and the governors of Jiangsu and Zhejiang. They would then forward the telegram to the court asking the throne to order the Foreign Ministry 'to do its best to insist on the Chinese position to preserve railway affairs and protect China's sovereignty." He ended the telegram by noting that "this is only my humble opinion. Please discuss it and inform me of your decision."[62]

It was in this context that the local governors-general and governors found themselves facing a dilemma. As provincial officials, they were pressured by the court to implement the proclaimed policy. As rulers of local areas, they faced direct pressure from the local elites. Caught in between, they often found themselves playing the roles of reluctant mediators seeking compromise between the central government and local elites. Concerning the loan issue, although the provincial officials were ordered by the edict of October 20, 1907, to "supervise the swift completion of planning and allocating of the loan and to persuade local gentry not to persist in their requirements for the sake of stabilizing the whole situation," local governors generally took a position leaning toward the views of the local elites.[63] The governor-general of Liangjiang, the governor of Jiangsu, and the governor of Zhejiang sent a joint telegraph memorial and informed the court of the strong resentment the loan agreement had stirred up among local people and suggested that Beijing consider local reactions and see if a deal more acceptable to the local elites could be negotiated with the British. When the court later issued sternly worded edicts warning local government officials to take swift action to persuade local gentry and noting that they would be held responsible if there were any incidents agitated by "rebellious groups," they jointly memorialized the court in telegrams, assuring Beijing that they were taking all necessary measures to keep the situation under control.[64] After receiving the edict, the governor-general telegraphed the Jiangsu Railway Company and the General Chamber of Commerce asking them to explain the court's intention to the gentry and merchants and to dispel public misgivings. He went on to say that "it is my daily hope that a good transformation of strategy can be drawn from your discussions. I shall make a factual report to the throne and try my best to remedy the situation. I request that you reply promptly."[65]

Significant here are not the details of interaction between high-ranking Qing officials or government ministries and local railway companies but rather the fact of this interaction itself. It set a precedent in Chinese dynastic history in that the railway company, as a new modern organization governed by private shareholders, was recognized by the government as a legitimate entity to negotiate and consult with in the process of decision making that concerned it. This represented a significant step forward compared to actions taken during the campaign to boycott American goods. Though the Shanghai General Chamber of Commerce played an important leadership role in the campaign, it was concerned that a business organization's involvement in diplomatic issues was not congruent with the political system.[66] Thus, the initial public telegram was sent, not in the name of the chamber, but in the name of a group of people led by Zeng Shaoqing. The railway companies of Zhejiang and Jiangsu certainly acted in a firmer and bolder way in dealing with the Qing court.

Furthermore, after the loan decision was furiously resisted by the Zhejiang and Jiangsu elite, the Foreign Ministry asked the railway companies to send representatives to Beijing and negotiate a settlement. This set another precedent, in that here, when the government and local elites were involved in a disputed issue, the latter were formally allowed to participate in policy deliberations with the former. From the telegram sent to the directors-general of the two provincial companies by the governor-general on November 13, we can see that when the Foreign Ministry first asked the companies to send representatives to Beijing to "examine records and to be briefed in person," the request was rejected by the two railway companies. The ministry then sent another telegram noting that the railway companies could send representatives to "explain the whole situation in detail to the ministry. If there is a way to uphold the request, the ministry will do its best in negotiating to meet the expectation of elders in Jiangsu and Zhejiang." After receiving this telegram, the railway companies finally agreed to comply.[67] From the cordial tone of the telegram and conciliatory position of the ministry, it is obvious that the atmosphere and environment for political participation had undergone a sea change in the first years of the twentieth century in China.

The widespread use of the telegraph as the main means of political communication also contributed to another significant development in late Qing politics in which many official telegrams between government organs and policymakers were reprinted in newspapers, thus making it difficult for either party to hide their positions on a particular issue. For example, the first sections of each of two compiled volumes on the railway loan unrest were devoted to "edicts and memorials" and "telegrams in official circles." These included a large quantity of correspondence between central and provincial officials and between ministries in Beijing and the provincial authorities.[68] Newspapers such as the recently reformatted *Shen Bao* also gave more space to print important official telegrams, memorials, and letters.

This change was significant, because monopolistic control of political information was vital to the dynasty's rule, and the political elites traditionally conducted decision making *in camera*. As described in Chapter 3, Sheng Xuanhuai and his co-conspirators in the "mutual protection" scheme were very keen to keep their scheme secret from the public by controlling telegraph transmissions. This time the situation was very different. Because of strong public resistance to the official policy, both central and provincial officials often felt pressured to make their stands on the railway loan issue known to the public. In the process, a great number of telegrams were reprinted in newspapers, including telegrams between ministries in Beijing and local officials in Zhejiang and Jiangsu; between central ministries and local railway companies; and between provincial governors and railway companies. Making these telegrams accessible to the public served the purpose of delineating and clarifying the positions of various parties on the loan issue, but it also placed them under more intensive public scrutiny. The result was an increased degree of transparency in late Qing politics.

In fact, from 1905 on, we encounter new users of public telegrams, with new motivations. Throughout the boycott movement, public telegrams were sent largely by chambers of commerce and other organizations that represented a significant proportion of the Chinese elite. It was through the mobilization of various local organizations that the boycott movement was launched so rapidly and propelled further by rising Chinese nationalism. In the case of the railway rights recovery movement, private railway companies and chambers of commerce were finally allowed to participate in policy discussions, representing the start of organized political participation by local elites. More significantly, compared to the case of the "mutual protection of the Southeast" several years before, an increasing number of telegrams between policymaking parties were not kept secret, thus making their positions on specific issues more open. All these new developments signified an enlarged space for political participation in the last days of the Qing dynasty, in which political dramas were performed by multiple actors, ranging from private individuals to railway companies, local elites, and high-ranking officials. Following this look at the history of the public telegraph in China, the next question is how it became such an important means of political communication, maneuvering, and mobilization in late Qing politics, which is the focus of discussion of Chapter 5.

CHAPTER FIVE

Telegraph Power

Textual and Historical Contexts

ABOUT EIGHTEEN centuries ago, various warlords assumed the reins of power from the dying East Han dynasty and engaged in a period of chaotic warfare. In 199 A.D., Yuan Shao, the most powerful warlord, decided to fight a decisive battle against his main rival in north China, Cao Cao, who controlled the dynastic capital and thus often legitimized his offensives against other warlords by issuing imperial edicts through a nominal emperor whom he controlled. After an army of 300,000 men had been deployed, an advisor suggested to Yuan Shao that "since your lordship resorts to arms in the name of the highest allegiance, it behooves us to spell out Cao Cao's crimes and circulate the indictment through all districts in order to publish his offenses and secure his punishment. Our claim thus will be valid and lawful."

Yuan Shao took this advice and instructed a renowned literary genius called Chen Lin to draft a public proclamation. As described in the famous Chinese historical novel *The Romance of the Three Kingdoms,* "Yuan Shao read Chen Lin's draft proclamation with great satisfaction and ordered it circulated through all regions, and [for copies to be] hung at key passes, fords, and other points of entry." The proclamation is a full-length denunciation of Cao Cao, and is too long to cite here in its entirety. The following is an excerpt:

Now the house of Han is dying a slow death. The social fabric hangs slack and torn. The court stands without a shred of support. The top administration is defenseless. In the imperial estates the elite look downcast, heads bowed, wings furled, having lost all hope of succor. Though loyal liegemen remain, how can they manifest their integrity when they are menaced by so cruel and violent a vassal?

Cao Cao controls a picked force of seven hundred that surrounds the palace. It poses as the residential guards, but in reality detains the sovereign, a sign of impending usurpation that we will find all too alarming. The time is ripe for those loyal to the dynasty to splash the ground with their life's blood, for upright men to make their mark. Let no one fail to rise to the occasion. . . .

Whoever takes Cao Cao's head will be made lord of five thousand households and awarded fifty million cash. Any commander of a unit, subordinate commander, military or civil official who surrenders to us will be welcomed without question. Let our generosity and bounty be widely published, together with announced rewards, so that by this proclamation the empire will know of the grave crisis facing the sacred court.

This order has the force of law.[1]

It was said "the document reached the capital at a time when Cao Cao was stricken with migraine and confined to bed. As he read it, he began quaking to his marrow and broke into an icy sweat. Suddenly his migraine passed and he leaped out of the bed" and demanded to find out who had written the proclamation.[2] Is it possible that a literary text could have had such power to shock a legendary warlord in Chinese history? Where did this power come from? The writer may have exaggerated Cao Cao's reaction, but the episode nonetheless shows that the public proclamation was an effective genre of political discourse and an important means of seeking legitimacy in historical Chinese political struggles.

The Public Telegraph and Textual Power

The above proclamation is an example of a special genre of traditional Chinese political texts called *xiwen*, which were often used to denounce usurpers or political rivals and as summons to arms in wartime. Yuan Shao's proclamation served both purposes. Compared to other Chinese political texts, *xiwen* had a number of unique characteristics. First, they were authoritative. In most cases, *xiwen* were issued by people in powerful positions who claimed the legitimacy and moral authority to issue such proclamations. A just cause was often elaborated on at length to enhance its moral persuasion. Second, *xiwen* were public. The majority of *xiwen* were intended to reach a large audience, serving as an effective means of publicizing political information. Even military *xiwen* were often used to exert public political and military pressure, and they were thus often made public as well.[3] Third, *xiwen* spread fast. In fact, in ancient China, feathers were often attached to the envelope of the *xiwen*, signifying that the document was an urgent dispatch that had to be sent by express courier. Finally, the text was often elegantly written, with a sophisticated mixture of rhetorical techniques whose solemnity, authoritativeness, and persuasiveness stirred readers' feelings to take the issuer's side and incited anger, contempt, and mobilization against the side the text intended to denounce. Writing *xiwen* was not an easy task, and such proclamations were often drafted by the best writers of their time.[4]

If we want to know why the public telegraph so quickly emerged as a new genre in the Chinese press in the last years of the Qing dynasty and was used by the Chinese elite as an effective means of political discussion and mobilization, we cannot neglect this new genre's relationship with traditional Chinese genres of public political discourse such as *xiwen*, imperial edicts, bureaucratic correspondence (*gongwen*), public notices (*gaoshi*), leaflets (*chuandan*), and notices put up on walls (*jietie*). Of all these genres, the public telegraph seems most like *xiwen*, and it went through a similar "authority-enhancing" process that forced its readers to take it seriously.

By their very nature, public telegrams were subject to scrutiny by a large number of people, which put pressure on the sender to ensure that the cause was a valid one. If a favorable response was not forthcoming, making the telegram public at least clarified the sender's point of view and thus shielded him or her from misunderstanding or attack. No matter how the telegrams were subsequently reprinted, their public status indicated that they were serious and not to be taken lightly. The public telegrams discussed so far fall into two broad categories: (a) telegrams proclaiming, petitioning for, protesting against, or promoting a particular issue and intended to be circulated widely, and (b) policy-related telegrams reprinted in newspapers and made public.

The fact that public telegrams were often issued collectively likewise contributed to what I call the "authority-enhancing" process. Some public telegrams were sent by an individual, but most had a collective signature, on behalf of either a group of people or an organization. These can be classified into several types:

(a) Telegrams jointly issued by a group of people. Examples include the telegram protesting the appointment of an heir to the throne sent by Jing Yuanshan and 1,231 co-signatories and the memorials to the throne on the railway issue sent by the governors of Jiangsu and Zhejiang.

(b) Telegrams with a number of lead signatures, but claiming to represent or to be issued on behalf of a vast number of people. Thus the "birthday-celebrating" and "well-wishing" telegrams sent by overseas Chinese to the court in 1899 were often sent by leaders of overseas Chinese communities on behalf of all community members. In the case of the Suzhou-Hangzhou-Ningbo railway dispute, retired Grand Councilor Wang Wenshao and 114 influential figures petitioned the court on behalf of all the gentry in Zhejiang.

(c) Telegrams sent with a general collective signature, without specifically giving the sender's name. Examples include the telegram protesting a railway loan sent to the governor of Zhejiang on behalf of "all gentry in Shaoxing" and one sent to a Beijing official on behalf of "fellow townsmen from Ningbo."

(d) Telegrams sent in the name of an organization or a number of organizations, which will be discussed in detail later.

Obviously, by using collective signatures, the senders of public telegrams intended to show that the points raised were of wide concern and did not merely represent an individual's opinion. In Chinese, "public telegram" is written with the characters *gong,* signifying public and collective, and *dian,* telegram. The term *gongdian* thus implies both that a telegram is public and open, not private and secret, and that it is a collective message, not an individual one. The extended implication is that it has been sent in a just cause, in the public interest, or on an issue of urgent public concern. *Gong* is the prefix in the words *gongdao, gongzheng* and *gongping* (fair, just, impartial, evenhanded, reasonable); *gongyi* (public good), *gonglun* (public opinion); *gongkai* (open, overt, public); *gongbao* (communiqué, bulletin); *gongbu* (promulgate, announce, make public); *gongde* (public morality, social ethics); and *gongshi* (public affairs, official business). All these terms have positive connotations. Being called a *gongdian* undoubtedly helped to enhance the authority of this new genre of political discourse.

The collective signatories of public telegrams did not appear out of a void. The practice closely resembled the preexisting genres of *gongqi* and *gongbing. Gongqi* were either open letters or letters signed by a group of people. Sometimes, *gongqi* were more like public notices. *Shen Bao* started to publish public notices on various affairs in the very early stages of its publication. *Gongbing* were derived from *jietie* (notes stuck on a wall). Historically, since they were a means of spreading unofficial information anonymously, *jietie* were forbidden by authorities. But when a *jietie* was signed by many people, it became a *gongbing.*[5] The public telegram with a general collective signature can thus be seen as a type bridging the anonymous and the public. However, when a public telegram was signed "all gentlemen in Ningbo," for example, its enhanced representativity was counterbalanced by the diminished authenticity implicit in the failure to specify the actual senders.[6]

A third characteristic of public telegrams was, as with *xiwen,* that the text possessed a unique rhetorical style. Since sending telegrams was a costly undertaking in the late Qing era, texts were usually very concisely written. Numerous abbreviations were used, and the message often went straight to the main points. The following is a telegram sent to a high-ranking official in Beijing by local people in Ningbo. The original text has twenty-eight characters in Chinese: "When the foreign loan agreement was reached, the railway rights were lost, and the Zhejiang people were shattered. Your honor is from Ningbo and should represent us. We beg you to memorialize the throne on our behalf and not let your fellow townsmen down." The telegram was signed "a public request by all of your fellow Ningbo townsmen."[7] The style of such public telegrams can generally be summarized as succinct and pointed. After telegraphic news was widely adopted by newspapers, the telegraphic style had a great influence in changing the traditionally ornate writing of Chinese political texts.

Although the authority of public telegrams was definitely enhanced by their concise, succinct style, telegraphy basically communicated point to point, and to be heard by a wider audience, a telegram needed to be amplified. This was done by newspapers. In fact, a telegram became a public or circular telegram only after it had been reprinted; otherwise, it was just a plain coded telegram read by a limited number of people. Newspaper editors thus played a key role in making public telegrams truly public.

Shen Bao is a good example. Because of the conservative position of its chief editor, it reprinted neither the telegrams that overseas Chinese sent to the Qing court in 1899 pressing Empress Cixi to restore power to Emperor Guangxu nor Jing Yuanshan's telegram protesting Empress Cixi's plot to appoint an heir to the throne in 1900. In contrast, these telegrams were widely reprinted in overseas Chinese newspapers, especially those run by followers of Kang Youwei and Liang Qichao. Besides their political positions, newspaper editors were motivated by several other factors in deciding whether or not to print telegrams, including their contents, political sensitivity, news value, timeliness, and the status of the sender or senders. Editors thus served as evaluators and filterers of telegrams. When a public telegram was finally reprinted in *Shen Bao*, the fact that it had appeared in a well-established mainstream newspaper itself enhanced the credibility and authority of its text.

Finally, among those telegraphic communications dealing with policy issues, a fairly large number were memorials to the throne by ranking local officials. This fact signifies an important change in the "communication-decision" structure of the Qing dynasty, which had previously been based on the unique palace memorials system (*zouzhe*) created during the Kangxi (1662-1722) and Yongzheng (1723-1735) reigns.[8] Initially, the Qing adopted the traditional memorial system (*benzhang*), a highly formalized bureaucratic communication system inherited from the Ming dynasty.[9] Since under this system, a memorial passed through the hands of many people, keeping it secret was very difficult, and an early leak of the contents often led to a power struggle among different court factions. To ensure the emperor's control of vital political information and also exert mutual surveillance among officials, Emperor Kangxi thus started by asking his most trusted provincial officials to provide secret reports on local conditions to him directly. This privilege was later extended to other high-ranking officials when the palace memorial system was perfected in Emperor Yongzheng's reign. The memorials were sent in sealed envelopes directly to the emperor, and after being read, they were returned to the original senders. Unlike the old *benzhang* system, which had provided an open channel of communication, most *zouzhe* were secret correspondence between the memorial presenters and the emperor.[10]

The original purpose of establishing the palace memorial system was to change the routine, formal communication-decision structure into an effective, secret personal structure that enhanced the throne's control over political information. When the telegraph arrived in China in the 1880s, the new technology was adopted to forward memorials and promulgate edicts. However, it did not cause any significant change in the system besides increasing the speed of transmission. *Jing Bao* (discussed in Chapter 2) was still the primary source of official political information. It was not until the turn of the twentieth century that more and more telegraphic memorials were reprinted in newspapers. It was not until 1905, for example, that *Shen Bao* deliberately started to carry a large quantity of telegraph news and memorials. In doing so, the newspapers changed the communication-decision structure, willy-nilly, from absolute secrecy to increased, if still limited, openness. Meanwhile, *Jing Bao*, the traditional method of disseminating political information, became obsolete. When memorials and official telegraphic communications became more accessible to the public, this not only enabled the Chinese elite to engage in politics in a more informed way but also attached seriousness and significance to the texts of public telegrams, thus making them more authoritative.

In summary, several characteristics of the public telegram helped establish it as an authoritative and effective new genre of political text in China. Public and collectively authored, speedily disseminated, dealing with issues of wide concern, having a concise yet pregnant style, issued mostly by the rich and powerful, and carried by major newspapers, public telegrams became accepted as significant texts. In addition, public telegrams drew their textual strength from their continuity with traditional Chinese genres of political discourse, such as *xiwen*, *zouzhe*, and *gongbing*, further incorporating the attributes of the public notice, official correspondence, and news writing. Possessing such textual power, they became a very effective tool of political communication and mobilization in modern China.

Institutionalized Usage of Public Telegrams

It will be recalled that when Cao Cao read the *xiwen* denouncing his impending usurpation of the throne, he started shaking and his migraine was dissipated by the shock effect of the proclamation. He asked where the *xiwen* came from. At this point, the story takes another surprising turn. When Cao Cao found out that it was from Yuan Shao, he was relieved, because he knew Yuan Shao lacked a sense of military strategy, and he was confident that he would be victorious in the battle proclaimed by the *xiwen*. This new development in the episode reminds us that textual power alone was not sufficient; the power relationships in real life, reflected in the position held by issuer, often played a more pivotal role. In early twentieth-century China, the increasingly organizational usage of public telegrams certainly enhanced their mobilizing power.

A fundamental change after 1905 was that public telegrams were issued more frequently by newly emergent organizations. The majority of the public telegrams discussed in Chapters 2 and 3 were initiated by influential social figures on urgent political issues, often on a spontaneous basis (i.e., the case of Jing Yuanshan) or on behalf of a generalized mass of people (i.e., all Chinese in Singapore or all the gentry in Hangzhou). The effects of these telegrams largely depended on public attention to the issue concerned and their senders' charisma. These telegrams had a strong effect, but were generally confined to protesting or appealing against a particular issue. Only after the telegraph started to be widely used by organizations did it come to function as an organizing and coordinating tool to launch national campaigns. The movement to boycott American goods was the first time that a well-organized public organization employed the public telegram in national politics. All of this was made possible by the emergence of new types of organizations at the beginning of the 1900s.

The Chinese elite clearly realized the new power they had acquired through forming organizations. As the famous modern Chinese educator Ma Xiangbo said at a specially convened meeting to discuss the American goods boycott on July 19, 1905, "China has had no organizations in her several thousand years of history. To respond to current foreign threats, educational and business circles are working together, which is a stroke of good luck in China's unfortunate situation." The meeting was initiated by the Shanghai Learned Society (hu xue hui) and attended by representatives of Shanghai business, educational, and industrial circles, as well as those of other cities. After passing the boycott resolution, the meeting drafted a telegram asking the SGCC to send it to the ministries in Beijing and cities nationwide.[11]

Ma was right, but the situation he described had not come about easily. It had been a long-standing policy of the Qing dynasty to prohibit private assembly and the formation of societies by intellectuals. Realizing that the tumultuous politics of the late Ming dynasty had been largely caused by struggles among partisan intellectual organizations, Emperor Shunzhi (1644–1661) issued edicts prohibiting them twice, in the seventh and seventeenth years of his reign. These prohibitions were not lifted until 1904, but they had been breached by reformers by the end of the nineteenth century. During the reform movement, Kang Youwei and his followers founded close to a hundred societies all over China. After the One Hundred Days Reform was crushed by Empress Cixi, the court persecuted members of the various reform societies and reiterated the prohibition of private societies.[12]

Nonetheless, led by Kang Youwei, the exiled reformers organized more than 100 Societies for Protecting the Emperor (in America called the Chinese Empire Reform Association) in overseas Chinese communities after 1899, and overseas revolutionaries were also involved in establishing anti-Manchu organizations. At the same time, open-minded intellectuals, social dignitaries, and students educated in the Western-style set up various organizations within China. These organizations were not officially recognized by the government, but given the much-weakened political and social control of the Qing dynasty after the Boxer Rebellion, they managed to establish themselves and multiply even before their prohibition was effectively abolished when the Qing dynasty permitted the establishment of chambers of commerce in 1904. Between 1901 and 1904, 271 new organizations were established in China (not including branches). Among them, 127 were located in metropolitan areas, 62 in prefecture and county seats, and the rest in small and medium-sized cities.[13]

The scope of these organizations was very wide, and they had diverse political and social agendas. They engaged in various kinds of activities, including promoting education, publishing newspapers and books, organizing newspaper reading rooms, setting up libraries, conducting physical and military training, propagandizing new ideas through drama, music, and slide shows, conducting surveys, engaging in modern business, introducing modern sciences, and sponsoring public speeches. Though many of these organizations were loosely organized and would be viewed as merely embryonic modern civil organizations in later years, they played an important role in modern Chinese history. Their appearance effectively enlarged the public space in Chinese society in the last years of the Qing dynasty, especially in the Yangzi Delta, as reflected by the fact that 170 out of 271 organizations were located in Jiangsu (77), Zhejiang (51) and Shanghai (42).[14]

The appearance of chambers of commerce in 1904 signaled the relaxation of the prohibition of organizations by the Qing court. From 1904 to 1912, more than 900 chambers of commerce were established nationwide.

In 1906, the Qing court proclaimed that it was preparing to adopt constitutionalism, prompting the establishment of a large number of societies advocating constitutionalism and local self-governance. Facing a de facto loss of control, but wanting to regulate these new organizations, the Qing court in 1909 issued laws legalizing the formation of organizations and regulating assembly and organization.[15] In this new environment, a large number of the Chinese elite joined the wave of organization formation. According to incomplete but revealing statistics, in addition to the chambers of commerce, there were 723 educational societies in China by 1909, and by 1911 there were at least 19 general agricultural societies,

TABLE I

Chambers of Commerce in China, 1904–1912

Year	General Chambers	Branch Chambers	Total
1904	6	23	29
1905	5	36	41
1906	14	91	105
1907	7	58	65
1908	3	84	87
1909	1	172	173
1910	4	177	181
1911	3	109	112
1912	2	162	164
TOTAL	45	912	957

SOURCE: Ma Min and Zhu Ying, *Chuantong yu jindai de erchong bianzou*, 45–46.

with 276 branches. Thus there were around 2,000 commercial, educational, and agricultural organizations alone.[16] The total number of organizations in all fields must have been significantly larger.

It was in this context that the telegraph was widely used by various organizations in the early twentieth century. When public telegrams were sent by organizations, their influence could be enhanced, not only by the status and reputation of organization members, but also by the organizations' greater resources and powerful position. The campaign to boycott American goods in 1905 clearly shows how potently the SGCC used the public telegram to mobilize and coordinate the campaign nationwide. The most important thing that set the chamber of commerce apart from other organizations at the time was that it was generally the nexus of activity of other organizations in an area. This can be explained in two ways. First, the chamber of commerce possessed significant political and financial resources compared to other civil organizations. Its leaders were usually *shenshang* (gentry-merchants), with distinguished social and economic status.[17] Secondly, the fact that many chambers of commerce were well organized and had a network beyond the local level certainly helped enlarge their influence. In Suzhou, for example, apart from the general chamber, eight local branches were established in surrounding areas.[18] The existence of these local branches enabled the general chambers to extend their reach, especially to small cities and towns.

With substantial social and financial resources and a well-established network of organizations, chambers of commerce could exert considerable influence on the nongovernmental power network composed of various civic organizations. In fact, most members of local business elites were often involved in a variety of activities and sat on the boards of many associations. You Xianjia, the president of the Suzhou Chamber of Commerce for the first three years of its existence, was also a board member of the physical education association, the school affairs association, the police society, the general chamber of agriculture, and the municipal self-governance society.[19] Because of the considerable political and economic resources possessed by local chamber leaders, they played a leading role in organizing activities of general concern to the area, often acting as the coordinators of these activities.

In the case of the movement resisting railway loans, the Jiangsu and Zhejiang Railway Companies played the roles of legitimate mediators between the government and local shareholders, thus becoming a nexus of communication and information. Since they were established according to government regulations, approved by the court, and did not receive official subsidies, these two companies were entitled to a full independent status.[20] As modern business organizations, their legitimate status was acknowledged by both Beijing and the provincial authorities, as shown in the numerous telegrams between two companies, ministries in Beijing, and the provincial governors in Jiangsu and Zhejiang. In addition, the directors-general and deputy directors-general of the two companies were members of the social elite.[21] The Chinese elite ran both the chambers of commerce and railway companies, and the accessibility of the telegraph greatly helped make their voices heard.

As a technology of communication, the telegraph did not go through the many changes in the first decade of the twentieth century that it had in an earlier period. However, it was clear that the telegraph was increasingly used, not only to express individual and collective opinions, but also as an important means of organizing large-scale, sometimes even nationwide, campaigns, which in turn contributed to wider and more frequent telegraph usage. Why did the role of the telegraph become increasingly important in public political participation? The answer may best be found by turning away from the telegraph itself. The difference in the effects of using the telegraph had, in fact, more to do with who used it and how it was used, rather than with its intrinsic qualities.

After 1905, well-organized legal organizations became the major senders of public telegrams in national political mobilizations. Before then, as we have seen, most public telegrams were sent either by individuals or by ad hoc groups.[22] The telegrams sent in the campaigns to boycott American goods and resist British railway loans were different from their predecessors in many ways. First, most of them were sent by chambers of commerce, railway companies, or other organizations. Legal, resourceful, and in a leading role, these organizations used the public telegram skillfully, giving them a great degree of influence on the national policy issues. Secondly, because these telegrams touched issues of broad public concern and were from authoritative sources, newspapers were eager to pick them up and reprint them, giving them wide circulation and maximum publicity. Concurrently, the first years of the twentieth century saw another wave of newspaper publishing in China, making public telegrams more likely to be reprinted. Finally, the last dozen years of the Qing dynasty were the most eventful period in its history. With the ongoing New Policies reforms and the rise of Chinese nationalism at the turn of the twentieth century, a new historical context provided a more receptive environment for political participation for Chinese citizens, thus making it possible for the public telegram to play a more active and effective role in politics at the end of the Qing dynasty.

By emphasizing the importance of the historical context in which the public telegram played its role, my approach challenges those who emphasize the role technology plays in social change. The key point I want to emphasize here is that it was not the telegraph that caused social and political changes, but rather ongoing social and political changes that made the telegraph more effective in facilitating information flow and helping to further expand political participation in late Qing China. Of course, this technology provided a dramatic improvement in communication and information dissemination, but the technological revolution could also be used to achieve very different goals. The fact that the public telegram as a new genre of political text only appeared after 1895 also illustrates the importance of historical context in affecting the way a technology is utilized. In retrospect, the much-loosened political control in the New Policies period provided the necessary context in which telegraphy's capacity to open up public space could be realized.

The New Policies and Chinese Nationalism: The Golden Age of Political Participation

From 1901 to the fall of the Qing dynasty in 1911, the so-called New Policies (*xinzheng*) period witnessed a series of dramatic reforms, including the abolition of the civil service exams and promotion of study abroad; the setting up of ministries of foreign affairs (replacing the Zongli Yamen), commerce, police, and education, as well as a bureau of military training; the prohibition of opium and discouragement of foot-binding among women; the drafting of commercial laws and promotion of the construction of railroads; and a plan to convert the dynasty into a constitutional monarchy.[23] These reforms touched all political, social, educational, and military aspects of Qing rule and in fact laid the basic framework for China's transformation into a modern state in the twentieth century. However, this period has not attracted a great deal of scholarly attention so far, given its undoubted significance in modern Chinese history. What interests us most here is the fact that in this period, the Chinese elite gained an expanded space for political participation they had never possessed before.

The New Policies were initiated from the top down and were undoubtedly propelled by the deep crises the court faced after the Boxer catastrophe. In the dawn of August 15, 1900, one day after allied foreign troops fought their way past the Boxers into Beijing, Empress Cixi, along with Emperor Guangxu and a small entourage, escaped from the capital. After enduring much hardship, they reached Xian on October 23, and the court temporarily settled there. On her way to Xian, Empress Cixi relied mainly on the telegraph to issue orders to the rest of China. *Shen Bao* and other newspapers reprinted telegrams issued from the so-called *xingzai* (emperor's temporary residence). On January 29, 1901, Empress Cixi issued an edict from Xian acknowledging responsibility for the Boxer uprising and the need to make changes in the stricken dynasty. In the edict, the court openly solicited advice on reform from ranking officials. Though it was not uncommon for the emperor to ask his subjects to participate in policy debates, it was very unusual for Empress Cixi to ask for advice on such a large scale and in such a humble way, indicating the unprecedented legitimacy crisis that Cixi and the court faced after the Boxer catastrophe.

The court's open solicitation of advice was responded to with enthusiasm. Among the various suggestions proposed by Qing officials, three joint memorials by Zhang Zhidong and Liu Kunyi, two of the most powerful governors-general at the time, were the most influential. They advocated more reforms in education and government administration and the adoption of more "Western methods" in commerce, agriculture, communication, and the military, basically following the thinking of the old

Western Affairs Clique. Others proposed more dramatic political reforms, urging the court to adopt constitutionalism and set up a parliament.[24] Before 1905, the court seems largely to have followed the approach proposed by Zhang and Liu, demonstrating reluctance to initiate large-scale political reforms.

Either the Qing rulers did not realize that in providing more room for political participation, they were opening a floodgate that let loose a current that would soon escape their control, or they more likely had no other choice. The Chinese elite became more active in participating in political discussion in the New Policies period, and their ability to exert political influence was greatly augmented by the new institutions at their disposal. Under the New Policies, they were allowed to form professional associations and societies to promote commerce, education, opium suppression, and many other social and political issues. Unlike the old-style organizations that had existed before, such as townsmen associations, commercial guilds, and disaster relief associations, these organizations were formally organized, more broadly based, and had clear purposes. Sanctioned by the government, they could conduct their activities openly and gain access to more resources. Furthermore, under loosened political control, more and more organizations, often prompted by a special event or formed to address a particular issue, appeared with or without official permission.

Another institution that played an important role in the changes was the modern newspaper. As a result of the reforms, the number of newspapers continued to increase. From 1902 on, the court allowed the publication of official newspapers both in Beijing and in the provinces, and the prohibition on private newspapers in Beijing was subsequently also lifted. Once again, actual developments went well beyond the court's initial intention. In addition to an increased number of newspapers that were not totally out of accord with the government position, a number of newspapers published by students studying abroad appeared, which tended to be prorevolutionary in nature. The Qing court tried to tighten control, but it was unable to prohibit them all, and the process quickly became a tug of war. In 1903, the government tried to shut down the prorevolutionary *Su Bao*, but the case grabbed national attention and eventually put the government into a very awkward position when confronted with inflamed public opinion.[25] The vast majority of newspapers, whether they favored revolution or reform, started to engage in political disputes that made for very active political participation in this period.

Armed with two new institutional tools, modern organizations and newspapers, the Chinese elite became the main political players in the New Policies era. However, one crucial question remains to be answered: Why did people participate in politics? In other words, what motivated the Chinese elite to involve themselves in politics in the early twentieth century? No answer can be complete that does not include the rise of modern Chinese nationalism at the time, which was a direct response to the colonial and imperialist threats China faced and the impending disintegration of the Qing empire.

A 1905 article titled "On Self-Survival" in *Dongfang Zazhi* (Eastern Miscellany) gives a very revealing summary of the deteriorating situation China had faced since 1894. It notes that after the Sino-Japanese War in 1894, "self-strengthening" (*ziqiang*) became the most popular watchword in public discourse. The word changed to "self-reliance" (*zili*) after the Boxer catastrophe in 1900 and changed again to "self-survival" (*zicun*) after 1903 when Russia and Japan engaged in war in China's northeast.[26] These three popular watchwords and their evolution in public discourse undoubtedly reflected collective anxiety about China's future. Following the perspective of social Darwinism, which was widely accepted as a law of social progress, Chinese perceptions of national and racial distinctions were deep and often highly emotionally charged. As scholars have pointed out, modern Chinese nationalism was very much a nationalism of "self-defense," yet its development had multiple components and trajectories following changing historical conditions.[27] It is beyond the scope of this study to give a detailed description of Chinese nationalism, and the following is only a brief account of key components of modern Chinese nationalism that played a substantial role in mobilizing political participation in the late Qing era. As we shall see, the main points of Chinese nationalism were often reflected in public telegrams reprinted in national newspapers.

The Rights and Duties of the "New People"

A nation consisting of *guomin* (nationals or citizens) was a new concept to most Chinese at the turn of the twentieth century. In China's long dynastic history, the sanctioned discourse demarcated the population into the emperor and his subjects, with the former as the paramount ruler and the latter as absolute subordinates. When Kang Youwei and Liang Qichao first introduced the concept of *guomin* at the end of the nineteenth century, their assertions that a nation should consist of a group of fellow countrymen who had the right to discuss national affairs, make national laws, pursue national interests, and defend against national threats stirred up a large following among the Chinese elite. Faced with the reality that these ideas were totally strange to the vast majority of Chinese, the elite made strenuous efforts to enlighten the emperor's subjects. Heated discussions were devoted to examining the shortcomings of the Chinese national character and finding a way to transform vast numbers of mentally enslaved Chinese into people with a modern consciousness, or into "new people," to use Liang Qichao's term.

Among the long list of qualities that such "new people" should possess, rights, duties, and responsibilities were held to be the most important.[28] On the one hand, the right to participate in national politics was elaborated as an inalienable right possessed by each individual. On the other, it was considered an individual's duty and responsibility to participate in politics in times of need. The spreading of this new consciousness provided the Chinese elite with a theoretical foundation on which to legitimize their political participation. In the case of the Suzhou-Hangzhou-Ningbo railway loan, the fact that the Foreign Ministry had reached an agreement with the British without consulting with the local elite received great play in agitating the public. The government eventually had to invite local representatives to Beijing to pacify public anger, signaling a de facto enlargement of space for the local elite to participate in the decision-making process.

National Sovereignty and National Interests

In public telegrams after 1900, the term *liquan* continued to appear frequently, but its connotations had changed. In addition to the old meanings of *li* and *quan* in public discourse, the concept of *quanli*, the same characters as *liquan* but printed in reverse order, was used more often to signify rights possessed by the "new people" and China. At the level of people, corresponding with discussion of how to act as "new people," the concept *quanli* focused on rights, especially the people's right to participate in the political process. At the level of the country, the phrase designated national sovereignty. When the two characters were used separately, the character *li* increasingly referred to national interests and the character *quan* to national sovereignty. In a time of constant foreign encroachment and threats, protecting national sovereignty and interests became very important to politically conscious Chinese.

The movement to resist railway loans is a good example of this. The motives of the Jiangsu and Zhejiang elite in calling for the abrogation of the preliminary Sino-British agreement were closely related to the fact that they viewed the right to construct the railway as a matter of national sovereignty. A telegram sent to the Grand Council on behalf of all Zhejiang gentry, led by Wang Wenshao, asserted that the gentry were afraid that "when the loan right is not in our hands, the railway right will be lost next too." In a telegram to the Grand Council from the Jiangsu gentry, railway rights were related to national sovereignty and to the lifelines of Jiangsu and Zhejiang provinces. A joint petition to the governor of Zhejiang by Wang Wenshao and 115 Zhejiang dignitaries further pointed out that "throughout history, railway loans have often been used as bait by those whose real purpose is to seize control of other countries." To those resisting the loan, the loss of the railway was thus tantamount to the loss of sovereignty in two provinces. The Zhejiang Railway Company proclaimed in a telegram that "the Foreign Ministry, to get loan kickbacks, has totally neglected imperial edicts, commercial law, and public opinion and voluntarily abandoned the Zhejiang people. The Zhejiang people will never follow the fate of Egypt, India, Korea, and Vietnam."[29]

Considering the cost of railway company shares, the majority of railway company shareholders were undoubtedly members of the elite class.[30] For example, the initial capital of 300,000 yuan for the Jiangsu Railway Company was raised mainly by members of the Suzhou Chamber of Commerce, and the first phase fund-raising of 2,000,000 yuan was completed by soliciting funds from gentry and merchants in Shanghai.[31] Thus the movement to resist loans was directly related to the local elite's economic interests. However, the drive to construct a self-financed railway was also motivated by the local elite's aim to compete commercially with the foreigners. Though ideas of conducting a "commercial war" (*shangzhan*) against foreigners had been raised by earlier figures in the Western Affairs Clique, such as Wang Tao and Zheng Guanying, by the early 1900s, private commercial interests were more closely related to national interests, helping the local elite to mobilize the public.[32]

"Civilized Anti-Foreign" Methods

Even though early twentieth-century China witnessed the rising tide of modern Chinese nationalism, nationalist mobilizations such as the railway rights recovery movements and the boycotting American goods movement were fundamentally different from the Boxer Rebellion of a few years previously. Quite strikingly, all these movements emphasized peaceful methods of resisting foreigners. Unlike the xenophobic Boxers who burned down churches, pulled down telegraph lines, and dismantled railroads, the elite protagonists of these subsequent nationalist mobilizations actively used the telegraph to mobilize the masses to strive for the right to construct more Chinese-built railroads, with the ultimate goal of saving the country—and themselves. The method they adopted was called *wenming paiwai* (civilized anti-foreign).

In the case of the movement to resist the Chinese exclusion treaty, its leaders emphasized opposing the treaty in a "civilized" way. On May 21, after a meeting, the Suzhou merchants and gentry came out with a fif-teen-article plan, article eleven of which stipulated that strict orders should be given to prevent ignorant people from using the boycott as an excuse to attack Westerners and missionaries. The Shanghai Civilized Society Opposing the Exclusion Treaty held a meeting on July 26 in which a public speaker claimed that the existing Chinese exclusion treaty affected the future and survival of the Chinese race. However, he admonished the audience that Chinese should treat American merchants and missionaries with civility, thus avoiding making the boycott an issue of international dispute.[33]

Although American goods were sometimes publicly burned, and one Chinese immolated himself to protest the American exclusion law, the boycott was very much a controlled mobilization. The campaign to resist railway loans in 1907 and 1908 witnessed a similar situation. Wang Daxie, the loan negotiator, was threatened with having his ancestral tomb dug up and even assassination, yet these threats were never endorsed by any of the associations resisting the loans.[34] In a special meeting held on October 31, 1907, the newly organized Suzhou Society for Resisting Railway Loans adopted a more combative position. It called on its members not to be constrained by the term *wenming* (civilized) when they came to punish those people who had misled the government for the sake of individual gain. Nonetheless, it admonished that the principle of taking such action was not to target foreigners.[35]

Constitutionalism and Anti-Manchu Revolution

Constitutionalism and anti-Manchu revolution were two different approaches to building a modern Chinese nation-state. Without doubt, in the early 1900s, many Chinese elites believed that adopting constitutionalism was the best way to assure China's survival as an independent nation. In 1893, Zheng Guanying published his famous *Shengshi Weiyan*, in which he proposed both a constitution and a parliament.[36] After the failure of the One Hundred Days Reform, Kang Youwei and Liang Qichao were exiled abroad and advocated the adoption of a constitutional monarchy in China, in opposition to the revolutionaries led by Sun Yat-sen who advocated a democratic republic.

After the Boxer Rebellion, the appeal of constitutionalism gradually increased. Newspapers started to discuss constitutionalism, and influential elite figures such as Zhang Qian were active in promoting this idea. Constitutionalism gained momentum after the Japanese victory in the Russo-Japanese War in 1904–5, in which an Eastern country with a newly established constitutional monarchy soundly defeated the tsarist empire. Using the outcome of the war as evidence of the superiority of the former to the latter, Zhang Qian and others intensified their advocacy of constitutionalism and succeeded in influencing a number of high-ranking government officials. In 1904, Zhang even drafted a memorial to the court for Governors-General Zhang Zhidong and Wei Guangtao that asked for the adoption of a constitutional monarchy in China.[37]

Under this pressure, the court decided in the summer of 1905 to send five high-ranking officials abroad to examine Western political systems. From the end of 1905 to August 1906, five ministers in two groups visited Japan, Britain, France, Belgium, the United States, Germany, Russia, Italy, and Austria. On their return, they all proclaimed that constitutional monarchy would be the best political system for China. After deliberations, on September 1, 1906, the Qing court issued an edict proclaiming the start of "preparation for constitutionalism" in China.[38] The seeming convergence between the court and public opinion further helped to make the idea of constitutionalism widely accepted by the Chinese elite at the time.[39] Use of the public telegram reached a peak during the subsequent movements to promote constitutionalism, which witnessed the largest political mobilization and widest participation by the Chinese elite before the fall of the Qing dynasty.

The Public Telegram in Petitions for Constitutionalism

The advocates of constitutionalism were initially euphoric after the issuance of the September 1, 1906, edict. Celebratory gatherings were held in cities nationwide, and numerous celebratory telegrams were sent to the court. On September 9, the SGCC and other organizations held a celebratory meeting and sent telegrams to Beijing. So did major Shanghai

Chinese newspapers, including *Shen Bao, Shi Bao, Hu Bao, Nanfang Bao*, and *Zhongwai Ribao*, a week later.[40] In addition, advocates of constitutionalism formed a number of organizations to promote the actual implementation of the proposed plan. In Shanghai, the Constitutionalism Study Association was established in December, with Ma Xiangbo as its head; and one week later, the Association for the Preparation of Constitutionalism was also formed, with Zheng Xiaoxu as president and Zhang Qian and Tang Shouqian as vice presidents.[41] Similar associations were established in Jilin, Guangdong, Guizhou, Hubei, and Hunan provinces. In Japan, Yang Du established the Public Association of Constitutionalism (xianzheng jiangxihui), and Liang Qichao established the Informed Politics Society (zhengwen she).[42] In February 1907, Kang Youwei changed the name of the Society for Protecting the Emperor to the Imperial Constitutionalism Association.[43] Constitutionalism was the centripetal force that held together different political groups—aside from the revolutionaries—in support of a common goal.

Yet the initial euphoria of the advocates of constitutionalism disappeared quickly. Because the Qing court did not commit itself to a definite date for adopting constitutionalism and always emphasized the fact that the educational level of the Chinese people was too low to introduce constitutionalism for the time being, the advocates gradually came to suspect that the court was doing everything to procrastinate on the issue. In response to public suspicion and disappointment, on July 8, 1907, the Qing court issued another edict, authorizing those "who really know the execution plan and implementation procedure" for constitutionalism to present their opinions to the court. Compared to the edict of January 1901, in which Empress Cixi solicited advice from ranking officials, this time the scope was much wider, including everyone from high-ranking officials to those who had only passed the county-level civil service exams.[44] Led by Yang Du, the constitutionalists started to petition the court to establish an elected parliament. In September 1907, Yang sent representatives of the Public Association of Constitutionalism to present a petition with more than 100 signatures to the court, but they got no response at all. Undiscouraged, Yang and his comrades solicited more than 4,000 signatures from his native Hunan province and presented the petition again in March 1908, asking the court to establish a parliament within one or two years.[45] Other constitutionalists and organizations followed Yang's initiative enthusiastically.

Once again, the telegraph was widely used. The overseas branches of the Imperial Constitutionalism Association used the telegraph to petition the court to set up a parliament, and within China, similar petitions were organized by organizations advocating constitutionalism in many provinces.[46] Under pressure, the court reacted in two ways. On the one hand, in July, it proclaimed regulations for the organization and election of consultative boards (Ziyi Yuan), ordering each province to set up such a board within a year. On August 27, the court proclaimed that it would gradually carry out preparations in order to compile a constitution and establish a parliament in nine years. This meant that the whole process would be complete by 1917.[47] On the other hand, the court did not want to allow the petition to get out of control, and on August 13, it ordered that the Informed Politics Society be shut down and effectively forced its dissolution.[48] Many constitutionalists felt that nine years was too long to wait for a parliament. Nonetheless, most of them spent the year 1909 focusing on the task of establishing provincial consultative boards. By October 14, 1909, twenty-one provinces had established such boards, Xinjiang being the sole exception.[49]

Though the boards did not have the authority of provincial assemblies and only served as consulting organs to the local governors, the constitutionalists saw them as political platforms from which they could exert more influence on provincial and central government. In fact, the boards are a good example of elite political participation in modern China. The voters' eligibility requirements in terms of birthplace, sex (male only), age (over twenty-five), profession, social status, education (the illiterate were excluded), and property ownership were so stringent that only a very small portion of the population were qualified. There were, for example, only 55,069 qualified voters, about 0.5 percent of the province's population, in Shanxi. The number of voters in Guangdong, Fujian, and Jiangsu was 141,553, 50,034, and 59,643 respectively, or 0.43 percent; 0.22 percent, and 0.18 percent of their respective populations.[50] Not surprisingly, the majority of the elected members of the consultative boards were members of the elite.[51]

After the establishment of the consultative boards nationwide, the attention of constitutionalists, who had gained control of many provincial boards, again shifted to the setting up of a national parliament. Starting in late 1909, constitutionalists initiated new waves of petitions to the court. In 1910 alone, three major petition campaigns were launched, in January, June, and October. Compared to the previous petition in 1908, the petitions in 1910 were notable for two things. First, the three petition drives were mostly initiated, organized, and led by members of the provincial consultative boards, the first time the Chinese elite were able to launch political mobilization upon a platform of elected representative bodies. After the first petition for a parliament failed, the representatives of the petition proposed a Conference of Consultative Boards to coordinate their activities. The conference formally commenced on August 12 and passed its charters, which stipulated that after a resolution was passed by the conference, it had binding power on all consultative boards.[52]

Secondly, petitions in 1910 saw a much larger, well-organized mobilization. In the period of the first petition, an Association of Parliament Petition Comrades was established as the coordinating organization to lead the petition drive.[53] In the third petition, not only were large-scale public gatherings held but they were often followed by public processions to submit petitions to the offices of local governors-general and governors. These petition proceedings were participated in by more than 1,000 in Zhili, 3,000 in Henan, 4,000 in Guizhou, 5,000 in Fujian, 6,000 in Sichuan, and 10,000 in Shaanxi, and in most cases, provincial governors received the petitioners and promised to "forward the petition" to the court.[54]

It is not an exaggeration to say that 1910 was the year that the constitutionalism petition as the focus of national politics was made "public" in an unprecedented way by public telegrams, newspaper editorials and reports, signature collecting, and public gatherings and proceedings. A new development was that the positions of local governors-general and governors on national politics were more explicitly stated, and they themselves used public telegrams to make them known to the public. *Shen Pao* regularly published their telegraphic correspondence with the central government on issues of national concern, such as the regulations for local autonomous administration.[55] Li Jingxi, the governor-general of Yungui (Yunnan and Guizhou), was an advocate of establishing a parliament and cabinet as soon as possible. He presented a memorial to the court in June 1910, but it apparently did not attract much attention. In September, Li telegraphed his fellow governors-general and provincial governors expressing his concern about the grim political circumstances the court was facing and asking for their opinions on the speedy setting up of a cabinet and parliament.[56] Li's telegram was well received. After further consultations by telegraph, on October 25, 1910, more than eighteen governors-general, governors, and Manchu generals sent a second joint telegram to the Grand Council urging the court to act swiftly to establish a parliament and cabinet.[57] On November 4, the Qing court eventually proclaimed that it would shorten the time for the introduction of constitutionalism from nine years to five years, which meant that China would have parliamentary elections in 1913.

Having described the power and effectiveness of public telegrams in national politics in the late Qing era as a result of their publication in newspapers, it is also necessary, however, to stress that one should not overstate the role of the public telegram in shaping late Qing politics. Although the public telegrams were employed as never before in the period of the constitutionalism petition, by the end of this political mobilization, the limits of the public telegram in Chinese politics began to be recognized, and the petitioners began to seek more forceful political means to attain their goal.

On March 20, 1911, *Shen Bao* published a public letter that appealed to various organizations nationwide to use the telegraph to ask the provincial heads of consultative boards to gather in Beijing in the following months to "make the grand plan of salvation." The letter was signed by Sun Hongyi, the secretary of the Beijing Constitutionalism Petition Comrades Society. According to him, among others, the reason for taking such action was:

The consultative board is the representative organ of people for a province, and the head of the board is the representative of the organ. Getting together the representatives of provincial representative organs is just like getting together 400 million compatriots. Therefore, the final plan for self-reliance coming out of their collective discussion will be more effective and powerful. . . . in a word, the proposed gathering has a direct bearing on the survival of our country. Why? Because it is not a crisis-handling action if the head of a board merely sends a telegram to warn the government. Furthermore, telegraph text is too simple to shake the government.[58]

This is quite revealing. Even though political activists had noted the limitations of the telegraph in national politics, its role as a main means of political mobilization was undeniable. It was a bit ironic that while declaring the ineffectiveness of merely sending telegrams to the government, Sun Hongyi urged his audience to use the telegraph to organize the gathering of heads of the provincial consultative boards.

In summary, it is in the constitutionalism petition period that we see both the culmination of the use of the public telegram and its limitations in the last days of the Qing dynasty. Players in national politics, whether revolutionaries, reformers, conservatives, students studying abroad, or reform-leaning Qing officials, all employed public telegrams according their different needs. The impact of public telegrams mainly derived from the benign historical "receiving context" constituted by the New Policies reforms. The ultimate goal of national and personal survival, the desire to protect national sovereignty and interests, consciousness of rights and responsibilities in political participation and of the need to adopt "civilized anti-foreign" methods, the belief that constitutionalism was the right way to save China—all these factors contributed to increasing political mobilization and participation by the Chinese elite. It was to this receptive audience that the public telegram was skillfully directed, and its effects were felt.

But after all, the public telegram was essentially only an effective means of conveying political information and could not in itself exert a decisive influence on national politics. The rapid fall of the Qing dynasty to republican revolution in 1911 shows us that when an information technology such as telegraphy is employed to advocate a political cause widely perceived as the right choice, such as constitutionalism, the final outcome is never inevitable: History should make those who believe in an intrinsic relationship between the Internet and democracy have second thoughts. In fact, even though the constitutionalists launched an impressive public political mobilization, the realpolitik of the Qing dynasty did not match the high hopes for a constitutional monarchy expressed in their numerous public telegrams. It was the alternative aspect of early twentieth-century Chinese nationalism, namely, anti-Manchu revolution and republicanism, that toppled the Qing dynasty shortly afterward. In a matter of a few months, the public telegram would be used more by republican revolutionaries than by constitutional monarchists. In the following years, public telegrams would continue to be employed by various players in the chaotic and turbulent Chinese politics until the establishment of the People's Republic of China in 1949, when a new era of Chinese politics began.

PART II

The Internet

CHAPTER SIX

China and the Internet

Proactive Development and Control

IN LATE APRIL 2002, there were two pieces of news closely re-lated to the topic of this book. On April 22, a Nielsen/Netratings press release reported that by the end of the first quarter 2002, China had the world's second-largest at-home Internet population: 56.6 million. But given the fact that this number amounted to only 5 percent of the popu-lation in China, the survey conductors predicted that China possessed a huge potential for further Internet growth. If China were to reach a usage rate of 25 percent, half of what the United States had at the time, there would be 257 million Internet users in China. As proclaimed by the press release, at a growing rate of 5–6 percent monthly, this could be a reality in the not too distant future.[1] Compared with the above eye-catching news, which was picked up quickly by both the media and researchers, another piece of news, on the telegraph in China, seems to have attracted little attention. On April 25, *People's Daily* reported that from May 1 on, China would abolish the government affairs telegraph and press tele-graph services, which signaled the end of the era in which the telegraph had played an important role in both governance and press, as we saw in previous chapters.[2]

Public Telegrams and Politics in the PRC

Before we begin the discussion on the Internet and political participa-tion in contemporary China, it is necessary to have a brief look back at how the telegraph faired in the earlier years of the People's Republic of China. From the very start, the telegraph was put under rigid government control. The Telecommunications Bureau was under the discretion of the Central Military Committee. In October 1949, the bureau issued "provisional regulations on domestic telegraph operation," which classified telegrams into the following five categories: government and military telegrams; telecommunication bureau business telegrams; private telegrams; public interest (i.e., meteorological, air-defense, flood warning, etc.) telegrams; and special (i.e., press, naval, etc.) telegrams. Of special interest to the present study is the so-called *gongyi* (public opinion) telegram, listed among special telegrams. According to the regulations, "public opinion telegrams are sent by public and private organizations, their representatives, or people's conventions to issue congratulations, condolences, proclamations, and circular telegrams that represent public opinions."[3] Obviously, the public telegram remained among the telegraph services available at the beginning of the PRC.

One would be naïve to think that the public opinion telegram continued to play the role it once had in Chinese politics. Under the rule of the Chinese Communist Party, it was simply impossible for anyone to use the telegraph to express political opinions publicly without official sanction. In fact, article 28 of the regulations clearly stipulated that "if the telegraph service station, based on fact, judges that the content of a telegram is harmful to the national or people's interest, the matter should be handed over to the local government," which effectively forbade the sending of any telegram that was perceived as off the party line.[4] Nonetheless, with limited accessibility, the telegraph still remained one of the few ways for ordinary Chinese to voice concerns or grievances or submit petitions to higher authorities. In June 1974, the Ministry of Posts and Telecommunications issued a notice instructing local telegraph bureaus on how to handle "situation reporting" telegrams sent to Chairman Mao and the central government by individuals or work units. Though it stated that these telegrams should be handled promptly, it also instructed the local telegraph bureau to decline to accept those whose content touched on national and party secrets, or were not made clear, if the senders refused to make modifications. Furthermore, if the content was "reactionary," the local bureau should contact the public security bureau immediately. The contents of these telegrams were not to be revealed.[5]

It is not surprising that the only public opinion telegrams that could be sent and then reprinted in newspapers were those sanctioned by the authorities. I call them "orchestrated public telegrams" because their contents and when and how they were to be made public were predetermined by political needs. These telegrams were often sent during mass political campaigns, such as the Cultural Revolution. For example, in the first half of 1967, public telegrams were used regularly to convey important political information by both the central authorities and local "revolutionary rebellion organizations." On January 9, *People's Daily* reprinted an Open Letter to the Shanghai People issued by local revolutionary rebellion organizations five days earlier. In the letter, the masses were urged to "accelerate production by practicing revolution," which was obviously an attempt to restore economic order, which had been severely disrupted by the "revolution." On the same day, another Urgent Public Notice was issued in Shanghai, reiterating the importance of maintaining economic and production order. Two days later, *People's Daily* printed a congratulatory telegram sent to these organizations by the Central Committee, the State Council, the Central Military Committee, and the Central Steering Committee of the Cultural Revolution, in which they sanctioned the local position taken in the Open Letter and the Urgent Public Notice. Both the congratulatory telegram and the Urgent Notice were printed in their entirety in *People's Daily* on January 12. In response, several hundred thousand people held a huge public gathering in Shanghai to celebrate the receiving of the "congratulatory telegram." In the end, a telegram of reverential greeting (*zhijing dian*) was sent to Chairman Mao, expressing their loyalty to him and their resolve to smash the "bourgeois reactionary line" in the strongest terms. The text of the telegram was printed in *People's Daily* the next day.[6]

The telegram of reverential greetings to Chairman Mao became a popular form of public telegram during the Cultural Revolution. Whenever "revolutionary rebels" took over a local government, it was a political ritual for them to send a telegram expressing their reverential greetings to Chairman Mao. At the same time, circular telegrams were also used, though much less frequently. For example, on January 18, 100,000 "revolutionary rebels" from the finance and trading systems nationwide held a massive gathering in Beijing. The gathering not only sent a reverential greetings telegram to Chairman Mao but also sent an "urgent circular telegram" (*jingjie tongdian*), instructing "revolutionary rebels" to fulfill their job responsibilities while participating in the revolution. It emphasized that the instructions needed to be carried out immediately and that local revolutionary organizations should mobilize all propaganda machines to publicize the contents of the telegram. Obviously, the central government felt tremendous pressure to keep a certain degree of order in the areas of finance and trading to prevent the economy from collapsing, as shown by the fact that Premier Zhou Enlai attended the gathering.[7]

Even though public telegrams were used in mass political campaigns, they were orchestrated in a way that made them quite different from those in the late Qing period. A rare window of opportunity for the public to express nonconforming opinions on the political situation in China was in a very short period during the student demonstrations in May 1989 that eventually led to the bloody Tiananmen Square crackdown on June 4. The college students started their hunger strike on May 13, and martial law was declared in Beijing on May 20. During the later part of the student hunger strike (May 16–19), the emotions of different strata of Chinese society were stirred up, and the divisions among the communist leadership made it possible for People's Daily to publish something not following the strict official party line. On May 16, People's Daily reported that intellectuals had held demonstrations in support of the students a day earlier. On May 17, it printed an open letter by ten university presidents in Beijing appealing for restraint on the part of both the students and the government. The next two days witnessed an unprecedented openness of People's Daily in reporting the hunger strike. Numerous "urgent appeals" by social dignitaries, renowned intellectuals, famous writers, mass organizations, and leaders of democratic parties were printed in the newspaper.[8] Though most of these "urgent appeals" were delivered in the form of written letters or directly through the news media, the telegraph was also used. According to Zhu Xuefan, chairman of the Revolutionary Committee of the Chinese Nationalist Party (one of the democratic parties in China), he had "telegraphically appealed" (dian qing) to the central government to adopt urgent methods to deal with the situation on May 16, and he issued another "urgent appeal" on May 18.[9] In retrospect, we can say that from May 16 to May 19, People's Daily contributed, along with television and other media, to making the students' hunger strike the central focus of public politics at the time.

This window was closed after martial law was declared. From May 22 on, People's Daily devoted considerable space to publishing "supporting telegrams" sent to Beijing by provincial party committees and governments and military units.[10] On May 29, People's Daily reported on its front page that a lot of people continued to send telegrams and letters to the Central Committee and the State Council, appealing to those students holding sit-ins on Tiananmen Square to leave. Obviously, these reported telegrams were carefully selected, and the practice of newspapers publishing telegrams returned to the "orchestrated" stage, as during the Cultural Revolution. It seems that the authorities never forgot the importance of maintaining control of the news media and communications. On May 24, Li Peng, generally perceived as a hard-line premier, sent his secretary-general to visit troops guarding the Beijing Telegraph Building, as well as television and radio stations.[11] After the June 4 crackdown, *People's Daily* once again devoted a lot of space to publishing "supporting telegrams" from provincial party committees and governments, central ministries, and regional military commands.[12] Ironically, this would be the last time public telegrams were sent in great quantities at a critical time in Chinese politics. As the 1990s commenced, China was about to see a dramatic decrease in the use of telegrams, and by the end of the decade, a corresponding increase in another means of communication that, like the telegraph, would have an enormous impact on political expression and participation. That technology, as we all know, is called the Internet.

Behind the Rapid Development of the Internet in China

There is a Chinese saying: "If you are one hundred steps away from something, you are far behind, and if you are one step away, you are almost there." In the same spirit, one Chinese scholar thought that if the gap between China and developed countries in traditional industries was "one hundred steps," China was only "ten steps" behind the leading countries in the Internet when it entered this new technological domain.[13] This statement reflects a genuine picture of the situation in China. As we know, the Internet originated mainly in U.S. government-sponsored military-oriented projects during the Cold War. It was not until 1982, with the maturity of FTP/IP technology, that the Internet became applicable to civilian global communication. The popularity of the Internet nowadays has a lot to do with the World Wide Web, which only became operational in the 1990s.[14] So, technically speaking, China was only a few years from the leading edge of the Internet, at least in terms of the applications of this new technology. The detailed history of the technological development of the Internet in China need not concern us here; the following list is a brief description of the major events in the process:

1986—The Chinese Academic Network (CANet) is initiated as a cooperative project between the Beijing Applied Computing Institute and Karlsruhe University in Germany.

September 1987—China's first email is sent out through CANet.

1988—The Institute of High Energy Physics of the Chinese Academy of Sciences (IEHP) becomes able to exchange emails with Europe and North America.

1990—China initiates the National Computing and Networking Facility of China (NCFC), later the backbone of the China Science and Technology Network (CSTNet).

October 1990—China registers the country's domain name, cn.

June 1991—The IEHP constructs the first 64K line connecting China with the Internet through the Stanford Linear Accelerator Center (SLAC) network.

1991—The first BBS appears in China. In August 1995, Tsinghua University opens China's first Internet-based BBS.

March 1993—The State Council approves the construction of the Golden Bridge Network project, China's first national public economic information network, which starts commercial operation in September 1996.

April 1994—China sets up the cn first-level domain name registration server and opens an Internet router, signaling that China is formally connected with the Internet.

May 1994—The IEHP sets up the first www server and develops the first home page in China.

January 1995—China's first online electronic magazine appears.

May 1995—China Public Computer Internet (CHINANET) begins to construct its nationwide network.

November 1995—China Educational Network (CERNET) opens.

January 1996—CHINANET begins service to the public.

June 1997—The China Internet Network Information Center (CNNIC) is set up.

November 1997—The first CNNIC survey comes out.[15]

In the early stages, only scientists, researchers, and university faculty located in major metropolitan areas could access the Internet in China. The situation was altered when China Telecom decided to enter the Internet service providing market. In March 1995, only 3,000 people in China were able to access the Internet. But only four months later, in July 1995, that number had increased to 40,000.[16] With the opening of Chinanet in 1996, Internet service was finally made available to the general public. By the end of 1996, the number of Internet users had reached 200,000.[17] From 1997 to 2004, China saw an explosive increase in the number of

TABLE 2

Number of Internet Users in China, 1997–2004

Date	Number	Under age 40 (%)	Male/Female (%)
10/31/1997	620,000	88	88/12
12/31/1998	2,100,000	95	86/14
12/31/1999	8,900,000	94	79/21
12/31/2000	22,500,000	91	70/30
12/31/2001	33,700,000	88	60/40
12/31/2002	59,100,000	89	59/41
12/31/2003	79,500,000	90	60/40
12/31/2004	94,000,000	88	61/39

SOURCE: China Internet Network Information Center, Statistical Reports on the Internet Development in China, www.cnnic.net.cn/en/index/oO/o2/index.htm (accessed April 26, 2005).

Internet users, as shown in the statistics in table 2, supplied by the China Internet Network Information Center, which has tracked growth since late 1997.

By any standards, this growth rate is phenomenal. In half a dozen years, China has attained the second largest number of online users. Much discussion of the Internet in China has focused on the government's efforts to control it, and it is less frequently mentioned that the Chinese government has been an active promoter of the Internet, based on its conviction that this new technology could be an engine for economic and technological development. In fact, the official response to the Internet was a continuation of the extant policy that emphasized the importance of the information industry, adopted in the early 1980s. Both Deng Xiaoping and Jiang Zemin had stressed the crucial role of development of the information infrastructure to China's goal of achieving the "four modernizations" in agriculture, industry, national defense, and science and technology. Developing information technology was listed as a priority in both the National Strategic Plan of General Development of Science and Technology of 1983 and the "863" High Tech Plan of 1986. The task of informization of the economy was once again emphasized in the Ninth Five Year Plan (1996–2000).[18]

In stark contrast to the initial telegraph policy of the Qing court, which focused on the loss of both *li* ("interests," "benefits," or "resources") and *quan* ("power," "rights," or "control"), the current Chinese government is confident of its ability to keep China's Internet infrastructure and services out of foreign control. It is obvious that it is the aspect of *li* that has attracted the government's main attention. Contrary to the case with telegraphy, in which foreign governments and companies made repeated pitches to sell telegraphy to China, today it is the Chinese who are eager to access this new technological wonder. The following episode is quite illustrative. It is said that in late 1991, Chinese and American physicists reached an agreement to establish a 64K high speed connection between the IHEP and the SLAC, thus linking China with the Internet. But the plan was blocked by the U.S. government, which was concerned that China would obtain significant scientific and technological information through the Internet. It was only after China agreed to stringent conditions laid down by the United States, including not using the Internet for commercial and military purposes, linking the IHEP line only with the ESNet (Energy Science Network), and not spreading viruses on the Internet, that the U.S. government gave the proposal the green light. By the time the link was finally established in March 1993, almost one and half years had passed.[19]

If the U.S. government worried about the possible "undesirable" consequences of letting the Chinese go online in the early 1990s, the Chinese government has been aware of the "harmful" effects that the Internet could bring, but with different focuses. This is revealed in China's general Internet principle: "Developing it actively, strengthening its management, seeking advantages and avoiding harmfulness, making it serve our purpose."[20] It seems that even though the Chinese policymakers have realized that the Internet could bring potential political challenges to the regime, they do not regard it as fundamentally different from newspapers, radio, and TV. Each of these has undergone rapid development and has become more commercialized in the reform era but nonetheless still remains under the tight control of the government. The Chinese government has been promoting the Internet using a similar approach, focusing on its technological and commercial applications, while keeping an eye on its political implications.

Besides government promotion, the market mechanism also contributed to the astonishing growth rate of the Internet in China. After a series of reforms in the late 1990s, China released entrepreneurial ventures in the telecommunications industry from direct government control, leaving it to the market mechanism. The Internet has since attracted a large amount of investment and generated fierce competition. Sometimes, control seems to have been relaxed or even dispensed with in the name of development. For example, in order to encourage more people use the Internet, China Telecom offers convenient no-application Internet access called "just dial 163." Any one can log onto the Internet over a telephone line by simply dialing 163, using 163 as both login name and password. The charge will appear on the telephone subscriber's monthly bill. As my fellow anthropologist Dru Gladney once told an American audience in a lecture he gave at the University of Wisconsin, China is the easiest place in the world to get an Internet connection, something far beyond our expectations.[21] Obviously, this is good for business but not good as far as control is concerned.

In fact, when economic development becomes the priority, market forces often function in ways that are contrary to the government's goal of tightening control. The rapid spread of Internet cafés is a very illuminating case. The first Chinese Internet café appeared in Beijing in November 1996, but it was not until three years later that the phenomenon really took off.[22] According to CNNIC statistics, by the end of 1998, only 3 percent of Internet users were going online in Internet cafés. That figure increased to 11 percent by the end of 1999 and jumped to 21 percent by the end of 2000. Since then, the figure has stabilized at 15–19 percent.[23] Considering that some people log onto the Internet at their homes or offices as well as at Internet cafés, the actual number using Internet cafés exclusively may be smaller, but still accounts for about one-sixth of the total population of netizens in China. Naturally, this creates a great demand for Internet cafés, and the total number has seen explosive growth. In Beijing alone, there were more than 2,400 Internet cafés by June 2002.[24]

On June 16, 2002, an illegally operated Internet café in Beijing caught fire and twenty-four people perished. The mayor of Beijing immediately shut down all Internet cafés and launched a "rectification campaign." Other places subsequently followed suit. This was widely reported by the Western media. The Chinese government, a report in *TIME Asia* magazine asserted, had "for several years staged periodic cybercafé raids. . . . to shut down what is, for many Chinese, the main artery to the Internet. Control-crazy officials are struggling to monitor an information-packed online world that by its very name, the Web, is a tangle of unmanageable links to 'cultural pollution.' "[25] In labeling Chinese officials "control-crazy" regarding the Internet, intentionally or unintentionally, the reporter neglected the other side of the story, however. As she pointed out, fewer than 200 Internet cafés were fully licensed in Beijing. Nationwide, only 46,000 out of 200,000 had permission to operate.[26] But if officials were really "control-crazy," as she claimed, how could the number of illegal cybercafés overwhelmingly outnumber the legal ones? One plausible interpretation is that Chinese officials have not done a good job of regulating cybercafés. Then the question is why and what factors have affected their control.

During my fieldwork in China, I conducted participant observation in an "illegal" Internet café that I shall call "Ocean" in Beijing's college district and acquired much in-depth knowledge of the complexity of running a cybercafé in Beijing.[27] Based on my observations, it seems more appropriate to label local officials "development-crazy" rather than "control-crazy," because their concerns about economic factors often outweighed all others. To them, the more Internet cafés there were, the better it would be for local (district-level) economic development, adding new jobs and expanding the base of local taxation. So lower-level officials were generally tolerant of the setting up of new Internet cafés, even when they knew that they were not fully licensed.

As the owner of the "Ocean" café explained to me, to set up an Internet café, one had to get a permit from the Public Security Bureau (fire and safety requirements); Cultural Bureau (Internet content control, especially pornography); Telecommunications Bureau (network connection regulations); and Bureau of Industrial and Commercial Administration (business operation license). To get all four permits could be a tedious process. With Internet fever raging in China and the lucrative returns the Internet cafés generated, many businessmen therefore opted to set up and operate cybercafés without a full set of permits. Furthermore, government regulations clearly forbade foreign investment (including overseas Chinese capital) in the area of Internet café startups. Yet the local officials had allowed the owner of the "Ocean," a Taiwanese businessman, to operate the cybercafé by registering the café under the name of a local resident.

Why was this practice of blatantly ignoring government regulations generally tolerated in Beijing, as well as in the rest of China? One has to understand the complexity of everyday life to make sense of many phenomena that otherwise seem incomprehensible on paper. First, we have to keep in mind that the Chinese state is not a monolithic entity. There are officials who see the Internet primarily as an engine of economic development, and others who see it as a threat to the existing censorship system. Local officials make their own interpretations of the central policies based on local interest, and in practice, all of these make government policy seem fluid and internally contradictory. At the local level, the implementation of concrete policies and regulations is further complicated

by the fact that written rules are often stretched or even neglected to ac-
commodate personal connections. And in a worse-case scenario, local officials are often bribed to allow illegal Internet cafés to do business.[28]

So far, most raids on the Internet cafés have been launched to crack
down on underage patrons; most of the cybercafés raided reopened, and
new ones are continually being established. Western reports that only emphasize the "political control" side of the issue have missed its complexity. As one puzzled observer wrote: "Here in the Netherlands the same
old 'news' appears once again in the newspapers: 17,000 Internet cafés in
China are forced to close down, another 28,000 must install software
that blocks certain information. If we are to believe these stories completely, it remains a mystery how it comes [about] that over time more
rather than less Internet cafés appear."[29] The explanation requires taking
into account both the government's promotion policy and the role of the
market. We should pay more attention to the role played by the flow of
capital in challenging the state's regulatory function. As economic development becomes the ultimate criterion of job performance, local officials
have adopted more pro-growth policies, which in part explain why the
growth of Internet cafés has been so rapid, and why even though most of
them are not fully licensed, they are still able to flourish.[30]

Proactive Control

The general Internet principle referred to above reflects the Chinese
government's ideal scenario, which is to promote active development and
take full advantage of the new technology while strengthening control
and avoiding negative effects. Though, as we have seen, the concern with
development has generally led to explosive growth. In a society where information (especially political information) has been subject to rigid control, the Chinese government has also moved quickly to regulate the Internet, aiming at minimizing the feared side effect of the free circulation
of information. In February 1994, when the number of Internet users was
still negligible, the State Council issued the Safety and Protection Regulations for Computer Information Systems, which put the Ministry of Public Security in charge of the job, and clearly stipulated that computer systems connected to the Internet have to be registered with the public
security bureaus of the local government.[31] This one was only the first of
many similar attempts at regulating the Internet. The following is a list of
major PRC regulations related to the Internet:

—Provisional Administrative Regulations on the Computer Network Connecting with the Internet (February 1996; revised May 1997)

—Administration of Internet Safety and Protection (December 1997)

—Telecommunication Regulations (September 2000)

—Administration of Internet Information Services (September 2000)

—Administration of Electronic Bulletin Board Services (October 2000)

—Provisional Administrative Regulations on News Service by Internet Websites (November 2000)

—Administration of Business Establishments Providing Internet Access Services (April 2001) [32]

After the issuance of the Telecommunication Regulations, which listed nine kinds of information not to be made available, copied, transmitted, or spread through the telecommunication networks, all the subsequently issued regulations adopted the same list of forbidden information, which includes:

1. That which is against the basic principles established by the Constitution

2. That which endangers national security, reveals state secrets, undermines state sovereignty, and injures national unity

3. That which harms national dignity and interest

4. That which provokes hatred and discrimination among nationalities and injures national solidarity

5. That which undermines state religious policy and advocates cult and feudal superstitions

6. That which disseminates rumors, disrupts social order, and injures social stability

7. That which disseminates obscenities or pornography or promotes gambling, violence, murder, or terrorism

8. That which defames or slanders others or impinges on the legal interests of others

9. That which is otherwise prohibited by the law and administrative regulations

As the Qing court did with telegraphy, the current Chinese government tries to control the Internet at the infrastructural, service, and content levels. Obviously, the focus of the control is on Internet contents. As far as the Internet infrastructure is concerned, as we have seen, all the major networks are state-owned, and the Telecommunication Regulations stipulate that a Chinese partner should hold at least 51 percent of shares in a joint venture involved in the telecommunications infrastructure business. In addition, all Chinese computer networks have to connect with the Internet through Chinanet, the national public information network, which effectively rules out any possibility of individuals and businesses connecting to the Internet independently. As far as Internet service is concerned, the license system establishes the first screen mechanism for Internet service providers (ISPs). A series of regulations issued in 2000 and 2001 give detailed guidelines on what services are permitted, and what is not, as regards BBS, news publishing by websites, and Internet café operations. Nonetheless, the ultimate goal of controlling Internet infrastructure and service by the government is to regulate the information that is carried by the Internet infrastructure and made available by ISPs to Internet users.

For example, the regulations on news services by websites put a stringent limit on who can publish news on websites. Only the websites of central and provincial-level news organizations have this privilege, thus effectively excluding the vast majority of websites from publishing news reports of their own. The regulations on BBS are more revealing of the state's concern with the manageability of the vast and fluid flow of seemingly unruly information in this particular cyberspace. To ensure that the nine kinds of inadmissible information are indeed excluded from BBS, articles 13–15 of the regulations require BBS providers to

(a) remove any inadmissible content immediately, keep a record of it, and report it to the relevant authority

(b) record the information posted on a BBS; the time it was posted, and the Internet address or domain name of the posting; these records should be backed up, kept for sixty days and shared with the relevant authorities when requested

(c) record the times at which users log on, the user's account number, the Internet address or domain name, the phone number of the caller, and other such information; these records should be kept for sixty days and provided to the relevant authorities when requested

Any action taken by the Chinese government to regulate the Internet hardly escapes the watchful eye of so-called Internet utopians who believe that the free flow of information can change Chinese society. For example, only five days after China issued the Internet Safety and Protection regulations, on January 6, 1998, Radio Free Europe / Radio Liberty reported the new regulations but cited an "expert" prediction that "China's attempts to control the Internet were destined to fail," because most Chinese Internet users are university students who "are also [the] ones fighting most for freedom and democracy within their country" and "the ones who can cause the most damage to the communist form of government." In addition, the same expert claimed, the key to China's success in today's information age is the ability to freely obtain and integrate information at all levels—"how does one control access to information and still provide the information necessary for them to compete? The answer is simple: they can't."[33]

Surprisingly, only four years later, the rosy "democracy-is-just-around-the-corner" rhetoric was replaced by the pessimistic question of whether or not the Internet is destined to be a tool of surveillance and repression of the Chinese government. Lamenting the fact that some American corporations had played a big role in providing needed hardware and technologies for the PRC regime to build firewalls to screen out inadmissible information, one American Internet observer wrote in the *Weekly Standard*: "The American business presence in China is deeply, perhaps fatally, compromised as an agent for liberalizing change. The Internet remains the strongest force for democracy available to the Chinese people. But it remains a mere potentiality, yet another American dream, unless we first grapple with the question: Who lost China's Internet? Well, we did."[34] His proposed solution is to make new firewall-evading technologies available to the Chinese and ask the U.S. government to make Internet freedom in China a high priority, which falls into the fallacy that, as we have seen, views the issue of the Internet in China simply from a perspective that combines ideological conviction with technological determinism.[35]

It is true that the Internet in China has been subjected to state control, but the picture presented to us has been too black-and-white in nature, which inevitably distorts the reality to some degree and does not allow us to grasp the complexity of the issue. The real situation is not so clear-cut, and the ability of the government to control the Internet is being challenged all the time. Though required to keep records of patrons, the "Ocean" Internet café I observed in Beijing simply asks users to sign their names and never bothers to check their authenticity. It also winks at underage middle school students who come to play online games. The owner told me that he usually did not intervene unless these youngsters refused to quit after using the Internet for an exceedingly long time. Asked about whether or not the café was required to install monitoring software provided by the public security bureau, the answer was no, because his café had its own system, and, like most Internet cafés in Beijing, was not fully licensed. He viewed this requirement more as a plot by the public security bureau to generate extra income than a control measure, because everybody was trying to get "rich" no matter what it took.

On a macroscopic level, generally speaking, the regulations on the Internet have lagged behind the rapid development of the technology. Regulations are often vaguely written, sometimes conflicting, interpreted in different ways by different Internet players, and not always implemented, just as happens with regulations and laws in other areas in China. In this context, different players on the Internet are competing, negotiating, and working with one another, witnessing increased political participation and steady, albeit gradual, change.

The main shortcoming of current discussion is that it tends to see the Internet as an independent entity and singles it out from other information media. Besides the·specific technological means used to control the Internet, the control mechanism used by the state is in essence no different from that which controls newspapers, journals, press, radios, television, and satellite TV. The control of the Internet is an integral part of a censorship system that functions to ensure that the power of the communist party is not challenged. It is not surprising that Internet controls have aimed mainly at clamping down on "subversive" activities by Internet users or the operators involved. In 1998, a Shanghai software company owner, Lin Hai, became the first person to be arrested for providing tens of thousands of email addresses to an overseas Chinese dissident online magazine, *V.I.P Reference,* and he was subsequently sentenced to a two-year prison term.[36] Since then, according to the list provided by the Digital Freedom Network, more than thirty individuals have been detained for online political or religious activity.[37] But few have pointed out the fact that individuals would be subject to the same kind of persecution if they expressed their dissident views in newspapers or on TV. Although the Internet is more easily accessible than the traditional media, both it and the latter can only become true means of political participation if the Chinese state changes its censorship system and allows organized dissent. The Internet cannot be free without a system change. Even though I do not see this happening immediately, there have been small changes in recent years that deserve our attention.

Never having been an Internet utopian myself, I do not believe Internet technology alone will convert China into a democracy. But I view the

Internet as providing an important new avenue for making politics more public and potentially more democratic. Since I am not a pessimist either, I do not believe that the state can simply use the Internet to serve its goals without making political changes, and in fact the Chinese state is changing and the Internet is part of those changes. Never a fan of political fortune-tellers who make Chinese politics a staple of their punditry, I do not want to make any prediction about the direction in which the Internet will lead China and leave the task of answering such questions to future historians. The aim of this book is, as has been noted, to historicize and contextualize the study of the Internet. It is not the technology per se, but the creativity, will, and intentions of the people that have opened up new vistas of political participation. So in the rest of this book, I shall present a series of case studies to show small, subtle, yet concrete changes the Internet has brought about in Chinese society, especially in its role in enlarging political participation. This in no way implies that the changes will automatically lead China to liberal democracy. In a word, the ultimate aim of this study is to present a picture that is complex, fluid, and less subjected to ideological propositions—a picture that is still being formed and that is constantly changing.

From this perspective, the government's proactive control policy means that suppressive control is not the only method. Along with suppression and regulation, the government also uses subtler and softer strategies to achieve its goal, as we shall see in the following chapters. Another aspect of the proactive policy is that the government is deliberately taking the initiative to occupy cyberspace. Unlike the Qing policymakers who reacted to the arrival of telegraphy passively, the current Chinese government has been keen to use Internet technology. Besides harnessing it as a means of developing the economy, the government has also been swift to use the Internet to its own political advantage. In addition to the Golden Bridge project focusing on economic information, in 1999, the PRC launched an e-government project aimed at using the Internet to improve the efficiency of government services and government transparency. A target was set that, by the end of the year 2000, 80 percent of state organs should be online. Though far from satisfactory, e-government had made more information available to the general public than at any time before in Chinese history.[38]

Realizing that the Internet technology has also revolutionized the traditional media, the state adopted a policy that, on the one hand, limits the right of disseminating online news to only a small number of portal websites and central and provincial-level news organizations and, on the other, invests heavily to set up several key online outlets of the most influential media organs in China, including the websites of the Xinhua News Agency, *People's Daily*, and China Central Television. In the meantime, comprehensive new online media websites have also been established, among them the two most influential regional online news networks, the Qianlong network (www.qianlong.com) based in Beijing and the Dongfang network (www.eastday.com) based in Shanghai, in both of which both government and media organizations have invested heavily. This reflects the fact that the state aims to dominate the Internet, as it has done the traditional media. Yet as we shall see, the state has had to adopt new strategies to achieve its goal and the changes are visible.

In addition to actions taken at the national level, a close look at the grassroots level shows that the Internet has also been used to serve the party line in various ways, sometimes even very creatively. In a volume compiled by the people involved in political indoctrination, several dozen cases are presented to show how the Internet can play a big role in indoctrinating youth with party ideology, ranging from setting up online "Youth Communist Schools" to online "psychological assistance." These "red websites" target university students, government employees, and the employees of foreign-owned companies, as well as social science researchers.[39] This is certainly not good news for those who believe that the Internet has regime-changing power. However, no matter how numerous these "red websites" are, they will soon be obliterated and forgotten if they cling to the outdated propaganda methods to which these "workers of political thought" are accustomed. In fact, few officially sponsored websites or chat rooms have attracted a wide public following in Chinese cyberspace, People's Daily Online's Strengthening-China Forum (qiangguo luntan) being a rare exception. In order to gain a deeper understanding why this particular BBS has become so influential among politically conscious Chinese Internet users, it is worth looking at it in more detail.

A State Initiative: The Strengthening-China Forum

There cannot be many politically conscious Chinese netizens who have not heard of People's Daily Online's Strengthening-China Forum (hereafter SCF), which is still by far one of the most influential political BBSs in Chinese cyberspace. The SCF was set up in May 1999, but People's

Daily Online has a longer history. In fact, on January 1, 1997, *People's Daily* became the first major newspaper in China to go online, and it started using its domain name, www.peopledaily.com.cn, on July 1, 1998. It subsequently added English and Japanese online editions, reflecting China's desire to use the new medium to exert its influence on the outside world. Considering that the number of Chinese Internet users was still very small at the time, one might conclude that the actual effect of People's Daily Online ought not to be very great. However, the appearance of People's Daily Online at such an early point in the timeline of Internet development in China shows that, from the very beginning, the central authority realized the importance of taking the initiative to position the party media organ in cyberspace.

The setting up of the SCF helped to enhance the influence and popularity of People's Daily Online. On May 8, after the bombing of the Chinese Embassy in Belgrade by the U.S.-led NATO forces operating against Yugoslavia, People's Daily Online issued the first Chinese report on the event. The very next day, a BBS named "Protesting NATO's Barbarous Action Forum" was established, which was immediately flooded by angry messages from Chinese Internet users denouncing the main culprit, the United States. According to the webmaster, from May 9 to June 19, more than 90,000 messages were posted on the Protesting Forum. By late August, the total number surpassed 200,000. Using the words of Jiang Yaping, the chief architect of People's Daily Online, the effect of setting up the Protesting Forum was "very good" and responses were "extremely strong."[40] On June 19, the Protesting Forum was renamed the Strengthening-China Forum. The change of name not only reflected the shifting focus of forum messages, which ranged from angry denunciation to more sober analysis, but also the purpose of the agenda set by People's Daily Online. Grasping the fact that many online participants in the Protesting Forum were motivated by patriotism, the webmasters chose Strengthening-China as its new name, which was a truly popular choice.

As an outside observer, I was amazed by the swiftness with which People's Daily Online reacted to the embassy bombing. My puzzlement was later resolved in interviews with Jiang Yaping and Guo Liang, an Internet usage survey conductor at the Chinese Academy of Social Sciences, who happens to be a friend of Jiang's. According to Guo, Jiang Yaping and People's Daily Online had been considering setting up a BBS forum with a "brand name" and had contracted with software developers to make preliminary technical preparations to do so. Nonetheless, they encountered difficulties in finding an entry point that would attract strong responses from Internet users, an issue further compounded by *People's Daily's* reputatation as the official organ of the CCP. The embassy bombing provided a perfect opportunity, and it was seized right away. "I want to thank the Americans for doing us such a huge favor!" Jiang Yaping said. "The forum we had conceived finally was established at the right time and fell right into place."[41]

The unexpected success brought the SCF great name recognition and concurrently enhanced the influence of People's Daily Online. The delighted higher authorities in turn put more resources into the online version of the newspaper. The first time I visited People's Daily Online in October 1999, the SCF had only two offices, which were jammed with about a half dozen webmasters. The next summer, when I visited again, its offices had been relocated in a much enlarged space. In summer 2001, I was amazed to see that the whole online operation had moved into a new building with a huge hall full of cubicles. In addition, the SCF had its own ultramodern online broadcasting studios. In the second half of 2000, People's Daily Online was expanded into the so-called People Net, with www.people.com.cn as its new domain name. As Jiang Yaping pointed out, *People's Daily*, as the largest-circulation Chinese newspaper, with well-established name recognition, and the support of government, aimed to make People Net the biggest comprehensive Chinese news website. By that time, there were more than 140 people working for People Net. It had websites in Chinese, English, Japanese, French, and Spanish. Russian and Arabic websites were added in 2001.[42] I was told that People Net employed more than 200 people after the new operations hall was finished.

What has been described above shows us one side of the proactive policy the Chinese state has adopted in dealing with the Internet. The other side is how to control it and prevent it from becoming a threat to the state. This side is equally complex, because in dealing with something as novel as online space, the state has to come up with new strategies, much like learning how to swim by actually swimming. As far as the SCF is concerned, control basically lies in the hands of webmasters, who constantly monitor the flow of messages. The lack of experience and expertise was felt immediately after the success of the SCF. Jiang Yaping admitted in August 1999 that his biggest headache was that he needed "at least ten webmasters who are competent at working online, have sound political judgment, are enthusiastic about the work, and at the same time are responsible to the forum participants. It is very difficult to find them, and we are working on it diligently."[43] I witnessed the recruitment process in high gear in October 1999 when I was conducting preliminary fieldwork in Beijing. Difficult though it was, it seems that the SCF was nonetheless able to establish a relatively stable team of webmasters shortly thereafter.

The methods and degree of control also underwent constant changes. One day, when the SCF was still located in the two-room office in 1999, I was chatting with the lead webmaster. While talking with me, he kept monitoring the screen and found two inadmissible messages and immediately removed them. Answering my question about what his criteria were, he explained to me that even though the criteria were not as rigid as they were in print editions of *People's Daily*, there were certain things that under no circumstances could be allowed. The two messages were removed not because of their contents, but because of the online personas their posters adopted. One had used "Li Hongzhi," the name of a prohibited cult leader, and the other "Zhu Rongji," the name of the Chinese premier at the time. Because of this, irrespective of their contents, these two posts had to be removed. This was later made clear in the SCF regulations.[44] Looking at several other webmasters working in front of screens, I realized that the job is both very stressful and tedious. This is one of the reasons why the SCF was only open from 10 A.M. to 10 P.M., and the webmasters were divided into two shifts.

Several months later, the SCF changed its monitoring method from allowing messages to be freely posted online in real time and then subjected to a webmaster's censorship to having them read by the webmasters first and then, if they passed the screening, allowing them to appear online. This change drew participants' criticism and protests. On April 5, 2000, one participant, whose online persona was "South Sea Monk," declared that he would "temporarily" stop participating in the SCF after his postings had been repeatedly removed by the webmaster.[45] Another participant, named "Kangaroo," wrote an "open letter" to the SCF lamenting that more and more original enthusiastic forum members had left because of the increasingly stringent monitoring policy. The author did not conceal that he/she had been a big fan of the SCF, yet it was exactly because he/she had wholeheartedly hoped that the forum would remain as open as it had been in the beginning that he/she was considering quitting. At the end of the letter, the author made an emotional appeal: "SCF, please rectify your mistake! SCF, let's travel through the clouds together!

Strengthen China! Strengthen China!"[46] Obviously such an appeal did not have much influence on the decision makers of People's Daily Online, as more censorship technologies, including IP tracking and blocking and key-word filtering, have since been implemented by the SCF. In addition, censorship was tightened in certain politically sensitive contexts. For example, on May 20, 2000, the day of Chen Shui-bian's inauguration on Taiwan, more than 12,000 messages were posted, but more than a quarter of them were deleted by the monitors.[47]

Nonetheless, compared to the print edition of *People's Daily*, which has been subjected to rigid control by the highest party authorities, People's Daily Online and the SCF represent a "loosened up" space that would have been inconceivable were it not for the arrival of the Internet. On the one hand, political news and information that usually could not have made it into the print edition, such as the whole text of George W. Bush's 2003 State of Union address, was put on the web edition, with follow-up comments.[48] On the other hand, People's Daily Online sometimes even publishes "tabloid-type" social and cultural news with the aim of attracting more viewers and competing with commercial news portal sites such as www.sina.com.cn and www.sohu.com.[49] Even with the control mechanisms mentioned above, if put into perspective, any casual visitor to the SCF would certainly be surprised by its unprecedented degree of openness and tolerance of online discussions of politics. First, within a broadly encompassing theme of "strengthening-China," the SCF virtually sets no limits on the scope of discussions. The content of the forum is extremely rich, ranging from breaking news around the world, critical comments on current affairs, nationalistic outcries on Sino-American and Sino-Japanese relationships, all kinds of views on the Taiwan issue, the suffering of laid-off workers, the corruption of local officials, expressions of individual grievance, rumors, and personal attacks. Though the webmasters make agenda-setting attempts from time to time by listing "today's focus-points," generally speaking, SCF participants have the right to post messages on nearly any topic of their own choice.

Secondly, the SCF webmasters have to walk a fine line in doing their job. They seemed to be very conscious of preserving the openness of the forum, on the one hand, and maintaining censorship, on the other hand. Because finding a balance between the two is the key to the continuous success of the forum, and nobody knew how to achieve it in the beginning, the webmasters had to be creative and risk-taking. As pointed out by a Chinese Internet observer, it was surprising to many Chinese in 1999

that with the approach of June 4th, the anniversary of the 1989 Tiananmen crackdown, while some Chinese BBS forums opted to shut down
temporarily during this politically sensitive period, the People's Daily Online Protesting Forum (before its name change to SCF) decided to continue to remain open, with enhanced monitoring. This decision delighted
Chinese netizens and attracted more enthusiastic participation. Furthermore, since these participants realized the political risk the Protesting Forum faced, they became more cooperative with the webmasters in keeping the forum in order.[50] This phenomenon does not mean that Chinese
netizens bent to the pressure of the state; rather, it shows their appreciation of the newly emergent space for much freer expression and their desire to help it keep growing in the Chinese context, where any radical and
irresponsible action would make it vulnerable to the more conservative
sector of the state and eventually result in it being shut down.

Monitoring cyberspace has also caused subtle changes in the SCF's
censorship practices. Because of the interactivity of the Internet, the webmasters have faced more direct challenges to their censorship from forum
members, and these protests seem to have made encouraging revisions to
their monitoring tactics. The webmasters could not simply delete messages; they often had to explain to complainants why they had done so.
Censorship of interactive relations with people is something new to both
sides. The SCF has made efforts to improve the sometimes contentious relationships between webmasters and forum members. The interactions
between the webmaster and online participants have generally remained
civil, with the webmaster often taking a friendly posture. After adopting
pseudonyms for a while, the SCF later tried to use the real names of webmasters in order to facilitate interactions between them and forum members. Since different monitors' criteria for interpreting regulations vary,
some forum members post "sharp" messages when a webmaster perceived to be "soft" is on duty. In addition, ordinary forum members have
adopted other strategies and methods, both practical and rhetorical, to
deal with the censorship. These include using false names to register online, inventing new terms only understood by fellow participants, and applying metaphor, satire, and mockery to make the writing more poignant
yet "admissible." It is such efforts on both sides that have made the SCF
the most influential political BBS in Chinese cyberspace.

The unexpected popularity of the SCF quickly caught the attention of
observers both in and outside of China. In an analogy to the special economic zones in China where market economies have been allowed to

emerge over the past two decades, a commentator writing on Singapore's Zaobao Online called SCF a "special zone online" because of its relative freedom and tolerance of political expression. The author classified SCF members' political positions roughly into five sets: pro-communist or anti-communist; pro-Western democracy or anti-Western democracy; pro-American or anti-American; supporting government policies or opposing government policies; and supporting reuniting Taiwan by force or opposing the use of force. Exclaiming that the SCF represented a rapidly changing China, the author concluded that vis-à-vis a BBS forum that encompassed open and multiple political positions and ways of thinking, "big character posters," the traditional means of free expression in the PRC, had become "outdated." Acknowledging that the SCF had its own censorship system, the commentator noted that other media forms also have censorship and that from the perspective of the SCF regulations, the restrictions were not that stringent. In conclusion, he stated that the SCF had become China's much needed "special zone of expression" and appealed for openness and tolerance from the authorities and understanding and cooperation from netizens to make this "special zone of expression" more prosperous.[51]

A comparison of the SCF's message boards with those of Washingtonpost.com shows that, on the face of it, the latter has control mechanisms very similar to those of People's Daily Online.[52] Nevertheless, I am not as optimistic as the above commentator and view the SCF rather as an ongoing experiment by the state. It is too early to say that a "special zone of expression" has emerged. In essence, the SCF is a result of the proactive policy the Chinese state has adopted on the Internet. It should be seen as one of the many small, subtle, yet constant changes Chinese society has experienced in the past quarter century. The opening up of some space in the Internet is both a reflection and extension of the changes China has made. It is not difficult to surmise that the nationalistic sentiment evoked by the embassy bombing was the main reason behind the initial success of the SCF. However, such sentiment leads to a further series of questions. What are the characteristics of nationalistic discussion on the Internet? Why is political discourse so closely intertwined with nationalism in contemporary China? And is nationalism being used by the state to divert discontent and build up a new consensus? As we shall see in the following chapters, contemporary Chinese nationalism is so complex that there is no one-size-fits-all answer. The case of the SCF shows that the Chinese state is taking proactive steps to establish a relatively controlled public

sphere on the Internet by selectively opening up some previously controlled space and trying to channel political discourse in the direction it
most desires.

Over the past six years, the SCF has remained one of the most influential political BBS forums in Chinese cyberspace. In 2002, according to
statistics provided by People Net, at the time of the Sixteenth Party Congress in November, the record of the number of participants in the SCF at
a given time was repeatedly broken and eventually reached 43,109.[53] The
degree of participation fluctuates according to political climate and
events. From May 1999 to May 2000, the first year of its existence, the
SCF got active responses on the issues of the embassy bombing, the claim
of state-to-state relationships between Taiwan and the PRC by the then
Taiwanese leader Lee Teng-hui, the crackdown on the Falun Gong,
China's efforts to join the World Trade Organization (WTO), and the
election of the pro-independence Chen Shui-bian as Taiwan's new leader.
All these events attracted Chinese Internet users to the forum, which provided a relatively free place to express their opinions in a society that put
limits on political expression in real space. The year 2001 witnessed the
Sino-American plane collision incident on April 1 and the terrorist attacks in the United States on September 11, and Chinese netizens reacted
explosively to both events. At the same time, the degree of control also
fluctuated, as shown in the SCF's reluctance to discuss a fireworks accident in a Jiangxi primary school in March 2001 and its more active involvement in discussing a mine-flooding accident in Guangxi in July
2001. As the case of the SCF reveals, though control of the Internet remains a main concern of the state, the process has become more flexible,
and the state does not always play a straightforwardly repressive role.
What the state is not willing or unable to see is that even with only small
cracks in it, the wall denying Chinese political participation will never be
the same. In fact, the online activities of many Chinese are contributing
to the enlargement of those cracks in various ways and from different angles, as we shall see from the concrete cases cited in the following chapters.

CHAPTER SEVEN

Negotiating Power Online

The Party State, Intellectuals, and the Internet

I WENT TO MEET Mr. Ma Lijun in July 2001 in a village about ten kilometers west of Beijing's Capital International Airport. It was a hot and humid day typical of a Beijing summer. After the taxi driver had circled the village a couple of times, I finally found the English-learning center where Ma's office was located. To my surprise, the center was a large compound of classrooms and dormitories, well-built and equipped with air conditioning. It was unusual, even in the middle of a village, to be submerged in the ever-expanding urbanization of Beijing. Aware of my puzzlement, Ma explained that the owner of this English-learning center was a Chinese American. Obviously far-sighted, he had bought thirty-acres of land cheaply in 1995 and established a center that aimed to attract students from the upper-middle echelon of Chinese society whose families wanted them to study abroad.[1] As we walked down a long corridor to Ma's office, I saw a couple of foreign teachers entering small classrooms, bearing out what Ma had told.

The purpose of my visit had nothing to do with English-language teaching. I was there to interview Ma on how he ran a very influential Chinese web site called sixiang geshihua (The Formalization of Ideas, www.pen123.net.cn, now defunct) that focuses on serious and scholarly discussions of political and social issues. "Here is my office," Ma said, and opened a door that led into a room about 100 feet square. My first impression was that the room was anything but an office. In the left corner sat a desk with a notebook computer, while on the right side there was a single bed littered with Ma's clothes. There was only one chair in the room. Ma insisted I take it, while he sat on the bed to talk to me. Before the interview formally started, he showed me another room where two part-time student assistants were working in front of two desktop computers. Having been to the ultramodern operations room of People Net and seen the impressive external appearance of the language center, I was surprised to hear that this was the sum total of the equipment and staff Ma used to run the Formalization of Ideas web site.

Asked why he had embarked on his project, Ma replied: "We need to have our voices heard and one of the best ways to do this is to possess an online platform." Ma's words are representative, because many Chinese intellectuals have realized that the Internet is a new and effective means of expressing their opinions. This chapter focuses on one particular unique niche in Chinese cyberspace—intellectual web sites. The term refers to Chinese web sites that focus on academic, critical, and theoretical discussions of diverse political, cultural, and other intellectual topics. These web sites usually have three major parts: a webzine for electronic publications, a BBS forum for the improvised exchange of ideas, and a digital academic archive for the effective dissemination and retrieval of scholars' works. Webzines can be seen as online editions of regular magazines, in which articles are selected and published by web editors whose editorial criteria often reflect differences in journal style, position, and degree of sophistication. Each BBS provides a platform for web surfers to engage in discussion and is a place for people to publish articles that may not be palatable to the webzine editors. Though most Chinese intellectual web sites started after 1998 and have thus had very short histories of operation, they have become popular outlets for many Chinese intellectuals to voice their opinions on a variety of issues concerning China in general and academic matters in particular. The Formalization of Ideas web site is thus only one of many of its kind.

The uniqueness and popularity of the electronic Chinese intellectual press can only be understood in the context of the PRC. Though the number of Chinese newspapers has increased from 186 in 1978 to 2,111 in 2002, and the total number of Chinese journals reached 8,889 in the same year,[2] each newspaper or journal has to have official sponsorship and submit to official supervision in order to receive publication permission. Under this control, independent publication and editorship were dreams beyond the reach of Chinese intellectuals before the arrival of the Internet. Since a web site can be easily turned into an online magazine (webzine) published on the Internet anywhere in the world, it is very difficult for the government to monitor them all the time. Furthermore, since such webzines do not need much start-up capital, Chinese intellectuals have enthusiastically embraced this new opportunity, and an increasing number of intellectual web sites are flourishing online.

This ever-growing intellectual web-based press in Chinese cyberspace is in direct contradiction to the government's plans to add online versions of traditional press organs while keeping control of publication and editorship. In a short period of time, observers of and participants in Chinese intellectual web sites have witnessed a complex process of evolution. On one hand, the newly emergent intellectual web sites have undoubtedly expanded the space of free expression for Chinese intellectuals; on the other, the state has also confronted the challenge of this new means of publication with refined strategies to control the new domain. Examination of this process requires us to ask a series of questions. What are the characteristics of the Chinese intellectual web press? Why does the state have to adopt "refined" control strategies? How have the intellectual web publishers responded to the state? What are the prospects of maintaining and enlarging this form of web-based press in China? In the following discussion, I shall try to present some preliminary answers by analyzing three representative Chinese intellectual web sites that I studied intensively during fieldwork in summer 2001 and fall 2002.

Pioneering the Intellectual Web Site: The Realm of Ideas

Before it was forced to close down in October 2000, the sixiang de jingjie (The Realm of Ideas) site was arguably the most influential intellectual web site in China. Created by Li Yonggang, a young political science teacher at Nanjing University on September 20, 1999, this site was one of the earliest web sites run by intellectuals and devoted to intellectual discussions. Happy to return to my alma mater, I interviewed Li in the summer of 2001 in Nanjing. Li told me that, like most Chinese, he had a very short history of web surfing. He had started to use the Internet at the end of 1998, mainly in search of academic reference materials. To his disappointment, there were few places to get scholarly materials, even though by 1999, Internet fever was under way in China and a great number of e-business sites had been established. This experience led Li to set up a web site to share academic materials with fellow scholars. After spending a week and half learning basic web-page designing, Li opened a site named Window of Public Administration (Li's academic specialty), where fewer than 100 articles that Li had found online were posted.

The new web site had few visitors in the following one and a half months, even though Li did his best to publicize it. After some hard reflection, he concluded that the scope of the web site was too narrow and too disciplinary in orientation to attract a wider audience. Thus in early November 1999, he redesigned the site, adding more space devoted to topics in the humanities, economics, and current affairs, and renamed it the Realm of Ideas. These changes seem to have had a marked effect, reflected in an increased number of visitors. According to Li's records, from September 20 to October 12, there were only 1,000 hits on the web site's visitor counter. The number reached 10,000 on December 17 and 20,000 on February 4, 2000. Along with an increasing readership, readers began to submit articles to the Realm of Ideas from December 1999 on. This was of great significance, because prior to this time, the articles on the web site had mainly been downloaded from other web sites. The issue of copyright was thus always at the back of the web editor's mind. The number of self-submitted articles increased steadily, and by May 2000, Li finally had the ability to choose to post most articles from those submitted rather than re-posting from other sites.[3]

Another turning point that further enhanced the popularity of the site was Li's decision to open a digital archive of collections of scholarly works by both Chinese and foreign intellectuals (in Chinese translation). This led more people to send in their writings, including some "independent" or quasi-dissident intellectuals. The increase in both the quantity and the quality of articles on the Realm of Ideas site in turn attracted a more cultivated readership. The web site thus rapidly gained fame, influence, and support. A web administrator from the Promotion Committee of the Chinese Education Net provided unlimited storage space for the Realm of Ideas on the organization's server. In May, Li opened up two BBS boards on the site, one named "Sharp Forum" and the other "Gentle Forum." The first of these attracted more participants, and its "sharpness" also brought it to the attention of the authorities. In retrospect, the "sharpness" was on two major fronts: the web site's strong liberal orientation and the often emotional and abusive tone of the discussions.

Both in his editorial notes and his interviews with me, Li made no effort to conceal his personal liberalism. The Realm of Ideas devoted a large space to publishing liberal-oriented articles and the works of liberal thinkers. Works by and about the idols of Chinese liberal intellectual life were hot spots on the web site and included selections from the writings of Václav Havel and a biography of Friedrich A. Hayek and his major writings. Cui Weiping, coincidently another Nanjing University graduate and an active liberal female literary critic based in Beijing, told me an illustrative story about how she had found a new avenue to publish online. In the late 1990s, she and her collaborators translated selections from Havel's writings into Chinese, but they were unable to find a press to publish the translation. Thus the translated copy only circulated among a small number of interested friends. After Cui logged on to the Realm of Ideas, she became not only an enthusiastic fan but also an active contributor to the web site. She was more than happy to have her translation published online.[4] Li told me that Cui was one of the first "well-established" scholar-patrons of the web site, and through Cui's social capital, Li was able to establish connections with other well known scholars and writers, thus further expanding his ability to obtain more submissions and generating publicity for and expanding the influence of the web site.

The liberal orientation of the web site certainly alienated certain elements of its readership, especially so-called new leftists and nationalists who did not agree with the tenets of liberalism. This disagreement reflects the complicated environment of Chinese intellectuals at the turn of the twenty-first century. In the late 1990s, after China entered a phase of comprehensive transition from a centrally planned economy to a market economy, Chinese intellectuals' attempts to gain a meaningful grasp on China's current conditions and future development resulted in a number of different evaluations, propositions, and theories, of which liberalism, new leftist thinking, nationalism, and new Confucianism were the most important. The heated theoretical exchange between the liberals and new leftists gained wide attention among Chinese intellectuals. Though a detailed discussion of the different schools of contemporary thinking is beyond the scope of this chapter, a brief introduction to the conflict between the liberals and new leftists is necessary to lay the foundation for the further discussion of intellectual web sites in China.

It is first necessary to caution readers that "liberals" and "new leftists" are terms broadly describing two intellectual groups whose ideas vary greatly from member to member. Some may be willing to accept a "new leftist" or "liberal" label; others may strongly protest against such labeling. The labels are used here mainly for the sake of convenience of discussion. A simple way to understand the groups' disagreements is to look at their general assessments of China's transformation up to the end of the 1990s. The liberals, while acknowledging the progress China had made toward a market economy, not only viewed this process as far from complete but felt that it had been impeded by the lack of political reforms centered on democracy, individual freedom, and the rule of law. From the same perspective, the liberals attributed rampant corruption, polarization of wealth, and social injustice to the powerless and poor to an unhealthy market economy operating, not according to the principles of the free market, but rather through top-down initiatives that protected vested interests forged between capital and state power. In brief, liberals advocated fundamental political reforms that would lead China to a fully free-market and democratic political and social system. In return, this system would provide the necessary conditions for China to rectify corruption and combat other social illness it faces today.

"New leftists" is a term coined to differentiate those it designates from the "old leftists," usually referring to Maoists and diehard communists.[5] New leftists' assessment of current Chinese social and political transformations is very different from that of liberals. They view China's economic transformation as an evolving incorporation into a larger process of globalization dominated by the Western world. During the last decade of the twentieth century, China was transformed in the direction of a capitalist society, and all kinds of social injustices have emerged, putting socially marginal groups at the mercy of all-encompassing market forces. China should not blindly follow neoliberal economic doctrine that worships the power of the "invisible" hand of the market, new leftists argue, but should rather try to find its own way, building upon the successful experiences of socialism and the Maoist past, to rectify the increasing economic injustice that the reforms have inflicted on many ordinary Chinese.[6]

Beneath their different assessments of China's recent socioeconomic transformation and its consequences, the two groups cherish fundamentally different values.[7] It was in this broad context that the Realm of Ideas web site unwittingly became involved in the ongoing debate between the liberals and the new leftists. Though the web site published articles by authors of different orientations, its liberal-leaning position was obvious, especially during the site's early months. Prompted by his friends who were concerned about this issue, Li Yonggang revised the site once again in mid-June 2000, trying to make the Realm of Ideas a more open and inclusive platform for the exchange of ideas. However, soon afterward, a controversy regarding the Cheung Kong–*Dushu* Awards transformed the web site into a battleground between the two camps.

Cheung Kong is a Hong Kong conglomerate owned by the tycoon Li Ka-shing, who not only has extensive business interests in mainland China but has also become a major donor promoting education and science in China.[8] In early 2000, Cheung Kong contributed 990,000 yuan to establish awards for outstanding work in the social sciences and humanities. The awards were to be jointly administered by Cheung Kong and the well-known Beijing intellectual journal *Dushu* (Reading) and were named the Cheung Kong–*Dushu* Awards. It is difficult to know whether Cheung Kong simply sought to make sure that social sciences and humanities were covered by its cultural programs, but given the influential status that *Dushu* has among Chinese intellectuals, it was money well spent. This is an example of what David Harvey has called the "flexible accumulation" method of doing business in the postmodern era.[9]

To the dismay of the donor, however, the subsequent choice of awardees provoked a huge controversy among the Chinese intelligentsia, both in the traditional print press and, especially, in cyberspace. The direct catalyst for the crisis was the fact that Wang Hui, who had been the joint editor-in-chief of *Dushu* since 1996 and had also served as the coordinator of the academic selection committee, was one of the recipients and was thus entitled to share a large sum of money with other awardees. When this news leaked out during late May and early June 2000, it immediately became a hot topic of discussion among Chinese intellectuals. Two camps with contrasting opinions rapidly formed. One camp, citing conflict of interest, accused Wang of sacrificing the credibility of the selection process and individual integrity in accepting this award. On the other hand, many voiced their support of Wang, claiming there was nothing wrong in his receiving the award as long as the selection process was conducted fairly and his work had the necessary scholastic merit.

The controversy would probably not have spiraled out of control had Wang Hui not happened to be one of the representatives of the new leftist camp. Indeed, it is said that his editorship has been a major contributing factor in transforming *Dushu*, originally liberal in orientation, into a new leftist stronghold. Wang specializes in the intellectual and cultural history of modern China, and in 1997, he published an influential article entitled "Contemporary Chinese Thought and the Question of Modernity," in which he gave a macroscopic review of the different schools of thought in the reform era, thus unavoidably making judgments that displeased a number of well-known intellectuals.[10] Wang was notably critical of the Chinese liberals, saying that "it is truly a naïve fantasy that many Chinese intellectuals optimistically think 'marketization' can naturally solve the issue of democracy in Chinese society."[11] Even though the debate on the award was not entirely the result of the factional division in the Chinese intelligentsia, it is safe to say that the existing divide between the liberals and the new leftists added much to the mutual resentment between the two camps.

Though the traditional print media played an important role in broaching the controversy, it was in cyberspace that the most heated exchanges occurred, and these often crossed over the thin line separating legitimate and illegitimate discussion of the matter.[12] At the time, there were few web sites devoted to intellectual discussion. The online debate on the Cheung Kong–*Dushu* Award was thus mainly concentrated in the BBS forums of three web sites, namely, the Realm of Ideas, Chinese Reading Net (zhonghua dushuwang, www.creader.com, now defunct), and the newly established Century China (shiji zhongguo, www.cc.org.cn). During my interview with Li Yonggang, I was told that from mid-June through early July, the "Sharp Forum" of the Realm of Ideas was full of messages on the subject, ranging from essay-length elaborations to one-liners written only in the subject heading column. With the heating up of the debate, the Sharp Forum became a rumor mill and a place for the venting of personal grievances. Unfortunately, as Li explained to me, because the Sharp Forum was set up on a rented server, no archive was preserved when Li later shut it down. Today, the only place one can revisit the debate is to log onto the Century Salon (shiji salong) at the Century China web site, which keeps all previous messages in its archive.[13]

Xu Youyu, a well-known liberal and arguably the most outspoken of Wang's accusers in the controversy, wrote, in a message originally posted on the Chinese Reading Net and subsequently reposted at Century Salon on August 8, that the significance of the debates on the Cheung Kong–*Dushu* Awards was to make people realize the importance of impartiality in the selection procedure. The whole debate, Xu said, was "not about whether or not a particular individual should receive the award, but about whether or not the award selection should obey certain rules in order to maintain fairness of procedure." He concluded, "We have reasons to ask the intellectual elite to modernize their ideas and behavior. Everything must be conducted according to the rules of game; this is the basic requirement."[14] Xu wrote in a restrained style, voicing his resentment of the other side within the "rules of game." However, not everyone in the debate followed the rules. In a posting entitled "Ten

Questions for *Dushu*" on July 27, 2000, a pseudonymous participant presented ten questions in the form of the American Jeopardy game, insinuating that Wang Hui was an "ugly, dog-like, perverted" new leftist.[15] Many of the debate's participants protested that this kind of personal attack was outside the bounds of normal debate on scholarly matters.

The controversy was perhaps the first test of Chinese intellectuals' ability to handle the unprecedented degree of accessibility and freedom of expression provided by the Internet, and their response was only a qualified success. It did not take long for new netizens to realize that the cyberspace forums' unprecedented openness to the expression of individual opinion has not necessarily led to the "public, rational and well informed" discussion of affairs of public interest identified by Jürgen Habermas as the "public sphere."[16] Even though Chinese intellectuals dearly cherished the freedom of speech that had eluded them for so long, the webmasters of the first Chinese intellectual web sites quickly reached the conclusion that they had to censor messages featuring personal abuse. Li Yonggang thus started removing abusive messages from the Sharp Forum in the Realm of the Ideas.

Li's monitoring apparently did not satisfy the authorities. Though I doubt that the authorities were directly interested in the controversy, they certainly grabbed the opportunity to point out that there were "problematic" articles in the Sharp Forum and that the web site needed to rectify itself. Under tremendous pressure, Li shut down his web site in early July, claiming technical difficulties. After carrying out a great deal of self-censorship, deleting all messages and articles on the Cheung Kong–*Dushu* Awards, and effectively closing down the site's BBS, Li reopened the Realm of Ideas a few days later. In an effort to change the Realm of Ideas into a more open, inclusive, and scholar-friendly webzine, he created an archive of works by young Chinese scholars and tried to turn the site into an online weekly.

By this time, the reputation of the Realm of Ideas had reached a new level among Chinese intellectuals. The visitor counter reached 100,000 on July 10, and 200,000 on September 4. Along with the growth of influence came increased pressure from the authorities to shut the site down. The pressure was conveyed to Li through administrators at Nanjing University, as well as by well-intentioned friends and colleagues. After Li came to the conclusion that his self-censorship efforts would in no way satisfy the authorities' demands, and seeing no way to preserve the integrity and independence of the web site, he shut down the Realm of

Ideas permanently on the evening of October 14, 2000. By the time the site was closed, it had had a total of 320,000 accumulated hits. The final month alone accounted for one-third of these visits, with the average daily number of hits reaching more than 4,000.[17]

In retrospect, Li Yonggang's personal endeavor was of significance in the development of Chinese intellectual cyberculture. First, the Realm of Ideas popularized web sites of the so-called "scholarship and thought" (*xueshu sixiang*) type, opening up an online space new to most Chinese intellectuals. Li was not the first to run such a web site in China, but he certainly was the first to successfully attract the attention of the Chinese intellectual elite so that the influence of his web site reached far beyond the small audience of the majority of similar web sites at the time. Secondly, the Realm of Ideas also signified a conscious effort by Chinese intellectuals to treat cyberspace as a new domain of intellectual inquiry and to break free from the existing constraints of censorship to pursue a larger degree of freedom of expression. This aim was manifested in the three headline banners that popped up alternately on the home page of the Realm of Ideas: "Scholarship is a Public Treasure for All under Heaven" (Xueshu nei tianxia gongqi); "Exchange, Communication, Sharing" (Jiaoliu, chuanbo, gongxiang); and "Inclusiveness of All Schools, Freedom of Thought" (Jianrong bingxu, sixiang ziyou). These open statements were not only the guiding principles of the Realm of Ideas but have been accepted by most Chinese intellectual web sites, no matter what their webmasters' ideological and personal preferences might be.

Third and possibly most significantly, the Realm of Ideals tested the limits of government tolerance of e-intellectual web sites, waging a Promethean struggle with the authorities for more free space online for intellectual exchanges. Although the web site was forced to shut down, its brief existence had effectively shown web site patrons the basic contours of the space that intellectuals could occupy. It is necessary to emphasize here that at that time, both individual intellectuals and state authorities were faced with an undemarcated new domain in which both sides were testing the water of freedom of expression. Online pioneers such as Li Yonggang tested the unknown space through courage and personal sacrifices, thus contributing to the subsequent flourishing of intellectual web sites in Chinese cyberspace.

Handling Tensions on the Web:
The Formalization of Ideas

When I mentioned the Formalization of Ideas web site to my liberal-leaning friends, a number of them dismissed it as a nationalist web site and thus not worth visiting. Since I knew that Ma Lijun, the webmaster, was one of the authors of the 1996 bestseller *China Can Say No,* a work that attracted much media and scholarly attention in both China and abroad because of its strong anti-American rhetoric, I at first took this at face value and was expecting to encounter a heavily nationalistic web site. To my surprise, however, I was immediately struck by the fact that its archives had one of the most comprehensive collections of works by contemporary Chinese scholars, be they liberals, new leftists, nationalists, or whatever. Based on my observations of the web site since July 2001, Formalization of Ideas is much more than the web site of a nationalist clique. In fact, the history of this web site reveals the tremendous difficulties and tensions some Chinese intellectual web sites have experienced in the past few years.

Formalization of Ideas differentiates itself from first-generation, individually run intellectual web sites in a number of crucial ways. First, it was initially created by a core group of intellectuals who held similar positions. Indeed, it was set up as a *tongren* (by and for close colleagues) electronic magazine, like similar journals in the traditional print media. My liberal-leaning friends were not totally incorrect in labeling it a nationalist stronghold. The main supporters of Formalization of Ideas are Fang Ning and Wang Xiaodong, two well-known advocates of nationalism in China. When the site was founded, Fang was a professor of political science at the Capital Normal University.[18] Wang Xiaodong, the most outspoken advocate of nationalism, was once an editor of the influential magazine *Strategies and Management* (zhanlüe yu guanli). In addition to Fang and Wang, Li Xiguang, a journalist-turned-professor at Qsinghua University, and Han Deqiang, an economist at Beijing Aerospace University, were also members of this intellectual circle.[19]

The Formalization of Ideas web site was set up to promote the group's ideas and works, and its founding resulted from the group's experiences with the Internet. Wang Xiaodong had majored in mathematics at Beijing University and had studied abroad both in Japan and Canada, venturing online much earlier than most of his peers. By 1999, most of the group members had become Internet-literate, and in the same year, they orchestrated an online promotion for the book *China's Pathway under the Shadow of Globalization* (hereafter *Shadow of Globalization*), authored by Fang Ning, Wang Xiaodong, and Song Qiang, when the conventional channels for book promotion were unavailable for political reasons.[20] This unique experience of online scholarly promotion undoubtedly encouraged the group to take full advantage of the newly available medium of the Internet.

Fang Ning gave me a detailed account of their online book promotion in an interview in November 2002. After the Chinese Embassy in Belgrade was bombed by the United States in May 1999, they were prompted to write and indeed to finish the book in a couple of months. Given rising Chinese nationalism and anti-American sentiment in the wake of the embassy bombing, Fang Ning and his co-authors were optimistic about the speedy publication of their book, and the manuscript was sought after by a number of editors from different publishing houses. However, not long after the bombing, the Chinese government reopened WTO negotiations with the United States. Apparently, too, it did not want the Sino-American relationship to break down irredeemably or for nationalism to spiral out of control. The editors thus rescinded their prior acceptance of the manuscript, obviously concerned about the book's strong nationalist rhetoric and its critical view of globalization and China's efforts to accede to the WTO. Fang Ning half-jokingly described how the manuscript had been turned down by virtually every Chinese publishing house. Eventually, at the end of 1999, the book was published by the Chinese Social Science Press, with the backing of the press's editor, who was also the editor of *China Can Say No*.

In contrast to the enormous publicity that *China Can Say No* received in 1996, the book's authors soon encountered another unexpected obstacle, in that few media outlets were willing to publish reviews of the book. It seems understandable that mainstream print media did not want to be involved with the sensitive issues that might potentially attract attention from the watchful eyes of the authorities. Finding the traditional avenues blocked, the authors turned to the Internet to promote the book. From December 1999 to March 2000, they posted lengthy excerpts from it on the Strengthening-China Forum, then the most popular and influential political BBS in China. With the help of other netizens, numerous messages about the book's authors, contents, and responses to it in both China and abroad were circulated on the Internet, thus stirring up more public interest and gaining a large audience.[21] This online promotion boosted sales of the book. According to Fang Ning, *Shadow of Globalization* sold more than 100,000 copies, an impressive number considering the difficulties the authors encountered. This experience of online promotion undoubtedly contributed to the authors' desire to have an online platform at their own disposal.

Perhaps more important, unlike Realm of Ideas, Formalization of Ideas is institutionally sponsored, not an individual endeavor. Li Yonggang ran Realm of Ideas in his spare time from his university teaching job, but Ma, the webmaster of Formalization of Ideas, devotes himself full time to the web site. From my conversation with Ma, I realized that he relied on a subsidy from the English-learning center to keep the operation going. The center provided Ma with two rooms free of rent, as well as paying the salaries of the three-person team for the first year of the site's operations. The financial and technical support that Ma received enabled him to run the web site in a more professional way. This in part explains how he had been able to construct a very comprehensive digital archive of scholarly works on the Formalization of Ideas site, as mentioned earlier.

In addition to noting differences between the Formalization of Ideas and Realm of Ideas sites, we might also notice intrinsic contradictions and tensions regarding the Formalization of Ideas site. First of all, it is perhaps ironic that the web site of a group of nationalist-leaning Chinese intellectuals is supported financially by an American-run cultural institution, or, to be more precise, by a Chinese American named Patrick Chang. According to a biographical sketch on the web site of www.pen123.com.cn, Chang was injured in a diving accident that paralyzed him from the chest down at age 13. However, with determination and hard work, he became one of the youngest Ph.D. candidate in economics at Stanford University.[22] Obviously, Chang has multiple statuses in China as a role model, a celebrity, and a cultural businessman. Trying to alleviate my curiosity about his benefactor, Ma explained Chang's background in detail, emphasizing that Chang had been well received in the Chinese media, had wide connections, and was well respected in China.[23] In addition, Chang is a personal friend of Fang Ning's and has promised not to interfere with the editing of the Formalization of Ideas site. His unique status is not only acceptable to Fang Ning, Wang Xiaodong, and their collaborators, but also to the authorities, an important consideration, since foreign funding of social and political activities has

always been a sensitive issue in China. Ma's explanation convinced me
that, however ironic, the relationship between his web site and the American-run English-learning center was just a coincidence without special
symbolic meaning.

I conducted more interviews with Ma in 2001. By the last time I met
him in November, we had gotten to know each other better, and our conversation had become franker. As a fellow anthropologist puts it, we
started "getting below the surface."[24] Though Ma was still optimistic
about the future of the Formalization of Ideas site, he also expressed
more concerns during our last conversation. With the expansion of the
web site, Ma had encountered increasing difficulties in running it according to his vision and plan. As we shall see, his frustrations in his role
as webmaster were innately derived from and to a certain degree determined by the nature of the Formalization of Ideas site—an institutionally
sponsored web site run by a group of intellectuals purposely trying to use
it to promote the ideas and positions they share. The many operational
dilemmas that Formalization of Ideas faces show the complexity of the
operating environment of contemporary Chinese intellectual web sites.

The first dilemma Ma had faced was how to give Formalization of
Ideas a "scholarly" identity in the context of a broad web site whose aim
was to promote Chang's sprawling English-learning network. In fact, the
Formalization of Ideas site, set up in early 2001, was a late addition to
the so-called Patrick Consulting Net, set up in 1998. Theoretically, Formalization of Ideas was only a part of Chang's ambitious language-learn-
ing promotion web site, but Ma made the banners of the two web site
names appear interchangeably on the home page, trying to ensure a semi-
independent status for his own web site.[25]

Ma was not only concerned about the fact that Formalization of Ideas
was located within a vaguely defined business-oriented web site but also
constantly worried about the financial viability of the site. Trying to
achieve financial independence, he came up with a plan to make his web
site a service provider to the scholarly community in late 2001. As he explained to me, there was no future for Formalization of Ideas if it could
not gain financial independence; yet he did not want to sacrifice the intellectual integrity of the web site to commercial interests by engaging in
activities such as publishing advertisements. Eventually, he decided to try
to generate operational funds by providing "scholarly services." For example, taking advantage of the huge collection of scholarly works in the
site's digital archives, Ma planned to provide "information consulting,

collecting and categorizing" services to scholars conducting research on specific topics in the areas of social science, popular culture, or news media. The financial insecurity of the Formalization of Ideas site reflects a general struggle that many Chinese intellectual web sites have encountered, which continues today.[26]

Apart from financial issues, another question that troubled Ma was how to define the character of the web site. The dilemma he faced was that his group's intellectual positions were well known to their contemporaries, which meant that the Formalization of Ideas site was seen by many as a "clique web site" from the very beginning. This was in contrast to Ma's vision of making it an open platform for exchanges of all kinds of ideas, a vision he forged after he became the webmaster. Ma said to me during an interview: "I am a nationalist; this term is fine with me if people like to apply such a label. But when it comes to running an intellectual web site such as the Formalization of Ideas, you have to put your individual preferences aside and make the site as inclusive as possible. If it appeals to only a special group of people, the web site will have little influence outside its immediate circle, which in turn is detrimental to the spread of the group's own ideas. I am a true believer in the freedom of thought." Despite their differing individual ideals, Ma and Li Yonggang seem to share the same principle of making their web sites as inclusive as possible.

Surprisingly, Ma had often had to resist pressure from friends within his intellectual group. From time to time, he had had to make hard choices in publishing articles from authors who were not members of his group, often resulting in damage to his personal relationships with friends. As he put it: "If I publish too many articles by authors from other thought camps, some of my friends will be pissed off. If I publish too many articles with the positions I endorse, the web site will lose its credibility as an open platform to exchange ideas." Ma ended up spending a lot of time trying to keep the delicate balance, though acknowledging that the final result might not be satisfactory to anyone.

Scholarly or commercial, inclusive or exclusive, tensions were always present to pressure Ma to keep Formalization of Ideas balanced between different orientations. I was extremely impressed by the site's inclusive collection of scholarly works representing a wide spectrum of Chinese intellectual discourses. Yet just as the Realm of Ideas site was clearly liberal-leaning, the intellectual predilections of the Formalization of Ideas site were not hard to detect. For example, looking at its responses to the

September 11 terrorist attacks against the United States, one can discover
the complex feelings of nationalist-leaning Chinese intellectuals at the
time. As Ma put it in his short editorial on September 11: "In the aftermath of our deep shock at the means the terrorists employed, and the disaster terrorists caused in this terrorist event, in the aftermath of expressing our deep sympathy to those who perished or were injured in the
attack, shall we not also undertake a deep examination of the current
world structure as well as the policies that put this structure into place?"

The layout of the home page of the web site after September 11 reveals
more subtle information through its visual presentation. In the center of
the page, two pictures showed people fleeing from the collapsed World
Trade Center. Under these two pictures were two subtitles that read:
" 'We will bomb them back to the stone age!'—Words used by Americans
in the Vietnam War" and " 'We will destroy everything they cherish!'—
Words used by Americans during their bombing of Yugoslavs." By men-
tioning these two historical events in which both Chinese and Americans
had been involved, and by juxtaposing the American war slogans with
pictures of the terror the country experienced on September 11, the Formalization of Ideas site was trying to provoke its readers to think further
about the tragic events in America.

The emergence of Formalization of Ideas shows that the process of
government censorship has evolved from the old totalitarian control
mechanism to a new, looser system with some room for maneuvering.
Though the Internet expands the space for political participation, the
newly emergent space has few clearly articulated rules of operation. Survival in this atmosphere requires subtle political skills, which are also
hard to stipulate in terms of definite criteria. Unlike editors in the print
media, Ma faced the daunting task of monitoring an unruly area of cyberspace. Ma confessed to me that he spent most of his time and energy
censoring online submissions, deciding what could be put online and
what could not. Because the area of cyberspace he controlled was still
very unclear, and censorship was mostly self-censorship, Ma took a very
cautious approach. "I don't want to bring trouble to Mr. Patrick Chang,
neither do I want to bring trouble to the authors," Ma said. "Most important, I don't want to see the Formalization of Ideas site shut down by
the authorities," he added. "That would be the worst scenario, in that we
would lose the platform on which we can express our opinions, even if
only to a certain degree."

In summary, Ma was running an intellectual web site under very difficult conditions. Backed by a particular group of intellectuals, and yet not financially secure, he had had to negotiate with both his friends and his institutional sponsor to run the web site as independently as he could. He had had to face many dilemmas and to try to negotiate a series of compromises to move forward. Such dilemmas included how to keep a "scholarly and thought" web site like Formalization of Ideas part of a profit-oriented online venture; how to resist narrow-minded pressures and keep the site open to all schools of thought; and how to take advantage of the Internet's expanded space of political participation, yet conduct self-censorship to ensure the survival of the site.

Ma certainly struggled heroically to keep his web site running. Indeed, we might ask whether anyone else could have done a better job of running an intellectual web site in Chinese cyberspace. The successful example of shiji zhongguo (Century China) is one possible answer to this question.

Century China: The Convergence of State, Capital, and Intellectuals?

Since its inception in July 2000, Century China (www.cc.org.cn) has arguably become the most influential intellectual web site in China. It has four major components. *Shiji zhoukan* (Century Weekly) is a webzine publishing original scholarly articles. What makes it unique is that it is one of few Chinese webzines that pays an author for the right to publish his or her articles online. *Xingqi wencui* (Weekly Digest) has scholars as its editors and publishes articles on a theme chosen at the editors' discretion. *Gonggong pingtai* (Public Platform), also monitored by the editors, provides an open space in which scholars can publish their works (new or previously published) online. Finally, *Shiji shalong* (Century Salon) is a BBS forum for improvised discussions. Century China seems to have quickly gained popularity among Chinese intellectuals. By March 2001, only eight months into its existence, the number of weekly hits on its web pages reached 194,125, far surpassing that of Realm of Ideas.[27]

It is no accident that the Century China site has been able to achieve this status in such a short time. Compared to most Chinese intellectual web sites, it enjoys unrivalled financial and academic resources. The Century China site is sponsored by the CSDN Information Technology Company (hereafter CSDN Co.) and co-sponsored by the Institute of Chinese Studies at the Chinese University of Hong Kong, which is in charge of editing the web site. The web site's co-sponsor provides a partial answer to its quick success. Anyone familiar with contemporary Chinese intellectual life knows that the institute has been publishing the magazine *Ershiyi Shiji* (Twenty-First Century) since 1990. In the 1980s, before its editors, Jin Guantao and Liu Qingfeng, moved to Hong Kong from mainland China, they had already established their reputations by advocating "cultural discussion" (*wenhua taolun*). Under their editorship, the magazine often publishes trend-setting articles and has become one of the most influential intellectual magazines both in China and overseas. The established reputation of *Ershiyi Shiji* certainly contributed to the quick name recognition of Century China.

It would be surprising, however, if many online readers of Century China knew much about its chief sponsor, CSDN Co. Indeed, it took me some time to find out how a seemingly commercial establishment became involved with this web site. CSDN turns out to stand for China Social Development Network, one of the main projects in the Chinese government's effort to use information technology to promote social development. Authorized by China's State Development and Planning Commission and under the direct auspices of the commission's Department of Social Development, CSDN was established in Beijing on July 19, 2000. With the avowed aim to "develop people, serve people, and protect people," CSDN is a very ambitious project. According to Chinese officials, the network covers areas as diverse as population, labor and employment, culture, education, public health, social welfare, radio and television, publishing, cultural relics, archives, tourism, politics and law, and civil administration. The net includes a number of portal web sites, such as China Medical Net, China Labor and Employment Online, Chinese Net for Continuation Education, and Chinese Legal Service Net.[28] Century China is thus only one of numerous projects that make up this huge government endeavor.

What sets CSDN apart from other government Internet-related projects is that it is a contemporary version of the "private business under official supervision" concept that first appeared in the Late Qing era. It is a "private business" because CSDN does not involve government investment, but rather relies on private funding obtained through market mechanisms. Correspondingly a number of independent companies have been set up to execute individual projects. On the other hand, it is "under official supervision" because the government is responsible for (1) making a general plan, (2) setting standards, and (3) establishing coordinating and evaluating systems. CSDN Co., the sponsor of Century China, is clearly thus a business company funded by private capital yet set up under the supervision of the government to carry out the CSDN plan. The Institute of Chinese Studies at the Chinese University of Hong Kong was then "invited" by CSDN Co. to edit Century China.

Century China is thus not an ordinary Chinese intellectual web site. It is a part of a grand government information technology project, supported by private capital, hosted by a business company, and subcontracted out to an established cultural institution outside mainland China. Ample financial resources, well-established intellectual authority, transnational elite editorial personnel, and the publication of material through both traditional and cyber media, are all key features that have made Century China a special intellectual web site in Chinese cyberspace.

"So theoretically CSDN Co. has the final say on the editorial decisions?" This was the key question I wanted to ask in a telephone interview in October 2001 with Xu Jilin, a well-known Shanghai-based scholar who has been in charge of Century Digest and Century Salon. "You could say so. But they rarely interfere with our editorial job," answered Xu, who was then at Harvard as a visiting scholar. "How come?" I pressed further. "Well, it all depends on the tacit understanding both sides have reached. We have known each other for some time and the other side knows our record." The issue was quite subtle, he added, and it was not possible to clarify it fully over the phone. I then changed topics by asking how he managed to do his job when he was away in the United States. He replied that it was not very difficult to monitor Century Salon in the United States because information technology has made physical location unimportant.

I met Xu again one year later in Shanghai after he had returned to China. When I raised the old question of how he monitored discussions on Century Salon and decided the admissibility of postings touching on sensitive issues, his answer was as subtle as the one given a year earlier. "Well, it all depends on your feeling [*ganjue*]." He didn't define what he meant by "feeling" but emphasized that it was context- and case-specific, fluid, and changed under different circumstances. Using the admissibility of discussions as an example, Xu elaborated on the multiple layers of censorship that have emerged in contemporary China. His remarks are worth quoting at length:

The question of what can be published and what cannot is extremely complicated today. Something that cannot be published by official party newspapers [*dang-bao*] may be published by evening newspapers [*wanbao*]. Items that cannot be published in newspapers may be published in journals. Scholarly journals can publish articles that cannot be published in general journals. Some material may not admissible in newspapers and on television, yet it is publishable online. Some material cannot be posted on portal news web sites (such as www.sina.com.cn) but can be put on other web sites. Something that is not suitable to be put on news web sites can be put on BBS forums. Something that not admissible on BBS forums run by *People's Daily* may be admissible on other BBS forums. In summary, the admissibility question is very complex. I wish the government could tell me what is acceptable and what is not; but to our dismay, there is no such definite stipulation. That is why we can only make our judgments based on our feelings.

This reveals the daunting task Chinese webmasters face on a daily basis. Webmasters need to have a strong grasp of the current political atmosphere to make sound judgments. For example, immediately before the party's Sixteenth Congress in November 2002, sensitive writings became less admissible. The most skillful webmasters often test limits by posting writings that are close to the line of admissibility yet do not quite cross it.[29] Xu admitted that one has to change one's "feelings" according to changes in political atmosphere and sense where the "forbidden areas" are. This is a skill that requires experience accumulated through years in Chinese politics, and there was no doubt that Xu was very confident of his and his colleagues' abilities on this front.

Xu and his assistants adopted several strategies to monitor Century Salon. In order to promote certain messages, they put recommendation marks besides their headings, thus enhancing the likelihood of their being read. On the contrary, messages that the webmasters deemed less relevant to the discussions were put into a special "leisure area" (*xiuxian qu*) viewed by fewer visitors. Xu told me that Century Salon generally does not delete messages aside from unsubstantiated abuse. But my own observation shows that only one month after the inauguration of Century Salon, the webmaster posted an initial Public Notice proclaiming that personally abusive messages would be removed. This was done in the name of keeping Century Salon a "public space" with "healthy rules of the game."[30] Given the fact that Century Salon has witnessed several intellectual controversies since the Cheung Kong–*Dushu* Awards, it is likely that the webmasters periodically hit the delete key to keep the participants playing by the "rules of game."

In a relatively short time, Century China has established a reputation for being a relatively neutral intellectual web site with a strongly elitist tone. It seems that Xu and his colleagues share a consensus that Century China should be an online public platform that allows the expression of ideas by different schools of intellectuals. So far, Century China has shown no apparent preference for any particular intellectual school. One reason for this is that Century China's webmasters occupy diverse intellectual positions. The Shanghai-based webmaster Xu, in the capacity of a general webmaster, calls himself a "left-wing liberal," while the two webmasters of Century Digest are often labeled "moderate new leftists" and the young webmaster of Century Salon, Wu Guanjun, is identified as a liberal. Their diverse backgrounds and consensus about the need to make Century China a public platform certainly contribute to its relatively neutral tone. It is also possible that the web site's indirect ties with the government are a factor making it avoid being lopsided in opinions, a safe position taken for the sake of the mutual understanding reached between the host and the academic subcontractors.

Century China is in a special position to obtain elite status because of the abundant resources at its disposal that most other web sites lack. It is clear that from the beginning, the authorities were determined to set a high standard for the CSDN project. Among the first members of the CSDN advisory committee were the Nobel laureate Yang Zhenning and distinguished mainland and overseas scholars such as Wang Yuanhua, Jin Yaoji, and Wu Jinglian.[31] In addition, the Institute of Chinese Studies at CUHK, its editorial office, is an established academic institution with which many well-known Chinese intellectuals are affiliated. One need only look at the editorial committee of *Ershiyi Shiji*, which includes two Nobel laureates and many famous Chinese intellectuals in the humanities and the natural and social sciences, to realize the prominence of the institute. These resources have helped Century China quickly gain the reputation, prestige, and authority that many other intellectual web sites have struggled to obtain.

Compared to other Chinese intellectual web sites, Century China is thus standard-setting and has elite status. This elitism inevitably decreases the degree of active participation by intellectuals. Though the web site does not oppose the discussion of current social and political affairs, it encourages discussion of these issues from "academic and theoretical" (*xueli*) perspectives. As a result, visitors of the web site will encounter more theoretical and abstract discussions on current affairs than the spontaneous and direct responses that often displease the official censorship. In my interview with Xu Jilin, he acknowledged that initially the webmasters of Century China had no clear intention of making it an elite intellectual web site, but that it had gained a reputation as such because many participants had stopped patronizing it after their postings did not meet with the expected response or were declined because they did not meet the standard of scholastic merit set by the webmasters.

Nominally part of a government-sponsored project, and based on mutual trust between a commercial company and an established academic institution, Century China and its webmasters are strategically positioned in the "elite" sector of today's Chinese intellectual landscape. After all, keeping a certain distance from current politics and limiting discussions to the elite is a safe position, likely to be sanctioned by both the sponsor and the editors, because both sides would stand to lose if Century China were to attract uninvited political censorship. The web site still continues to promote cutting-edge intellectual exchanges and trend-setting theoretical inquiry, however, and thus represents an expansion of the existing space of freedom of discussion in China. By so doing, nevertheless, it also excludes the voices of the majority of politically conscious Chinese citizens who do not belong to elite intellectual circles. Those excluded have to seek alternative venues for online participation. As a result, a number of *minjian* (literally, unofficial, or private) web sites have emerged, representing online writers who seek to have their own place within cyberspace, as we shall see in the next chapter.

Expanded Space, Refined Control

The above three cases are representative enough to reflect the complex developmental contours of Chinese intellectual web sites over the past few years. Generally speaking, the majority of the first generation of Chinese intellectual web sites were run by individual intellectuals and operated on a very limited scale. Later on, the number of institutional web sites increased. These sites are sponsored by cultural establishments such as academic institutions or existing intellectual magazines, and in many cases, they are edited by nonconformist intellectuals. The increasing marketization of the Chinese economy also provides more opportunities for intellectuals to gain financial support rather than relying on state resources. The state has also been quick to realize the importance of utilizing and controlling this new domain. Chinese web sites will thus continue to develop through a series of complex interactions between the state, market mechanisms, intellectual establishments, and new technologies. Even though their interaction has had only a very short history, it is safe to say that so far both Chinese intellectuals and the state can claim to be winners in the process.

As far as Chinese intellectuals are concerned, the Internet has certainly enabled them to expand the space they need to engage in the exchange of ideas and free discussion. In contrast to the regularly published academic and intellectual magazines in China, Chinese intellectual web sites show an unprecedented degree of openness, frankness, and tolerance. As we have seen, the content of these sites is extremely rich and reflects general concerns in Chinese intellectual circles in recent years, ranging from critical commentary on current national and international affairs, debates between the New Leftists and the liberals, the introduction of Western social theories, the promotion of nationalism, and the staging of controversies between different intellectual factions.

No matter whether intellectual web sites are individually or institutionally run, most of them try to differentiate themselves from the traditional print press by proclaiming their "independent," "private" (or unofficial), and "noncommercial" status. Such claims derive from the fact that most of these webzines have been set up without going through the conventional approval procedure of print journals, and more important, the webmasters have exercised more discretion in editorial decisions. The most obvious illustration of this status is that intellectual web sites have increasingly become a place for nonconformist Chinese intellectuals (sometimes even dissidents) to publish works that are usually banned in the print press. Their status as unofficial intellectual sites is certainly these web sites' main attraction for viewers seeking fresh ideas and information that are hard to find in academic and cultural publications under state control in contemporary China.

The emergent electronic intellectual press has also facilitated the formation of a group of public intellectuals in China. This development is significant because while Chinese intellectuals played an important role in enlightening the general public in the 1980s, many of them chose to "return to study" after the Tiananmen crackdown in 1989. Avoiding being labeled as having too many thoughts but not enough scholarship, scholars in the 1990s have emphasized the study of concrete social issues and sound scholarship rather than grand theory building, thus creating a division of labor between academics and intellectuals. Although the intellectual web sites differentiate themselves by focusing on serious and thoughtful discussion, most of them prefer short, interesting, eye-catching articles to purely theoretical inquiries, mainly in order to make their sites more attractive to general viewers. This provides a new space for nonconformist intellectuals to publish thought-provoking essays that would not appear in either strictly academic journals or the mainstream print press. Thanks to the interactivity, speed, and unlimited space of e-publishing, in addition to the well-established academics who are also frequent writers online, a great number of new Internet-based writers and commentators have appeared and established their reputations in cyberspace. They have become China's new public intellectuals, aiming to facilitate the exchange of ideas, or—more optimistically—the formation of a public e-sphere in China.

Yet the greater freedom of expression and the possibility of quickly becoming famous online has also exacerbated the existing factionalism of the contemporary Chinese intelligentsia. Intellectual web sites have thus often become arenas for different factions to engage in heated disputes that have often gone beyond the norms of legitimate academic exchange. Worse still, abusive styles of argument suppressed by the print press have flourished online, as shown in the controversy about the Cheung Kong–*Dushu* Awards. Frequently, BBS forums have become places for the venting of personal attacks, and thus the online equivalent of the "big character posters" of the Cultural Revolution. If an intellectual web site becomes a cultural tabloid, this decreases the authority and credibility of the forum, often discouraging existing readers from participating in discussions again. Thus, although the embryonic Chinese intellectual electronic press holds great promise for the future, it is uncertain whether an independent electronic press will emerge. This will depend on both the maturing of Chinese cyber-intellectuality and the relaxation of state policies.

As far as the state is concerned, though, this new development challenges its concern with controlling the press and media, and thus the state is trying to catch up with the rapid pace of Internet development, gradually devising an effective policy to deal with intellectual web sites. The closing down of the Realm of Ideas web site by official pressure illustrates the state's early concern about the problems posed by an uncontrolled electronic press, but the frequency of the closing down of intellectual web sites is generally much lower than the frequency of new sites being set up. It seems that the state has resorted to a more refined control mechanism than that used against the print press, allowing a greater degree of tolerance to web site editors.[32] Faced with an increasing number of intellectual web sites, the state has mostly opted to exert pressure on web site editors to conduct self-censorship rather than attempting to close down the sites outright, even though the latter course of action is always an option if it chooses to do so.

The ever-present threat of being selectively punished by the state for crossing boundaries results in the fact that no matter how "independent" or "unofficial" a web site claims to be, various degrees of self-censorship exist to ensure the physical viability of the site. The most difficult point that editors need to bear in mind is that there are no clear regulations as to what can or cannot be published on the Internet, and thus editors have constantly to exercise their own judgment on the admissibility of submitted articles. Like a sword of Damocles hanging over editors' heads, the ambiguity of government policy in this area has turned out to be very effective. In the process, virtually all intellectual webmasters in mainland China have come to the consensus that no mention of organized political dissent will be allowed by the government. Topics such as Falun Gong, independent labor unions, and other political parties are thus virtually untouched by mainstream Chinese intellectual web sites.[33] As long as the state does not dramatically change its policies, web site editors will be under pressure to impose self-censorship, and a truly independent intellectual electronic press will thus not emerge in the near future.

An interesting development in Chinese intellectual cyberspace is that the state has taken the initiative in entering this domain by enlisting cooperation from intellectual establishments, as shown by the case of Century China. This seemingly unlikely marriage is made possible by mutual understanding on both sides. Though the state does not interfere directly with editorial decisions, it achieves its goal by trusting elite intellectual webmasters to conduct self-censorship. Intellectuals gain by being able to access political and financial resources provided by the state, while enjoying their "independent" editorial policies in order to make the web site influential and indeed the most prominent of its kind. The case of Century China shows a new trend in Chinese intellectual web sites, in which, after an initial stage of free development and brave challenge to government control, mainstream intellectual web sites have come to the realization that their expanded space has a vague yet tangible boundary. For the sake of the web sites' viability, their editors have to "dance in chains" and not overstep a set boundary. In this process, private capital has emerged as an increasingly important mediator between the state and intellectuals. Century China can be seen as a more complicated example of what Mayfair Mei-hui Yang calls "tension between state and capital in the cultural realm," in which the capital not only plays the role of challenging state regulations by providing alternative resources to intellectuals, but also a regulatory role tacitly requiring intellectual web sites to operate in ways acceptable to the state in order to safeguard its investment.[34]

Given the rapid technological development and new players (i.e., market mechanisms and capital) entering Chinese cyberspace, it is hard to imagine how a Chinese electronic intellectual press will fully emerge. On the one hand, intellectuals will continue to take advantage of Internet technology and expand the space of free exchange of ideas and information online. Conversely, the state will continue to try to monitor developments, most likely using more refined measures of control but refraining from outright suppression. Thus the process will involve negotiations between intellectuals and the Chinese state. For intellectuals, the desired goal is to have a free press online and be able to use it to create a public e-sphere in which they can engage in the rational discussion of all sorts of issues. For the state, even though it has accepted the fact that the Internet has opened up a new space to intellectuals, this new domain must stay under its control and not become a threat to its authoritarian power. Since both sides' abilities to achieve their desired goals are constrained, the final result will in all probability be an expanded space under more refined control.

CHAPTER EIGHT

Living on the Cyber Border

Minjian Online Political Writers in China

I F THERE WERE NO INTERNET, it would never have been possible for me to have my words heard," Lu Jiaping told me in an assertive
tone during an interview at his home in the summer of 2001. The sixty-
year-old Lu lived with his wife in a rented house in a village at the foot of
Xiangshan (Fragrant Mountain) in the western suburbs of Beijing. His
two-room home was crammed with outdated cheap furniture and
books—living conditions that reminded me of those that were common
in China twenty years ago. A desk was placed in front of the window of
the room that served as his combined bedroom, study, and living room.
On the desk was an old computer, on which Lu wrote articles on a broad
variety of topics concerning China's foreign policy, military strategy, corruption problems, and political history. Since he had no formal academic
training, it was very difficult for him to publish his articles in mainstream
scholarly journals and newspapers. He thus increasingly relied on the Internet to circulate his articles and gradually gained a growing audience in
cyberspace. After initially getting to know his name through surfing, I interviewed him in summer 2000 for the first time.

But the Internet had also brought him trouble. I met Lu again in July
2001, only a month after his elder son was arrested and jailed for seventeen days for creating and maintaining his father's web site, and helping
to post Lu's articles on the web. Lu was just barely computer-literate and
could only use his computer to do word processing and receive email. After finishing his articles, he had to send them to his son in Hunan
province, who would then post them on his web site or send them out to

a group of recipients, of whom I am one. According to Lu, the timing of his son's arrest was no coincidence. His son was arrested on May 18, 2001, and released on June 4, the twelfth anniversary of the Tiananmen crackdown, which is always a sensitive time for the authorities. The official charge against his son was "distorting facts, spreading rumors, and disturbing social order," but Lu thought that a couple of articles he had written on taboo topics, such as the events of June 4, 1989, and dissenting voices in official newspapers in the preceding months were what had actually prompted the authorities to take action.[1]

Nevertheless, to the puzzlement of many observers, nothing happened to Lu Jiaping himself. His life in Beijing was normal, and he kept writing statements on and appeals against his son's arrest. Though access to his previous two individual web sites was blocked, his other two web sites currently in use were not interfered with, and he could still get his writings sent out by email with the help of sympathizers. The news of his son's arrest obviously attracted further sympathy and attention, not only from ordinary Internet users, but also from the Western media. Lu Jiaping was interviewed by the Associated Press and Agence France-Presse. The *New York Times* even published a report on the subject, thus further publicizing Lu's name and increasing his influence.[2] Obviously, the authorities in Beijing and the local authorities in Hunan were not acting in a coordinated way. It was rumored that the arrest had been made because his son had joined an underground Chinese democratic organization. However, according to Lu, his son had nothing to do with any "reactionary" democracy-advocating organizations and had only filled out an online form to join an Anti-American Hacker Federation after the military plane collision incident on April 1.

We may never know the real thinking behind the authorities' action in arresting Lu's son for spreading his articles on the web, while doing nothing to prohibit Lu's writing or to block access to his web sites. Nevertheless, this episode reveals contradictions in the government's handling of individual political writers such as Lu Jiaping. This difficulty not only reflects the divide between Beijing and local authorities but also stems in part from the complexities of Lu's writing, which does not follow the formal style of intellectuals. Often it is difficult to decide whether his writings are scholarly or casual, serious or wishful thinking, politically admissible or inadmissible. Since Lu Jiaping does not have the credentials of a trained academic writer, he is usually labeled an "amateur" (*yieyu*), "private" (*siren*), or "unofficial" (*minjian*) online writer and generally excluded from mainstream intellectual discussions. Yet in contemporary China, this kind of marginalized writer is voicing social and political opinions that pose a direct challenge to the state. Often courageous and risk-taking, such writers are constantly testing the limits of government tolerance, a sacrifice that often goes unappreciated by elite intellectuals. In addition, there are plenty of valuable ideas in "amateur" writings that warrant notice. By discussing three "amateur" online writers who produce political writings, this chapter seeks to draw attention to an extremely colorful and active realm in Chinese cyberspace that will help expand understanding of political participation in contemporary China.

"Crank Writing" by a Stubborn Old Man

Lu put his name on the map in Chinese cyberspace with his April 2000 article on China's strategic mistakes in responding to the American-led military campaign against Yugoslavia, which chronicled the major events between March 20 and June 10, 1999, and presented his analyses and evaluation of China's handling of the Kosovo crisis. It was a long article of more than twenty-four single-spaced pages. The major events Lu listed included Chinese President Jiang Zemin's European trip from March 20 to March 30, the start of the NATO bombing of Yugoslavia on March 24, Chinese Premier Zhu Rongji's trip to the United States from April 6 to April 14 and to Canada from April 15 to April 20; the bombing of the Chinese Embassy in Belgrade by American-led NATO forces on May 8, and China's casting an abstaining vote on the Kosovo crisis in the United Nations on June 10, 1999. In addition, he also gave a detailed description of Russia's response to the crisis and American maneuverings worldwide during the military campaign.[3]

Lu presented his analysis and arguments to illustrate his main premise: in the current international order, the United States, as the only superpower, aimed to unilaterally dominate the world and would take whatever measures necessary to prevent the rise of potential challengers, namely, Russia, China, and the European Union. Since Russia and China were too weak to confront American hegemony individually, the only option was for the two countries to forge a "strategic cooperative partnership" to counterbalance American pressure and thus to form a multipolar structure in international geopolitics. In this "strategic cooperative partnership," Russia's main task was to resist the expansion of NATO in Europe and China's was to resist American attempts to organize Japan,

Korea, Taiwan, and the Philippines into a "little league NATO" to contain China. China and Russia should coordinate their actions with each other to gain a strategic superiority over America, since the latter was reluctant to wage (or perhaps incapable of waging) war on two fronts simultaneously.

Without giving much justification of his premises, Lu detailed the "mistakes" committed by the Chinese leadership that had proved detrimental to the consolidation of Sino-Russian "strategic cooperative partnership." First, Jiang Zemin should have discontinued his Europe trip when the NATO bombing campaign started on March 24, in the middle of his visit to Italy. But Jiang did not, only issued a statement of protest, thus giving no substantial help to Russia when the latter needed it most. Worse still, according to Lu, the Chinese leadership committed a bigger "mistake" by letting Premier Zhu Rongji go ahead with his planned visit to the United States and Canada on April 6. At that point, the Sino-American relationship was at a low point because of a rash of "China bashing" in the American media because of alleged Chinese involvement in illegal campaign donations and the stealing of American nuclear secrets. In a news conference before his trip, Zhu made an infamous remark that the purpose of his trip was to let Americans "diffuse their anger." This "anger diffusing diplomacy," from Lu's perspective, was equivalent to "kowtow diplomacy." Though the Chinese leadership might have hoped to use this trip to gain American concessions in accepting China's accession to the WTO, from Lu's perspective, this trip destroyed Russia's confidence in the Sino-Russian "strategic cooperative relationship" and even sent Russia an alarming signal of China's seeming diplomatic drift toward America.

To Chinese surprise, the United States and China did not reach an agreement on WTO accession during Zhu Rongji's visit. According to Lu, Clinton's refusal of China's WTO proposal dealt a blow to China's "kowtow diplomacy" and was part of a larger plot to create further rifts in the Sino-Russian relationship. By not granting the Chinese request to join the WTO, the United States assured the Russians that it had no intention of teaming up with China to isolate Russia and thus persuaded the Russians to work with NATO to press Yugoslavia to accept a Western-imposed settlement. Lu pointed out that the result of China's strategic maneuver was disastrous. China not only lost the trust and confidence of Russia but also did not gain anything from the United States. Worse still, the Americans were increasing strategic pressure against China by encouraging the Japanese to pass new legislation that included Taiwan within the scope of a Japanese defense perimeter under the name of a "surrounding sphere."

Lu continued his analysis by claiming that the Chinese Embassy bombing was not a "mistake" at all but a deliberate act by the Americans to find out China's bottom line on the Kosovo crisis. In the meantime, America postponed the United Nations vote on the settlement to give NATO more time to carry on bombing and to continue its maneuvering to make sure China would not veto the Kosovo agreement in the Security Council. Lu blasted those Chinese who believed that the embassy bombing had been a "mistake." He even speculated that the Americans had informed the Russians about the bombing plan. The fact that the Russians had kept silent signaled the total collapse of the Sino-Russian "strategic cooperative partnership" and the total triumph of American strategic maneuvers in the triangle of relationships between China, Russia, and the United States.

Though it was obvious that Lu had given serious thought to this article, it can by no means be considered scholarly writing. Lu collected his sources mainly from Chinese newspapers, and the paper was written in a journalistic style. Citations were generally not given and only a few references were listed, the article mixing factual narrative and analysis with subjective suggestions and speculations. However, after his article was posted on the Internet, it was well received, frequently forwarded, and widely circulated. After the Chinese Embassy was bombed in May 1999, there were countless comments, messages, and articles providing all kinds of explanations of the event on the Internet, and among them there were plenty expressing hawkish nationalistic statements. Why did Lu's article stand out? Apart from the fact that Lu's article echoed a widespread sentiment among politically conscious Chinese that the government had been too "soft" with the Americans in the embassy bombing incident, I think it was his unusually sharp critical style that made his article popular reading.

Lu's article distinguished itself from numerous other writings on the same topic from different perspectives. It offered a very different interpretation of China's diplomacy during the Kosovo crisis from that given in official statements; it provided a more detailed account and sophisticated explanation of what had happened than run-of-the-mill simplistic, emotionally charged popular responses; and, finally, it was more readable than most scholarly articles. Even though a number of scholars were skeptical of the effectiveness of the strategies adopted by the government, they were not allowed to challenge the government openly and thus could only imply their doubts in subtle ways.

In contrast, Lu Jiaping aimed his critique directly at the Chinese leadership, especially at President Jiang Zemin and Premier Zhu Rongji. When I read Lu's article for the first time on the Internet, I was struck by the sharpness of his critique and worried that the article might bring him trouble, especially since he always posted all his personal contact information at the end of his articles, and the authorities would thus have no trouble finding him if they decided to do so.[4] He was aware of this danger and always seemed ready for the worst to happen. "I am not afraid of anything," he told me during the interview in July 2001. He had been jailed twice before, once in the 1950s and again during the Cultural Revolution. In fact, only several days before our interview, he had been summoned by the local police to have a "talk." Having just experienced his son's arrest, he asked his wife to pack him a toothbrush, soap, and some clean clothes just in case he was not able to return home. Fortunately, the local policemen simply questioned him on what he had been writing recently, and nothing happened to him.

Writers like Lu Jiaping are challenging the limits to political writing set by the authorities. As a person with no institutional affiliation, title, or position and receiving no wage, housing subsidies, or health insurance— benefits that most Chinese mainstream intellectuals are entitled to from the government—Lu writes in a style more critical of the authorities than most self-described "critical" Chinese intellectuals. Lu depends mainly on moral correctness to protect himself. By insisting that he writes "for the country and the people," he effectively claims patriotic scope for his views. After reading his article on China's strategic mistakes during the Kosovo crisis, few readers would disagree that his motivation for writing was "for the sake of national interests," as illustrated by the article's strong opposition to the United States, Japan, and the idea of an independent Taiwan. Any radical action taken against him would thus make the authorities look bad. After the online publication of his article on the Kosovo crisis, he has become well known, and on average his web sites are visited more than one hundred times every day, which is a fairly high number of hits for a personal web site devoted to political writing.

What impressed me most was that Lu continued to challenge the limits of admissibility of political writing online by touching on more taboo topics and presenting eye-catching arguments. From late 2000 to early

2001, he wrote a series of articles discussing corruption in contemporary China, an issue of concern to many Chinese. The primary differences between his position and official propaganda, journalistic reports, and scholarly analysis were that he openly asserted that widespread corruption had occurred after June 4, 1989—in other words, that it had increased under Jiang Zemin—and that the fundamental reason for it was the single-party dictatorship of the Communist Party.[5] These are assertions one does not see or hear in the mainstream media. Lu further called for redress for the Tienanmen Square crackdown, saying it had suppressed what was predominantly an anti-corruption movement. In a two-part paper titled "Anti-corruption, June Fourth, and the Cultural Revolution," Lu argued that in suppressing the Tiananmen movement, the government had also suppressed the anti-corruption momentum among students and ordinary people at the time. As a consequence, the crackdown effectively encouraged, tolerated, shielded, and protected those engaging in corruption in the following years. In order to eradicate corruption, Lu argued, it was necessary to reassess the Tiananmen movement, something that would benefit party, government, country, and the people.

Lu also presented a detailed analysis of why the current leadership is unwilling to reassess the problem of corruption and the events surrounding the Tiananmen crackdown for the time being, concluding that the main obstacle was that the reassessment of either would endanger the legitimacy of the post-Mao leadership and the vested interests they had accumulated in post-1989 years. Lu openly mentioned Zhu Lin, the wife of former Premier Li Peng, a hard-liner during the June 4th suppression and still second in rank in the Communist leadership as late as fall 2002, as someone who had taken huge amounts in bribes. Lu went further, saying that it was impossible that Jiang Zemin had had nothing to do with and no responsibility for the rampant corruption in recent times while serving as the leader of both party and country for the past twelve years.[6] Such writing tested the nerves of the authorities. Lu must have realized the potential trouble this article might create for him. As he put it in an endnote to the first part of the article, he had encountered some "interference" and was worried about whether or not he could finish the article. The authorities did not take action, however, until almost three months later.

After the collision between an American spy plane and a Chinese jet fighter on April 1, 2001, Lu wrote a couple of articles predicting that the incident was the beginning of a "new cold war" and condemning the "soft" position taken by the Chinese leadership toward the United

States.[7] As he later admitted, it may have been his May 14 article that finally led the authorities to take action against him and his son. The title of Lu's May 14th article was "Finally There Are Different Voices in Official Newspapers." The piece itself contained his enthusiastic response to an article published in *Global Times* (*huanqiu shibao*), a popular international news-oriented newspaper published by *People's Daily*. Lu's enthusiasm for the article can be explained by its title, which was "Closely Observing American Strategic Initiatives—We Must Think of Our National Security Strategy Taking into Account the Worst Possibility." Lu therefore thought his criticism of the Chinese leadership's "appeasement" and its "soft" and "naïve" attitude toward the United States was finally being echoed by an official newspaper.

Four days after helping to put his father's article on the web, Lu's son was arrested by local authorities in Hunan. The police showed him printouts of his father's articles on the Tiananmen movement and the Cultural Revolution, the military plane collision incident, and the May 14th article. A second, subsequent episode is a good illustration of the differences in treatment received by mainstream intellectual writers and private writers with no official institutional affiliation. Lu's praise of the *Global Times* article's author, and of the paper for daring to publish "different voices," made *Global Times* very nervous. On May 20, a deputy editor-in-chief of the newspaper called Lu. After thanking Lu for his support and praise of the newspaper, the editor told him that because he had spoken out about his real thoughts, the authorities might not be happy to hear such true words. There was a possibility that Lu's article would bring the newspaper and the author "trouble" and "negative consequences." Finally, the editor asked Lu not to distribute his article on the Internet or give it to other parties and noted that it would be better if he could delete the article from his personal web sites. When Lu told him that his son had already been arrested for posting the article on the Internet, the editor was obviously surprised and expressed his regrets at the situation.[8]

The arrest of his son for posting his writing on the Internet was the price Lu paid for the right to speak in a "different voice" in China. The good news is that when I interviewed him again in the fall of 2002, Lu still lived with his wife in his cramped home in west Beijing, and continued to write articles on a variety of topics concerning Chinese politics and foreign policy. Nonetheless, the authorities have kept a watchful eye on him, and the local police substation summons him to have a "talk" from time to time. I remember vividly that on November 6, 2002, Lu called me to cancel an interview in the afternoon that same day, because he had been ordered to leave Beijing immediately by the local police. He told me this was a preemptive action taken with "sensitive figures" like himself to ensure nothing would disrupt the Sixteenth Party Congress, which was to open two days later. Ironically, the police seemed to have hinted to Lu that they were conducting these "talks" and ordering his temporary expulsion on instructions from higher authorities and had nothing against him personally. After the dust of the party congress had settled, Lu came back to Beijing and continued writing as he had done over the past few years.

Ji An: Seeking an Alternative in Zhongguoism

Ji An is very different from Lu Jiaping. He is more a "man of the cyber era" and thus more comfortable using email. Though I have regularly received his articles by email since I first contacted him in summer 2000, Ji has repeatedly turned down my requests for a face-to-face interview. I can only guess, based on the scattered personal information revealed in his online writings, that he is a man in his mid-forties, has a good command of English, and probably resides outside China, because he seems to have ready access to foreign news media and frequents web sites not based in China. Ji has refused to give me a definite answer about where he is based, saying that "he is a Chinese often traveling around the world." When I told him that my research plan focused mainly on political writers within China, he replied that I could see him as based in China.[9]

Ji An is well known for his prolific online writing. During my interviews with other online writers and intellectuals in China, many of them acknowledged that they had heard Ji's name and/or read his articles online. A number of them were apparently also on Ji's email list and received his articles regularly, although some expressed resentment at receiving so many unsolicited emails from the writer. Like a print-based commentator on social and political affairs, Ji writes a lot of short pieces on a broad variety of topics. The prolific nature of his writing makes it very difficult to summarize his positions on many issues, and indeed his improvised writing style often makes his arguments less credible to mainstream intellectuals. Nonetheless, in his online writings, one can easily find some important points in his observations on the conditions and future of ever-changing Chinese society. What attracted me to him first was the conscious promotion of Zhongguoism by Ji and his online comrades. To understand this philosophy, we need to consider a substantial extract from one of Ji's articles titled "Basic Principles of Zhongguoism":

> Zhongguoism advocates that the Chinese struggle for the prosperity of China and the Chinese nation through the path of self-reliance; it advocates that all Chinese enjoy happiness in life and maintain self-confidence, self-esteem, self-strength, and independence.
>
> Zhongguoism advocates that the Chinese working people obtain and enjoy the fruits of their labor fairly and equitably. . . .
>
> Zhongguoism advocates constantly raising the general level of science, culture, and knowledge of all Chinese to eliminate illiteracy in the whole country as soon as possible. . . .
>
> Zhongguoism advocates the unity of the Chinese nation and reunification with Taiwan at the earliest possible time. . . .
>
> Zhongguoism advocates that China establish and maintain strong national defense forces that can defeat all foreign invading forces at any time.[10]

Ji An knew that Zhongguoism as he presented it was a new concept and a new theoretical framework. As he acknowledged in the article, in order to avoid translation mistakes, he intentionally tried to coin an English word, "Chinaism," to be the translation of Zhongguo Zhuyi, and to call those who practiced Chinaism "Chinaists."[11] It is unclear why Ji later adopted the name "Zhongguoism" instead of the original "Chinaism"; in all probability, it is because the new term is more "Chinese" and less "foreign." He optimistically predicted that Zhongguoism would become an ideology shared by all Chinese in generations to come.

Though Ji emphasizes that Zhongguoism is a concept open to all ideas beneficial to China, it is only too obvious that he does not mention or include concepts of "democracy," "freedom," or "human rights" in his definition of Zhongguoism. This is intentional. In fact, in Ji's writings, "democracy" is often ridiculed as an instrumental concept employed by Westerners (particularly Americans) in their own interest. Ji therefore does not give much serious discussion to "democracy" and "freedom," but often completely rejects these ideas, viewing them as pretexts for American hegemony in the world. Several days before his Zhogguoism declaration, he wrote an article in which, in his trademark, free-flowing, half-sarcastic style, he asserted that in the term *minzhu* ("democracy," literally, *min* [people] + *zhu* [control]), *min* (people) lacks substance.

Putting quotation marks around the word "democracy," Ji denies any possibility that there is true democracy either as an idea or in practice. He defiantly says in his article: "[I]n summary, if you ever encounter someone associated with 'democracy,' you should say to him or her firmly and confidently: 'My friend, don't talk 'democracy' to me; what do you want to say, what do you want to control [*zhu*], how you want to control [*zhu*] it? Please speak using your own name and your own words. It is not necessary to use 'democracy' as trademark to sell your goods; it will be fine if you sell them using your own brand-name.' If everybody does this, then the word 'democracy' can be put to rest."[12]

Although Ji An's assault on democracy has been unsystematic and improvisational, he is representative of the growing element in China that has become more suspicious of Western discourses of democracy within the current international power relationship, especially in the framework of Sino-American relations, because they suspect that the Americans are not simply promoting ideas of democracy, freedom, and human rights to the Chinese, but rather employing them as ideological tools to promote and pursue tangible U.S. interests, thus compromising their appeal as universally accepted values. I believe the ostensible abandonment of ideals of democracy by some Chinese does not symbolize their general rejection of democratic pursuits but is a by-product of the anti-Americanism that has risen in China since the mid 1990s.

Ji An's article "Thank You from the Bottom of Our Hearts, Clinton!" is illustrative of this. It was written on May 15 1999, one week after the Chinese Embassy in Belgrade was bombed on May 8. Ji proclaimed that "American style democracy, American style human rights, everything American instantly revealed their repulsive appearance. This unprecedented American-style bombing has unparalleled effectiveness in patriotic and nationalist education on the Chinese in general and on Chinese youth in particular." Ji asserted that the bombing had smashed Chinese illusions about the Americans. The effects of the bombing would influence the Chinese for at least five generations and meant that the Chinese would not be lured or misled by the United States and other Western countries for at least several hundred years. For all these reasons, he thanked Clinton for the bombing and sarcastically labeled him the best American in 200 years.[13]

About one year later, Ji wrote an article, "From May 4 to May 8? From Democracy to Nation?" in which he reiterated his anti-Western rhetoric. He raised the question of why China was still so weak almost a century after the May Fourth Movement of 1919, saying:

Is it because we have not talked enough of Western "democracy?" No, on the contrary, it is exactly because we have talked too much of Western "democracy." In the past hundred years, we have talked about Western "democracy" so much that we have forgotten the "Chinese nation." Many Chinese have had the illusion of having become Westerners while continually talking about "democracy." From May 4 to May 8, it was not until bombs had fallen on their heads that they finally remembered that besides Western "democracy," there was a nation called the "Chinese nation"; and they finally understood that Chinese were Chinese, Westerners were Westerners. It was impossible for the Westerners to treat you (Chinese) as Westerners simply because you tried to learn their way of talking about Western democracy. They would always treat you as Chinese.[14]

It is not surprising that Ji An has been labeled an "extreme nationalist" by other online discussants on the issue of nationalism, and he himself has acknowledged this description. As a matter of fact, Ji has claimed that "nationalism is most fundamental" in the Zhongguoism he advocates. Apparently, even though he does not like the label extreme nationalist because it carries negative connotations in both the Chinese and Western media, he has not been very self-defensive about the description. Furthermore, he claims that he has contempt for the idea of "wholesale Westernization" but is not worried about its materialization in reality. This is because of his conviction that Chinese culture cannot be successfully Westernized and that Chinese nationalism is superior to Western culture. It is thus an open question as to who will prevail in the long run in the battle between Westernization and Sinicization.[15]

Knowing the connection between Zhongguoism and nationalism, it is not difficult to deduce Ji's stance on other issues that have attracted his attention. In 2000 and 2001, he wrote a series of articles on the Taiwan issue and China's efforts to join the WTO. His position on Taiwan was exceptionally hawkish, especially after Lee Teng-hui, Taiwan's former leader, claimed in July 1999 that the relationship between Taiwan and China was a "special state-to-state relationship." To Ji, this was the equivalent of a declaration of Taiwanese independence and thus violated all the conditions that China had placed on peaceful reunification with Taiwan. Obviously, he was not satisfied with the Chinese government's reactions to Lee's statement, because he viewed actions such as requesting Lee to "take back" his statement as "too soft" on the mainland side. He thus advocated in his article "An Outline of Taiwan Unification" that a military attack should be launched against Taiwan in order to solve the problem. Like a tumor found in the national body, Taiwan should be operated on at the earliest possible time.[16]

On March 18, 2000, Chen Shui-bian, the candidate of the Democratic Progressive Party, which advocates Taiwan's independence, won the Taiwan general election and became the first non-Kuomintang leader in the island's history. This prompted Ji to reiterate his proposition that the mainland should achieve reunification by launching a military campaign against Taiwan immediately. In a hastily written article the next day, Ji assailed official Chinese government policy on the Taiwan issue, described as "peaceful unification under the one country, two systems principle." Ji noted that such an appeasement policy on the part of the PRC had helped the Taiwan independence movement to develop from an underground force into an overt part of the political mainstream and predicted that "without resorting to military action, Taiwan cannot be reunited with China."[17] Ji's sentiment reflected the disappointment, frustration, and anger shared by many online discussants at that particular historical juncture.[18]

Ji An seems to be skillful in employing the Internet to arouse public attention regarding the Taiwan issue. For example, he even filed a "public lawsuit" online against Wang Daohan, chairman of the semi-official Association for Relations across the Taiwan Straits, which has served as the main channel for exchanges across the strait between Taiwan and mainland China. In his suit, he accused Wang of committing treason by suggesting to the Taiwan side that even the name of a unified China and the form of a future national flag were open to negotiation. In a "cyber-action" only made possible by the Internet, Ji called for this high-ranking government official to be sentenced to death.[19] In another case, Ji was so angry at Lee Teng-hui's suggestion of a "special state-to-state relationship" that on the very same day he put online a "Declaration of National Reunion by the People's Republic of China," in which, following the model of the Hong Kong Special Administrative Region, he proposed a Taiwan Special Autonomous Administrative Region and presented a draft constitution for its new government. If the Taiwan authorities did not accept the proposed constitution, a detailed military and economic blockade plan was also included.[20]

Without the Internet, it would have been inconceivable for someone like Ji to speak out on behalf of China in an unauthorized manner such as this. If he had adopted the traditional genre of writing a public notice, his audience would have been limited, and his action in posting a politically sensitive unauthorized "declaration" in the name of the government would probably have caused the authorities to take action against him. In this case, then, ever-expanding cyberspace certainly provides online writers such as Ji with a more effective means to express their opinions on national affairs.

If Lu Jiaping has tested the official limits of tolerance by discussing the mistakes of President Jiang Zemin's American policy and by touching on the taboo of the Tiananmen movement, Ji has surprised me by his personal and sometimes vicious attacks on Premier Zhu Rongji's dealings with America while negotiating China's accession to the WTO. Ji has been a staunch opponent of China joining the WTO, and he has maintained that the direct consequence of joining the WTO would be tens of millions Chinese workers being laid off, resulting in a drastic shake-up of the Chinese financial and agricultural sectors.[21] Ji has legitimized his concerns in the name of protecting the interests of 1.3 billion Chinese people. In his opinion, the Chinese people need in the first place to realize who owns the WTO, who controls it, what its true intention is in accepting China, and what the real effects of China's accession will be. Given his strong anti-American stance, Ji concluded that the hidden hand behind the WTO was the United States, whose ultimate goal was to use the WTO to gain political and economic control of China, this strategy being more crafty than the older method of colonialist conquest.[22]

From this perspective, Ji was therefore extremely upset by the concessions Premier Zhu Rongji made to Americans on WTO entrance conditions in his U.S. trip shortly before the embassy bombing. He ridiculed Zhu's trip as a mission "to show a smiling face," to deliver an apology, and to concede sovereignty to Americans and sarcastically labeled Zhu as a *sanpei* (three-accompanying premier) to describe his "soft" attitude toward Americans.[23] Given the fact that Premier Zhu is generally respected both in China and abroad, Ji unsurprisingly encountered a lot of angry online rebukes and protests.

In general, Ji An is another example of how *minjian* online writers have expanded their maneuvering room on the Internet. Ji's online writings are a mixture of leftist, nationalist, and anti-Western (i.e., anti-American) positions. Ji's style is trenchant, improvisational, combative, and sarcastic, and he is outspoken in his disagreement on important national policy issues. As Ji has acknowledged, his messages have been deleted by monitors of the Strengthening-China Forum, but generally speaking, he has not been subject to severe harassment by the Chinese authorities.

Ji is still busy churning out provocative messages and articles in Chinese cyberspace. An article written on September 30, 2002, ridiculed the Australian government's willingness to send troops to join America's proposed war against Iraq. Pointing out that Australia had stopped carrying out the death sentence because of humanist concerns but was willing to commit to more killing in war, Ji argued that this action revealed the hypocritical characteristics of humanism in Australia. Compared to the writings of mainstream "nationalist" Chinese intellectuals, Ji's articles lack sophistication and clear articulation. Nonetheless, his provocative and unusual arguments and his fluid and complicated opinions have contributed to the online political discourse in Chinese cyberspace, and some of the most insightful parts of his writings, such as the concept of Zhongguoism, can be refined, enriched, and strengthened into valuable ideas that deserve more elaboration by Chinese thinkers.

Anti: Symbol of Rebellion

"Liberals don't read Ji An's articles, neither liberals nor leftists read Lu Jiaping's articles, but both leftists and liberals read my articles online. I am the most representative *minjian* online writer in China," Anti told me. We were sitting in a McDonald's on Beijing's West Side in early November 2002. This was the first time I had met him in person, though his online writings had shown up on my radar screen for a while, thanks to a recommendation by Professor Gao Hua, my friend and former colleague at Nanjing University.

Realizing that he had not convinced me, Anti explained why his articles were widely read. "To liberals," he noted, "not only are Ji An's nationalist views unacceptable, but also his writings are often illogical and free-flowing. He does not even recognize the basic rules and format of serious writing [*yansu xiezuo*]. Lu Jiaping's positions on different issues are so self-contradictory that nobody knows what he is talking about. How can his articles be readable?" Anti did not even express sympathy for Lu when the authorities arrested the writer's son. He explained to me that it seemed to him that Lu was criticizing the current regime ultimately with the aim of defending it and making it more sustainable. How could Lu ask for sympathy when he was harmed by the regime he was trying to assist and uphold?

I then asked Anti why his articles were read by both camps. "Because I acknowledge the rules and forms of serious writing," he replied, "even though I am not and have no desire to become a member of the mainstream intelligentsia, I am a *minjian* writer adhering to established writing codes." "What makes you a *minjian* writer?" I asked, becoming more intrigued with each response. "Because I am an outsider to the system," Anti answered. Then he elaborated to me his criteria for classifying the different camps of contemporary Chinese intellectuals. These criteria centered on whether or not one acknowledged the legitimacy of and supported the current regime, or "system." Supporters of the current regime are insiders to the system, and others are outsiders to the system. Anti further classified Chinese intellectuals through three main binary oppositions: insiders versus outsiders; elite academics versus nonacademics; and dissident activists versus nonconformist thinkers. By "dissident activists," he meant mainly the "democracy activists" who faced suppression by the current regime. Anti admitted that even though he was an absolute outsider to the current system, he was not an activist. As long as one was an outsider, one could be called a *minjian* intellectual in China even if one held an academic position.

In his twenties, Anti has experienced a complex life compared to many of his contemporaries. He attended a three-year college in Nanjing and trained to be a computer engineer. However, upon graduation, he deliberately went to Wuxi, a city about 100 miles west of Shanghai, to be away from his parents, where he found a job as a reception desk manager at a local hotel. He then went through a succession of jobs seeking higher pay, working as a software salesman, computer programmer, and also an entrepreneur in China's Internet boom in the last years of the twentieth century. At the time I met him, he held a job as the Beijing correspondent for a Guangdong-based newspaper, *Ershiyi shiji huanqiu baodao* (the *21st Century Global Herald*).[24]

By all standards, as shown by his name, an uncompromising stand of being an outsider to the current system is Anti's trademark. At first I did not notice that his name had special implications, because the two Chinese characters making up the name are not uncommon. He explained to me that Anti was not his original name. After he had undergone a series of life transformations, in which he became a Christian and a skeptic about everything that the current system condoned, he had changed his Chinese name to An Ti and adopted Michael Anti as his English name. The name was a symbolic proclamation that he was determined not to accept anything established, sanctioned, or promoted by the current "system" in China.

In retrospect, his ability to access information outside of the "system" played a decisive role in his personal transformation. Born in 1975, he had no memory of the Cultural Revolution, and was still a teenager at the time of the events of June 4, 1989. As he himself admitted, he was a normal kid within the system and had joined the communist youth league in high school. Anti's worldview, forged by the Chinese education system and government propaganda, was gradually shattered when he was exposed to new information and ideas from outside the system. His interest in Christianity started in high school when he was attracted to gospel broadcasting by a Hong Kong "good companion" radio station. After entering college, instead of concentrating on his major in computer engineering, Anti read extensively in the humanities and social sciences, and this prompted him to do much soul-searching and self-reflection. His final transformation into a Christian and an absolute nonconformist in relation to the current system came after his online reading about the Tiananmen movement in early 1999. When the Internet allowed him to access versions of the tragic events of 1989 that differed from the official version, Anti's remaining confidence in communism, and indeed in humanity and humankind, was shattered. He became a devoted Christian and sought refuge in God.[25]

The appearance of the Internet also made the transformed, rebellious, and cynical Anti known to hundreds of thousands of people through his online writing. Though he was computer-literate, it was not until December 1998 that he had the necessary equipment to go online and become an active participant in BBS forums. Anti frequented Xici Hutong (www.xici.net, literally, "Lane of the West Ancestral Temple"), an influential Nanjing-based virtual community, partly because of its convenience and partly because of its reputation for open-mindedness. Subsequently, in August 2000, dissatisfied with the unfocused, empty discussions that filled many BBS forums, Anti started his own BBS forum on the Xici Hutong, Ruisi Pinglun (Re-see Review). It was intended, as he outlined it, to be an original, critical magazine of sharp, independent ideas with a rational, tolerant attitude.[26]

Anti took a classically liberal stand concerning the government. His deeply rooted skepticism regarding the virtue of government was reflected by his posting with the title "Let us guard against government as we guard against a thief, no matter whether it is Chinese or American."

Anti pointed out that the "government is like a monster eager to invade citizens' rights. Even though we cannot get rid of this monster, what we can do is to guard against it all the time and make it less evil in the world." He used Watergate and McCarthyism as examples to show that the U.S. government was capable of becoming a monster if not controlled. But he differentiated the U.S. government from the Chinese government because the former was always checked by the courts, Congress, and the media, as shown by the Clinton sexual scandal. Anti had no confidence in the Chinese government at all, claiming that since the Chinese government is the government of a Communist Party that has the courts, People's Congress, and media all under its control, there is no way to resist it if it wishes to infringe on citizens' private rights.

Anti was optimistic, however, about the role the Internet might play as a check on the Chinese government. He thought that unlike the traditional media, which were under tight government control, the Internet offered some independent space and functioned as a public opinion platform from which to watch over the government, provided everybody told the truth. Under such conditions, the government would have second thoughts before committing new crimes. Step by step, a democratic system would someday appear in China without war and turmoil. Anti made it clear that he was against revolution and violence. What the Chinese people should do was take advantage of existing rights given by the Communist Party and exercise criticism within the limits of its tolerance. Anti acknowledged that only two years previously, his posting would have been deleted by the Xici Hutong webmasters for its open criticism of the government, but by 2001, such postings had become very common, signaling an expanded space of political participation and thus the progress of tolerance in Chinese society.[27]

Viewing free access to information as one of the most important preconditions for China becoming a democratic society, Anti has enthusiastically advocated "new journalism" since he became a newspaper reporter in 2001. Though he has not given a clear definition of this term, in the context of China, it requires journalists to report on events from an objective, neutral position, without value judgments. His position has evolved in the past few years. In a short essay that he wrote on September 11, 2001, on the issue of the professionalization of Chinese journalists, Anti proposed that professionalization requires Chinese journalists to have a social conscience, to have a macroscopic view of China's problems, to adhere to professional ethics, and to pursue enhanced self-culti-vation—all criteria that are clearly value-oriented. His elaboration on what journalistic ethics are gives additional clues about his ideas regarding the new journalism in China:

The professional ethic of journalism is "truthfully to report all important news that is worth reporting," which is to say, to write news that is important and truthful, without taboo and prejudice. This is not only an idea; it is also a principle that we are required to fulfill every day. . . . This is also my principle in reporting news: I am reporting news, nothing can obstruct me. As long as I firmly believe in my professional ethics, those who try to obstruct me are damned assholes. In the worst-case scenario, I'll change my career or go abroad. But as long as I stay in the media for one more day, I won't change my position. Anyway, this fucking system is bound to collapse; it is better to assume it has already collapsed and be prepared earlier than your peers. Otherwise, if you choose to change after its collapse, it will be hard not to make a fool of yourself.[28]

Anti writes in a scathing and unorthodox way that is not permissible in traditional print journals, and this has brought him a large number of admirers online. In his equating of today's Chinese journalism with official propaganda, it is not difficult to notice that Anti's real aim is to promote "new journalism" in China. Anti has been trying to build a basic infrastructure to promote his ideas regarding new journalism. In addition to hosting a "voice of new journalists" BBS forum on Xici Hutong, he set up an individual web site (www.newjournalist.com) to discuss this idea in December 2002 and has put a "self-study guide for new journalists" online, in which he gives a comprehensive list of Chinese and English news media web sites worldwide that are accessible from China.[29] Anti is a big fan of the American system of journalism, especially newspapers such as the *New York Times* and says:

Whenever the *New York Times* is mentioned, I cannot help but salute it. I have nothing but praise for this newspaper. It is this newspaper that has established real journalism, real journalists, and really journalistic quality and style. The history of the *New York Times* is the history of the American freedom of journalism. Down to the present day, it has featured the most outstanding journalistic writing and perspectives and taken a neutral political position. That is the reason why our party and government has granted special permission to allow Chinese to read its web site online.

I am not sure of the details of how Anti was attracted by and convinced of the freedom of journalism in the United States. Certainly, however, the Internet played a big role. When he is reading the Pulitzer Prize web site (www.pulitzer.org), he says, "I thank the Internet, which enables us to get rid of the garbage of Chinese journalism education."[30]

Anti can be classified as a liberal in the Chinese political context because of his yearning for freedom in journalism, his belief in freedom, democracy, and justice, and his open stance of nonconformity in relation to the government. His seemingly pro-Western position puts him on a collision course with many net surfers who have strong nationalist sentiments. After the military plane collision incident on April 1, 2001, some accused him of keeping silent. His response would certainly have reinforced his image as a pro-Western "liberal" in others' minds. Excusing himself as busy and lacking knowledge of military affairs and international law, he took a couple of days to read a textbook on international law and browse related international treaties on the web. When he felt confident enough to speak out, Anti did not pay much attention to the event itself, but rather took painstaking efforts to scrutinize related press statements by the Chinese government. He pointed out that in fact the American spy plane did not enter "Chinese air space," since China did not have "sovereignty" over the 200-mile "Exclusive Economic Zone," and that the landing of the American plane on Hainan island had been brought about by an emergency and not been a deliberate invasion.[31]

From his position as an outsider to the "system," Anti worried about the government taking advantage of this opportunity to enhance its political legitimacy by provoking a wave of nationalism. Though Anti also acknowledged that the United States should apologize to China, and felt that George W. Bush's handling of the plane incident was inadequate, he was perceived by some other BBS forum members as unacceptably pro-American. One posting on the Xici Hutong accused him of acting like a spokesperson for George W. Bush, and another doubted his prediction of government-sponsored nationalism, pointing out that the government might actually be more afraid of rising nationalism than desirous to promote it.[32] He confronted these BBS members again after the events of September 11, when some online postings showed a malicious joy at the tragedy that horrified him. "I am ashamed of such an action by my compatriots," he wrote. "I feel ashamed of being a Chinese for the first time in my life. I say without any hesitation: American people are great, they have paid a heavy price for world peace."[33]

Anti's position was ridiculed and attacked by others in the Re-see Review forum. As the webmaster, he responded by deleting the offensive postings from the forum. In a public notice to all "patriots" in his forum, he asked them to go to other forums or face the risk of having their postings deleted.[34] This was not the first time Anti had exercised such power, and he intends to do so again in the future. The issue of how to monitor the BBS forum created a dilemma for Anti, as often pointed out by other forum members. On the one hand, he protested strongly in October 2001 to the higher-level webmasters at the Xici Hutong at their deleting postings in his forum. He acknowledged that Chinese cyberspace had a "bottom line" set by government, yet he was angry at the Xici Hutong webmasters for removing "unproblematic" postings from his forum.[35] Ironically, only one month later, he reiterated once again to members of the Re-see Review forum that he would "always keep my ax shining, because Re-see is mine, a point that needs no discussion. . . . My BBS forum is going to be run according to my rules."[36] In fact, Anti was running his forum in a way no different from others, including those involved in official censorship.

In response to Anti's criteria for deleting posts right after the opening of the Re-see Review forum, one forum member pointed out that it was unfair when one's opponent in the game was also the judge of the forum's ground rules.[37] Anti's seemingly contradictory position on Internet censorship has attracted attention from net surfers in the Xici Hutong. A short comment posted in November 2002 attributed Anti's celebrity status to his ability to use online writing to challenge the dominance of traditional writing contexts. Yet it noted that a dangerous trend would occur if successful online writers like Anti opted to establish a new hegemony over online discourse to defeat their challengers. If this trend continued, the message suggested, Anti and his peers would form a new elite controlling online discourse and thus would be the real masters of the seemingly free and democratic discourse in cyberspace.[38]

Anti's success in online writing and the praise and criticism he has subsequently faced reveal another aspect of the complexity of Chinese cyberspace. He is basically a challenger of existing rules rather than a setter of new ones. He has played the first part of his role quite well, and his writing style and his strong anti-establishment spirit have pushed back the government's line of tolerance to a certain degree, resulting in more room for freer political discussion online. While constantly testing the limit of official censorship, he knows what might be the final straw that would break the camel's back. He possesses the fine "feeling" cherished by elite intellectuals and exceeds the latter in his aggressiveness and willingness to take risks. However, when it comes to practicing freedom of expression in his own BBS forum, he defaults from time to time by deleting postings that he does not consider suitable. Though censorship may be a necessary means of keeping the forum viable and discussion focused, the action itself is in contrast to the principles of freedom of expression that Anti cherishes so much. Anti is conditioned, like anybody else, by the unique characteristics of cyberspace. How can one keep a BBS forum discussion free and democratic yet at the same time meaningful and focused? This is a difficult question. Anti is not to be blamed for not coming up with a new set of perfect rules, but he deserves admonishment if he uses his newly gained dominant position (as a famous online writer and the webmaster of a BBS forum) to suppress others' rights to express legitimate but different opinions.

Negotiating *Minjian* Identities

Minjian is the antonym of *guanfang*, but while *guanfang* can be translated as "official," it is more difficult to find an English word corresponding to *minjian*. It can be translated as "private," "nonofficial," or "unofficial," with connotations of "independent," "marginalized," or "outside the system," depending on the context in which it is used. Before the reforms began in the late 1970s, Chinese society was under a totalitarian regime and social space was to a large extent "statized," leaving little room for "private" or "unofficial" elements. It is only since the 1980s that a *minjian* sector has developed, a fact that prompted some scholars to proclaim that a civil society was emerging in China. The so-called *minjian* intellectuals also emerged from this historical period.

There has been little study done on the *minjian* intellectual group in China. Xiao Gongqin, a well-known Shanghai-based scholar, wrote a short newspaper article in which he used the term "marginal intellectuals" to designate this newly emergent group in Chinese urban centers. Xiao narrowly defines urban "marginal intellectuals" as simply those free-lance writers, artists, and professionals with a humanistic spirit who do not rely on state employment to make a living, made possible by the economic diversification and more employment choices in a growing market economy.[39] Nonetheless, during my interviews with several online *minjian* writers, I was struck by the fact that they also emphasized that no political affiliation or forms of independent thinking mark their identity. Lu Jiaping prefers to identify himself as a "self-supported unofficial researcher." The term "self-supported" means that he does not rely on any institution as a regular income source, while "unofficial" means he does not have any government connection or any affiliation with political parties. Lu can be seen as a typical *minjian* intellectual by any standard.

The complicated contexts of contemporary Chinese intellectual politics have made the phrase "*minjian* intellectuals" fluid and ambiguous. I use the term "negotiating" in the subtitle of this section to refer to the fact that even though all three of the above-mentioned online writers are proud of their identity as *minjian* writers, this does not exclude them from adopting "non-*minjian*" tactics from time to time to make themselves more acceptable to and less marginalized within Chinese society. After all, being *minjian* writers in China often means having to live an uneasy life. Pressures are felt on two fronts. On one hand, they have generally been neglected and marginalized by the mainstream Chinese intellectuals who control most resources, such as newspapers, scholarly journals, and academic accreditation. On the other, compared with mainstream political writers, they generally lack formal and informal connections with the authorities and often face the ever-present danger of having their sites shut down or being shut out by the authorities. In this unfriendly environment, they have to adopt strategies to protect themselves from "trouble" and to break out of the marginalization that they face most of the time.

Besides putting his articles online, Lu Jiaping also uses traditional ways of disseminating his writings, sending them out to friends, enthusiastic readers, officials, and newspapers, as well as to government organs. He would be very pleased if his writings received positive responses from the authorities or from persons of power and status. For example, in the printout of the article in which he proposes "strategies" on how to "liberate" Taiwan, he adds a note saying that he had received a telephone call from the secretariat of the Military Committee of the Central Committee of the CCP praising his suggestions and informing him that they had been conveyed to higher authorities for consideration. This search for official approval is, indeed, one reason why he is looked down upon by other writers such as Anti. Lu Jiaping is also willing to accept interview requests, mainly from foreign media outlets. He also makes it known that his book on the Cuban missile crisis has been published (in Chinese) in the United States. Apparently, however, it was not published by a reputable academic press. Anti has ridiculed Lu Jiaping and Ji An for depicting themselves as anti-Western defenders of national interests, while in reality being eager to be reported on by the same Westerners for whom they express contempt.

Lu Jiaping's self-aggrandizement and his attempts to reach media outlets that possess the hegemony of "authoritative discourse" should not be overly criticized. Under the circumstances that he faces on an everyday basis, these may be necessary techniques to enhance the credibility and authority of his writings. A more conscious manifestation by Lu Jiaping of a desire to become more acceptable to mainstream intellectual discourse is that he has started to put endnotes and a list of citations at the end of his articles. Though his notes and citations are still not formatted in the way editors of academic journals would require, they represent a big step forward for a writer without formal academic training.

Unlike Lu Jiaping, Ji An has stuck to his free-flowing writing style and shows no sign that he will make any changes. But this does not mean that he has made no effort to disseminate his writings to larger audiences. Ji An seems to have an advanced knowledge of how to use the Internet, and he has been able to send out his articles en masse through email lists. It is quite possible that he puts his articles on different web sites and BBS boards simultaneously to gain greater exposure for his writing. Establishing an electronic magazine on the web is another way of breaking out of the monopoly on resources possessed by mainstream academics. The concrete step taken by Ji An and his comrades to set up the online magazine *Zhongguo Zhuyi (ZGZY)* to publicize their ideas is an example of this kind of effort. The magazine has more than half a dozen editors and has published many issues since its inception in 2000.[40] Ji's online writing has also attracted the attention of a number of mainstream Chinese intellectuals, including Wang Xiaodong, Fan Ning, and Cui Zhiyuan. Ji's alliance with Cui Zhiyuan is more significant. Cui is an American-trained political scientist who has taught at MIT. He has been known for advocating a "third way" for China that shuns the undesirable aspects of both capitalism and communism. Cui is also listed as one of the editors of the ZGZY webzine, though it is difficult to know how active a role he has played in editing it.[41] If Cui has indeed played an active role in editing the ZGZY webzine, this is an encouraging development, indicating that mainstream Chinese intellectuals have started to pay attention to *minjian* political writing online.

Unlike Lu Jiaping and Ji An, Anti's position is closer to the boundary between the mainstream and the marginalized. The anxiety of being marginalized has always haunted Anti, especially in his early days as an online writer. Mixed feelings of self-confidence and a sense of inferiority often troubled him then. In one of his online essays in 1999, Anti claimed that so-called *minjian* science enthusiasts "possess outstanding ability in transmitting and analyzing materials, but we are also in a sad position, because we don't possess resources."[42] In August 2000, he lamented that in a close reading of many intellectual web sites, he had not found a single one in which his name appeared. After one and half years of online writing, this was so discouraging that Anti even thought of giving up his writing.[43]

However, self-confidence and strong anti-establishment sentiments are usually Anti's trademarks. Anti and his comrades online believe that the Internet provides the best way to challenge the existing "system." As enthusiastically predicted by Zhu Haijun, a well-known online writer who died at an early age, more and more academic resources will become accessible online, and eventually "the next generation of writers and scholars will most probably rely on the Internet to establish themselves."[44] Anti, in response to criticism by a scholar at Nanjing University, went further, claiming that traditional training in collecting and analyzing academic materials was obsolete in the age of the Internet. With many materials online and strong search engines, some traditional disciplines would die. Anti claimed that if all the classic Chinese texts had been online, he could have written the *Guanzhui Bian* (Pipe-Awl Collection [of literary and critical essays]) by the famous Chinese scholar Qian Zhongshu (1910–1998).[45]

Anti's assertions may be vainglorious and iconoclastic, but they certainly have some merit. China is in the process of a profound upheaval that has transformed many existing domains, and the boundary between the mainstream and the marginalized has and will continue to become more blurred. Anti did not try to deny that only after he had become famous online was he able to get his current job. By 2002, calling himself a "famous online commentator," Anti was able to participate in cultural events usually only open to "intellectuals," such as being one of the invited speakers in a forum commemorating the fifth anniversary of the death of Wang Xiaobo, a popular Chinese writer.[46] Given the rebellious position against the current system that Anti takes, it seems that it is unlikely that he will become a member of the "mainstream" unless the trajectory of China's transformation accords with his liberal ideas. One interesting episode that reveals tensions is that after Anti discovered that the Century China web site had put a collection of his online writings in its archive of scholars' works, he made a public statement that he did not feel comfortable with being labeled as a "scholar," and in early 2002, he requested that the webmaster remove his collection from the site.[47]

It is not my intention to be judgmental about the different strategies adopted by these three online writers. Each has made strategic choices in response to an environment in which they have to fight against daily political pressure, mainstream prejudice, and inaccessibility of resources. These choices often result in extreme complexity and frequent contradictions in both their writings and lives. There have been two kinds of responses to the appearance of Anti-style *minjian* online writers. The first is simply to treat them as the outbursts of lunatics. As the above-mentioned scholar at Nanjing University pointed out, the *minjian* identity Anti attributed to himself reflected his ever-present sense of inferiority because he was not a member of the mainstream. This scholar admonished Anti not to focus on the dichotomy between *minjian* and elite, but to equip himself with knowledge that would gain him acceptance in scholarly circles.[48] This response was basically from an elitist perspective. Another kind of response was represented by Xiao Gongqin, who appealed to mainstream intellectuals to treat recently emergent marginal intellectuals with greater sympathy, understanding, and care. Society as a whole, he felt, should provide these intellectuals with more space in order to include them in the "system." He further suggested that if the marginal intellectuals did not receive acceptance, their frustration and discontent could converge with that of the disadvantaged classes of society and subsequently become a cause of social unrest. It is obvious here that Xiao is discussing the marginalized intellectuals from a condescending perspective.[49] To me, despite his good intentions, he should pay more attention to the undeniably important role played by marginal intellectuals in challenging the existing ideological system through their much needed courage, sharpness, and sacrifice.

By any standard, the political writings of *minjian* Chinese writers are equal to those of mainstream Chinese intellectuals in terms of originality and desire to participate in political discourse. Many *minjian* writers write in a style more critical of the authorities than most self-described "critical" Chinese intellectuals, demonstrating their courage in testing the limits of censorship and enlarging the space of free speech. "This is all made possible by the Internet," to use the words of Lu Jiaping. It is the availability of the Internet that has been instrumental to the emergence of a group of *minjian* online political writers. A positive note is that all three of those described here are thriving in Chinese cyberspace. Lu Jiaping continues to write from his small rented house at the foot of the Fragrant Mountain; Ji An keeps pouring out numerous articles online, and Anti is busy advocating "new journalism" both on- and off-line. The products of these three *minjian* writers are only a small part of an enormous realm of ideas that not only deserves more attention from mainstream academics and political thinkers but also demands that the members of the mainstream take more initiatives to reach out to them, open resources to them, and to make them less marginalized.

CHAPTER NINE

Informed Nationalism

Military Web Sites in Chinese Cyberspace

O N JANUARY 18, 2002, China-related articles appeared in two major Western media outlets. One was a commentary by Nicholas Kristof in the *New York Times* noting how Chinese Internet chatters had reacted unsympathetically to the September 11 terrorist attacks against the United States and attributing the rise of Chinese nationalism to the "result in particular of 'patriotic' campaigns planned by President Jiang since 1990 as a way of knitting together the country, of providing a new 'glue' to replace the discredited ideology of Communism."[1] Late in the evening of the same day, the online version of the *Financial Times* reported that "[m]ore than 20 bugging devices have been discovered by Chinese intelligence officers in a Boeing 767 delivered from the U.S. and due to serve as the official aircraft of Jiang Zemin, China's president, according to Chinese officials."[2] This news was published on the front page of the *Financial Times* on January 19 and was also reported by the *Washington Post*, CNN Web site, and ABC's *World News Tonight* on the same day.[3]

While following the stories through Western media, I simultaneously logged onto the Strengthening-China Forum of People's Daily Online to observe Chinese responses. Since Beijing is thirteen hours ahead of U.S. Eastern standard time, it was already the morning of January 19 in Beijing when the news broke, and the forum started to open up discussion on the topics at 10 A.M. Surprisingly, little appeared on the Strengthening-China Forum about the bugged plane. Its monitors had clearly blocked messages directly addressing the issue, and since the site is affiliated with and under control of the official Communist Party newspaper, they must have done so at the direction of the higher authorities. The Chinese and American governments both tried to downplay the incident. On January 20, appearing on NBC's *Meet the Press*, Donald Rumsfeld, U.S. secretary of defense, said he had no knowledge of the spying devices, while Colin Powell, U.S. secretary of state, appearing on ABC's *This Week*, said the issue had not been raised by the Chinese in his recent conversations with them. It was not until January 22 that a spokesman for the Chinese Foreign Ministry acknowledged that he had heard of the report but said that he had no direct knowledge of the incident. He added that it would not have any effect on Sino-U.S. relations. Obviously, he was trying to downplay the issue.[4]

By prohibiting public discussion of the bugged plane incident in China's mainstream media, including newspapers, television, radio, and major online news portals, the Chinese authorities effectively prevented the incident from becoming a focus of public opinion. Nonetheless, it was beyond the government's capacity to police cyberspace in the way it controlled the traditional print press. Even though the monitors constantly deleted inadmissible postings, traces of the discussion of the incident survived on the Strengthening-China Forum. By closely following the ongoing discussion, I found that the bugged plane incident was raised repeatedly by forum members. One lamented the practice of the monitors, protesting that "the incident is such a good opportunity for our media to show through factual information that the U.S. is a rogue country. It would be such a pity if this opportunity were to slip away if we keep silent." Later, he/she called on forum participants to discuss why the SCF had forbidden mention of the Boeing 767 incident. When I revisited the same web page one and half hours later, the posting had been deleted.[5] One forum member proclaimed that the position taken by the SCF showed that it had lost its patriotic nature and said that he would cease participating in the forum.[6] Others reacted in more subtle ways and appealed to the monitor to be more careful in deleting messages.[7] One posted an article entitled "New Strategic Thinking and Implementation Plan to Develop a Chinese Jumbo Jet," suggesting that China should develop its own commercial aircraft with the same resolve it had shown in developing the nuclear bomb in the Mao era, thus making China less dependent on Boeing. Subjecting George W. Bush to the same treatment he had given the Chinese leadership, another message suggested forcing him to ride in a Chinese-made Red Flag car during his upcoming visit to Beijing in late February.[8]

To the Chinese government's dismay, its effort to suppress the news
was bound to be a failure because the availability of the Internet made it
impossible to achieve a total blockage. It was obvious that news about
this incident was readily circulated on the Internet and that Chinese web
surfers had many places to obtain the news from the outside world. Unlike the closely monitored SCF, many individually run web sites discussed
the issue openly. After I logged out from the Strengthening-China Forum,
I entered a popular web site named "Iron and Blood" (www.v-war.net or
www.tiexue.net), which is frequented by Chinese military enthusiasts. In
its BBS forum, the bugged plane incident had already become the focus of
discussion. Almost immediately after the news was broached by the Western media, a lengthy message containing a detailed Chinese translation of
the report in the *Financial Times* was posted on the V-War BBS.[9] The initial response by V-War members to the news was disbelief and shock, one
commenting, "don't talk nonsense," a second noting "this must be a false
posting, and a third asking "who could have done such a stupid thing?"
But other members thought the news was true, citing the history of U.S.
intelligence spying on the Soviet Union as proof. After the question of the
authenticity of the news was solved, the titles of messages became more
emotionally charged. One message briefly repeated the report from the
Financial Times, with the heading "Special Extra! Shameless Americans!"[10] And many similar ones followed.

One day later, another V-War forum member posted CNN's report
"China won't confirm, deny reports of bugged plane" in its entirety in
English online, adding his comments in Chinese. Obviously, this member
had been able to watch CNN television news. Quoting CNN's report that
"it is not uncommon for countries to spy on each other to preserve national interests, which prevail in any bilateral relationship," the poster
commented that CNN was resorting to sophistry and trying to cover up
America's shameless actions, a point that was echoed by many others.
One poster claimed that the words of all American politicians and media
were "crap" and completely unreliable. Another elaborated further: "it is
only an idiot who completely believes media, no matter whether American or Chinese. The only difference between the two is that when reporting about China, the American media is more shameless than the Chinese
media in reporting about the United States."[11] The majority of postings
on the V-War forum had a completely different attitude to the American
media from that of Anti, cited in Chapter 8. Given the fact that many V-
War forum members are both Internet- and English-literate, and some of

them have direct access to Western media outlets, why had they come up with such a different judgment of the Western media?

This phenomenon is frequently explained in terms of rising Chinese nationalism, as in Kristof's comments on Chinese Internet surfers' reactions to the 9/11 terrorist attacks, but the online Chinese response to the plane-bugging incident presents a complex picture of online politics in China that contradicts some common sweeping claims about Chinese nationalism. First, the blocking of Western media web sites by the Chinese authorities has been unable to prevent many Chinese from getting news from the outside, thanks to the rapid development of the Internet, which the government itself has helped to promote. Second, the Chinese state has not always been an unrestrained promoter of rising Chinese nationalism. In fact, it is sometimes eager to put a brake on such nationalism, because it is a double-edged sword. Third, while many observers of the development of the Internet have assumed that the increasing flow of information will have a positive influence on Chinese minds and enhance a Chinese quest for democracy, they have been disappointed by the fact that Chinese cyberspace has become a place to vent the strongest nationalistic sentiment against the West, especially the United States.[12] It illustrates that the Internet does not intrinsically have a democratizing function, and many China observers often forget that the flow of information is subject to different interpretations, as demonstrated by online Chinese nationalists, who have access to the Internet and are well informed about the outside world, yet are still very anti-American.

The "rise" of Chinese nationalism in the 1990s has attracted much scholarly and media attention in recent years. Many have pointed out that contemporary Chinese nationalism has become more "assertive," "aggressive," or "chauvinistic" and have tried to provide explanations. Some attribute the rise of nationalism to the need of party-state to fill a void left after the collapse of communist ideology; others think of it as a defensive reaction to external challenges.[13] While some pay special attention to the promotional (and manipulative) role of the state and call it "a state-led nationalism," others think that the newly emergent Chinese middle class became nationalistic because their encounter with the West and Western media has been restricted and superficial.[14] In analyzing the popularity of Chinese nationalist writings in print in the late 1990s, two media studies scholars made the interesting point that nationalism in today's China has considerable consumption value, that the media sells "packaged nationalism" at huge profits and with official blessing.[15]

While the above analyses touch on different aspects of contemporary Chinese nationalism, they share a common focus which emphasizes the "external" shaping factors, be it the manipulative state, the need for a new legitimizing ideology, the perceived foreign threats, the profit-seeking market, or inaccessibility to Western media. What I propose below is that to address the complexity of contemporary Chinese nationalism, we need also pay sufficient attention to the role of human agency, and acknowledge that Chinese nationalists are not merely subjects who submit to the "external" factors passively; rather they are individuals engaging in active thinking. What is of particular interest to us is that the availability of the Internet makes many of them well informed about the outside world and less prone to state manipulations. In fact, the cyberspace has quickly become a new domain in which nationalism is being redefined, expressed, and exercised, as scholars in various disciplines have noticed.[16] We must accordingly look at Chinese nationalism in the information age from new perspectives.

This chapter tries to tackle the issue of contemporary Chinese nationalism from a different perspective by addressing the formation of the new interest-driven game-playing paradigm in terms of which the Chinese have come since the late 1980s to perceive their position in the world. The paradigm did not appear overnight, nor is it the product of a single sponsor; rather, it has evolved from a long process of reflections, conceptualizations, and popularizations on the part of the Chinese state, elite intellectuals, and the general public in the 1980s and 1990s. The rise of contemporary Chinese nationalism cannot simply be attributed to manipulation by the hidden hand of the Communist Party, given the fact that the persuasive power of communist ideology has been seriously weakened in the era of reform and opening-up. Neither does the rise of Chinese nationalism have much to do with lack of exposure to the outside world. Ironically, as we shall see, much of the new interpretative framework has been borrowed from Western concepts and ideas, which have then been used by the Chinese to substantiate their nationalist rhetoric. The seeming convergence of many Chinese with the state on the issue of nationalism is based on this shared new de-ideologized paradigm, though often used with different emphases. Using this interest-driven game-playing paradigm to interpret information received about the world, the more informed Chinese are, the more nationalist they may be, as demonstrated by the responses to the plane-bugging incident by Chinese net surfers.

In the following, I focus on the so-called military web sites (*junshi wangzhan*) in Chinese cyberspace to examine the complexity of contemporary Chinese nationalism. The term "military web site" refers to web sites that concentrate on discussions of military affairs, weaponry and equipment, military history, and war games and often publish military fiction. I have chosen this particular type of web site because strongly nationalistic and anti-foreign discourse is perennial on them. Chinese military web sites, mostly run by individual military enthusiasts, number in the hundreds, if not more. Few of them last very long, and because of their very high turnover rate, they are relatively less subject to focused government monitoring than most other sites.[17] I use the V-War website, which I have been observing since late 2001, as an example.

The V-War site was set up by a college student at Tsinghua University at the end of 2000. With only a dozen registered members, and operated from student dormitories, the V-War site was only one of many "amateur" web sites set up by Chinese net surfers in the days of the Internet boom. On January 17, 2002, there were 4,257 registered members. One year later, the number had increased to more than 28,800. By June 10, 2003, the number had increased to 49,907. By November 21, 2004, the number had reached 233,451. In the meanwhile, the scope of its BBS forum expanded beyond purely military-related topics. The V-War web site has since grown into one of the largest military web sites in Chinese cyberspace.[18]

An Imagined Military Community

What distinguishes the V-War site from other military sites is that it is constructed as an imagined military community, and every member is viewed as a soldier. This virtual identity is imposed on a surfer from the very beginning. When one registers for a membership, one is given the option of being a soldier in either the Northern Corps or the Southern Corps, the two opposed military groups on the website. New members are free to choose either of these, and most make their decision based on which part of China they are from, since China is generally divided by the Yangzi River into northern and southern parts. Both the Southern and the Northern Corps are well organized, each having a headquarters, general staff, logistics department, and even a company for new recruits to give basic training to the newcomer. A more important status signifier is the rank a member holds in this virtual military community. When a new member is accepted by V-War, he or she is given the lowest rank, that of private. Promotion largely depends on the degree of participation in the web site, measured mainly by the number of online postings. For example, a private with more than fifty postings is promoted to private first class.[19] The time of joining the virtual community serves as another yardstick by which to judge the seniority of V-War members.

One's online name and byline are also important marks of identity in the V-War community. There are names that are historical or political allusions, such as Dragon Blood, Emperor Hanwu, and Bin Laden, and also names that seem to be random combinations of characters and numbers, such as Last2000, bin885179, and gundamzaku, to mention only a few. Though online names may have specific implications, the short sentences used as bylines often provide more clues to the personality and position of a member. For example, the byline of a member named Sun reads: "The East turns red when the sun rises, which brightens the East and blackens the West." From the online name and byline, it is not difficult to tell that this V-War member has strong anti-Western sentiments. The byline of Cold Blood reads: "Peace only exists on top of war. We need war for the sake of peace," clearly indicating belligerence. A webmaster named Emperor Hanwu (a 140–87 B.C. Western Han Dynasty ruler renowned for his wars against the nomads) quotes the emperor's words as his/her byline, which reads: "Be famous in military affairs and let barbarians acknowledge allegiance; be just and fair in government administration, let the people enjoy prosperous lives. The Chinese shall be the rulers of all under heaven." Obviously, this webmaster has strong nostalgic feelings for China's glorious past, a position shared by many Chinese nationalists.

The multimedia functionality of the Internet provides new ways of defining and presenting one's identity. In addition to creating a distinctive online name and byline, one can also use audio and visual presentations to supplement text postings. It is still not common for a V-War member to attach an audio file to supplement his/her personal profile, but everybody is given the option of providing a picture as a personal logo. Pictures used as logos range from animal cartoons to abstract figures. The member named Bin Laden uses the terrorist's portrait as logo. A member named April uses a portrait of Peng Dehuai, a famous Chinese marshal who was a victim of Mao's political purges for his outspokenness and thus commands a lot of respect among Chinese. In addition to these, images of soldiers, police, and generals are also often adopted, with noticeably frequent use of pictures of World War II German soldiers and generals. Other members use images of weaponry as their logos, such as tanks, guns, and aircraft. Sometimes these individual logos are animated—a jet fighter firing missiles, for example, or a rocket blasting off.

The creator of the V-War web site has made great efforts to make members feel as though they are in an all-encompassing military environment. In addition to the Northern and Southern Corps, the community also has a hospital, bank, its own currency, shop, chat room, and court-martial. Members can use virtual currency to buy weapons from the shop or engage in light conversation with others in the chat room, but they can also be court-martialed if they fail to follow the rules of the community. For example, a member has been put on trial for using a female portrait as his logo. V-War webmasters are conscious of the need to keep the web site sufficiently "masculine," given its military theme. They not only prohibit the posting of pornographic pictures but also any female pictures as part of postings or as individual logos. Only female members whose gender has been verified by webmasters can use their own portraits as their logos. In this particular case, the offender outraged the webmasters not only by posing as a female member but also by using a picture of a Japanese porn star as his logo. After the true nature of the logo was identified, he was subject to court-martial. Even though he made a public apology to community members, he was eventually "sentenced" by the court to a one-month expulsion.[20]

BBS Forums: Informed Discussions

No matter how "militarized" the V-War community is, textual expression on BBS forums is still the most important aspect of the life in this virtual community, reflected by the constant flow of message postings and subsequent feedback from readers, which is then replied to by the original poster. Under the general name of Tiexue Luntan (V-War or Iron and Blood Forum), by 2002, the web site had more than ten BBS forums that covered a wide range of topics, such as military fiction, war games, virtual military confrontations, weaponry and equipment, politics and economy, and military history, as well as a soldiers' club forum to host less relevant messages posted by members.[21] By January 2003, V-War had expanded to include subforums focusing on topics such as parachuting and flying, military-related multimedia products, and Chinese culture. Discussions in these BBS forums often show that participants are not only military enthusiasts but often are able to engage in informed and timely discussions of issues well beyond military affairs per se.

One good place to start is the forum on military weaponry, in which the majority of postings are about the development of new weapons and military equipment both in China and internationally. From a layman's point of view, many of these postings are very sophisticated, showing a mastery of technical details and the latest information, often from overseas sources. Many participants do not try to conceal their desire for China to have strong, modern armed forces. They thus lament the fact that China does not have the advanced weaponry possessed by the United States and Russia; they worry that the upgrading of Chinese military equipment is proceeding too slowly; and they feel proud knowing that China has achieved advances in weapon development. Their focus is mostly on China's potential rivals in the twenty-first century, namely, the United States, Japan, Russia, and India. Needless to say, Taiwan is also a center of attention, but the Taiwan issue is discussed mostly in relation to the United States and Japan, two countries that back Taiwan independence in the perceptions of most V-War BBS forum participants.

Heated debates are common on this BBS forum. Whether China should build aircraft carriers has been the longest-lasting and most hotly debated issue online, and there is no sign that either side of the debate will concede in the near future. Supporters of aircraft carriers propose that, politically speaking, China has to have aircraft carriers to win "big country" status in the new century. From the military perspective, having aircraft carriers is the best way to deter possible American military interference if China resorts to force to reunite Taiwan with the PRC, and to secure China's claim to sovereignty over the Spratly Islands in the South China Sea and its ocean transportation lanes for foreign trade and oil imports. Those who oppose aircraft carriers are not in disagreement with the ultimate aims laid out by the aircraft carrier enthusiasts but disagree on the tactics necessary to achieve them. They feel that China should not waste its limited resources building aircraft carriers that will be a financial and technical burden on the Chinese navy and think that a more efficient way to achieve the above-mentioned goals would be to develop and build a fleet of modern submarines. No matter how heated the debates are, both sides claim that their aim is to maximize the national interest and that they are arguing from patriotic standpoint.

Compared to the BBS forum on weaponry, the politics and economy forum focuses more on "strategic" issues from a geopolitical perspective.

It is in this forum that sensitive topics touching on China's current affairs are often discussed and debated. Here is a list of postings on the first page of the politics and economy forum on December 30, 2002:

1. Is another Sino-Japanese war inevitable?
2. American timetable to solve world problems
3. On nationalism, strengthening China, and other issues
4. The fight for world hegemony
5. I appeal to your rational faculties
6. Be alert to the danger of the V-War politics and economy forum becoming a forward position of propaganda and subversion by democracy advocates
7. Making another China—introduction to the Sutian Canal
8. Please cite where the transferred postings are from
9. I weep for you, good-hearted people
10. On China's position toward North Korea
11. Reflections on online "hawkish thinking"
12. Public notices of the politics and economy forum
13. Who are the members of the real "axis of evil?"
14. Group pictures: 109th anniversary of the birth of Mao Zedong
15. Why are the Chinese police disliked?
16. Why has the United States started to try to please China?
17. The rise of China—neglected important events in 2002
18. The new Chinese leadership possesses a steady and balanced style
19. Thoughts about the V-War politics and economy forum
20. Rich people have quietly changed China
21. Had I known, I would not have done it (selections from Stainless Steel Mouse's online writings)
22. We want freedom, not democracy
23. Perspectives of laid-off workers in the Northeast
24. Fantasy of Taiwan idiots—bombing the Three Gorges Dam
25. Pulling back North Korea's iron curtain
26. Breaking reports on corruption inside the Hope Project by the Southern Weekend reporter Fang Jinyu
27. Do we still have confidence in the Chinese Communist Party?
28. The big changes in China in 2002
29. Hu Jingtao: We shouldn't suppress dissenting voices in society by dictatorial means
30. U.S., Japan, and Taiwan hire thugs to occupy Chinese BBS Forums

Even though the above page has been randomly chosen, its contents are fairly representative of the majority of postings on the BBS forum. According to my rough classification, postings nos.1, 8, 12, and 19 are directly related to the forum itself, nos. 7, 14, 15, 18, 20, 21, 23, 26, 27, 28, and 29 are concerned mainly with domestic issues in China, and the rest, about half the total, concern international relations. Of the postings on domestic issues, no. 7 purports to be a transferred posting by Lu Jiaping on a grand plan to divert waters from rivers in southwestern China to North China, most likely in response to the commencement on December 27, 2002, of China's ambitious project of "Diverting Water from South to North," which will take fifty years to complete. No. 26 touches on the sensitive issue of the Hope Project, which is China's biggest government-sponsored fund-raising program to support school-age children in poor areas. Irregularities in the program management were broached earlier but have since been forbidden as a topic of public discussion in official media. Obviously, the reporter is resorting to the Internet to get her message across.

Postings no. 18 and 29 are more politically oriented, commenting positively on China's new leadership less than two months after it was appointed. Posting no. 18 praises the new CCP leadership's style because it pays more attention to China's national interests, balancing different national priorities and engaging in concrete problem solving. Posting no. 29 hints that the new leadership may loosen the government's policy toward the expression of political and social discontent, which is based on the author's interpretation of a recent speech by Hu Jingtao, the newly inaugurated general secretary of the CCP. Posting no. 21 reposts two articles by Stainless Steel Mouse, the online persona of Liu Di, a female Beijing Normal University student who was arrested for posting "national-security-endangering" messages on the Internet and participating in "illegal organization." Since her arrest on November 7, 2002, the case has been extensively publicized online, and many have seen it as a signal of the government's intention to tighten Internet control. As a means of protest, her writings have been widely circulated on Chinese BBS forums. The V-War forum is only one of these.

Of the postings on international affairs, two postings on North Korea (no. 10 and no. 25) reflect China's concerns over the standoff that was unfolding at the end of 2002 between the United States and North Korea over the latter's nuclear program. There are also postings expressing strong nationalist sentiments. The heading of posting no. 24 reveals the poster's stance against Taiwan independence. Posting no. 13 is a simple online survey. Of the ten listed countries (Iraq, Iran, North Korea, the United States, Britain, Japan, Russia, Nazi Germany, France, India, and Australia), the United States (26), Japan (22), and Britain (15), got most votes (out of a total of 96) as members of "the real 'axis of evil,' " reflecting the generally negative attitude of the majority of forum members toward them.[22]

Nonetheless, what makes the V-War forum different from the extreme nationalist stance often cited by the Western media, such as the commentary in the *New York Times* quoted earlier, is that there are also plenty of postings that are highly informed and thoughtful in nature. In fact, many of the above postings on international affairs have differing orientations. The first posting maintains that China and Japan are not necessarily poised to have another war. The author even suggests that if China and Japan let their deeply rooted memories of war and hatred go and become partners in establishing the engine of the world economy, both countries will benefit from this cooperation, surpassing America and Europe and becoming the third pole of a new world order.[23] Postings no. 3 and no. 11 both caution against the danger of extreme nationalism. Equating extreme nationalism with Nazism, posting no. 3 advocates the equality of all fifty-six nationalities in China, as well as the equality of all nations in the world, and criticizes Chinese who indiscriminately hate Japanese.[24] Denying that the rise of extreme nationalism is a result of government promotion, and instead attributing the phenomenon to a psychological reaction to China's marginal role in world affairs in the 1990s, the author of posting no. 11 claims that China has become more mature in recognizing the dangers of extreme nationalism and appeals to fellow forum members to be true patriots by making China "prosperous, moderate, responsible, friendly, nonaggressive, cooperative, rational, and participatory" in its dealings with other countries.[25]

Generally speaking, postings on the politics and economy forum are multifaceted, well informed, and often very timely. Though many V-War members are nationalistic (or patriotic, as most of them describe themselves) and hawkish, they are exposed to discussions of China's current domestic and international affairs from many different perspectives thanks to the Internet's unrivaled capacity for information transmission. Close scrutiny of the thirty postings on December 30, 2002, listed above, shows that the majority were re-postings from other web sites and BBS on the Internet. The Internet makes it possible for information to circulate rapidly over a wide area, which the traditional media cannot do. The webmasters of this forum seem to admit most postings that do not deviate widely from the forum's focus, thus making it a site of informed discussion.

What are most V-War members like? There are no comprehensive and scientifically conducted surveys available, but online surveys on their age and education conducted by V-War members themselves give some idea. In October 2002, a member named "Lurker" conducted a survey of members' ages. A total of 77 responses gave the following results: under 16 (1); aged 16–20 (12); aged 21–25 (35); aged 26–30 (21); aged 31–40 (7); and aged over 40 (1). The survey shows that most V-War members are in their twenties and thirties, which is congruent with the general demographic distribution of China's online population in 2002.[26] Two months later, another member conducted a survey of members' highest level of education. A total of 100 responses gave the following results: middle school (11); high school (9); three-year college and current college students (25); bachelor's degree (40); and postgraduate degree (15). This survey shows that the overwhelming majority of V-War members have higher education qualifications.[27]

The majority of V-War members are thus well educated and well informed, yet nationalistic and anti-Western. This raises a key question: if these Chinese Internet surfers are informed about the outside world, why does nationalistic thinking appeal much more to them than ideas of democracy and freedom, and, worse still, why do they treat these ideas with disbelief and sarcasm? I would suggest that even though the Chinese have become more informed, they have also adopted a new interpretative framework in which the once-cherished values of democracy and freedom are reexamined and scrutinized in the context of Sino-American relations, in which the two rival powers often find themselves on a collision course. These well-educated, well-informed young Chinese have become nationalists, not on an ideological basis, but rather based on a new interpretative framework that has gained popularity only in the past two decades.

The Key Concepts of a New Paradigm

It is worth emphasizing from the start that because of the fluidity and complexity of the new paradigm, it is virtually impossible to present a complete picture. What this chapter aims to do is examine several key concepts that comprise this paradigm, trying to reveal how these widely accepted concepts have provided Chinese with relatively coherent analytical tools. Among numerous concepts that Chinese often use, "comprehensive national power" (zonghe guoli), "national interests" (guojia liyi), and "rules of the game" (youxi guize) are three phrases that we often encounter nowadays in Chinese mass media, intellectual writings, and messages in Internet chat rooms. These are the three key concepts that are the backbone of the new paradigm that Chinese use to perceive their position in the current world. Understanding these key concepts will help us make sense of seemingly often-contradictory positions in and expressions of Chinese nationalism.

Before exploring details of these three key concepts, a brief account of previous paradigms employed by Chinese nationalism is necessary. At least two paradigms exerted widespread influences prior to the 1980s. One was formed at the turn of the twentieth century, based on social Darwinism, and emphasized the imminent danger of the destruction of the Chinese nation and race by the surrounding imperialist powers. Though the ultimate goal was to seek national strength and power and to protect Chinese interests and sovereignty, the immediate aim of this paradigm was the "salvation" of China in a world of jungle law. "Salvation" became both the aim and means. Both the nationalists and the communists were propelled by this urgency in their revolutionary mobilizations. The framework lost its appeal after the People's Republic of China was established, since, from the communists' perspective, the task of national "salvation" had been accomplished when Mao Zedong proclaimed that the Chinese people had stood up on October 1, 1949.

From the inception of the People's Republic, the Chinese communists followed an ambivalent position in relation to nationalism. While they were nationalists in essence, the communists avoided using the concept because nationalism was in conflict with the proletarian internationalism of Marxist doctrine. Thus, after 1949, even though the Chinese leadership never formally endorsed nationalism, policies were pursued within a bipolar framework of anti-imperialism and internationalism. Under this paradigm, fighting Americans in the Korean War was interpreted as an act of internationalism and anti-imperialism. After its split with the Soviet Union in the early 1960s, China faced virtual isolation from the rest of the world. Being self-reliant became the main means of warding off foreign pressure at that time, while a large amount of foreign aid was provided to third world countries in the name of internationalism, triggering endless discussions today of how "irrational" China's foreign policy was in the 1960s and 1970s.

Comprehensive National Power

The concept of comprehensive national power (CNP) was introduced into Chinese academic discourse in the mid 1980s. Huang Shuofeng, a strategic studies scholar for the Chinese military, who was arguably the first one to use this concept, was inspired by strategic studies by Western political scientists, such as Ray Cline and Joseph Nye, in which "national power" was a well-established concept.[28] Huang coined the term "comprehensive national power" in 1984, most likely under the influence of systems theory, which was a hot topic all over Chinese academia at the time.[29] According to Huang, "Comprehensive national power is the combined force, including both the material and spiritual power possessed by a sovereign nation, which ensures its survival, growth, and ability to exert international influence."[30]

This concept was soon widely accepted not only by academia and the mass media but also by the Chinese leadership, because it suited China's "big country complex"—the dream of national wealth and power. No matter how CNP is defined, population, territory, and natural resources are generally included in the calculation to China's advantage; a Chinese truism is that China has "[a] vast land, rich in natural resources, and [a] large population." The concept of CNP was widely used in the 1990s, and serious studies of the subject were conducted. The collapse of the Soviet Union led the Chinese to realize that the essential competition among nations was not limited to individual areas such as the military, economy, and polity, but was a competition based on the CNP of each country. Correspondingly, a broadened concept of national security emerged, which emphasized the protection of multiple aspects of national security, including the political, economic, military, environmental, and financial safety of a state.

With China's phenomenal economic development since the 1980s, the concept of CNP has been used by the Chinese to assess their current world position and set future goals, boosting increasingly strong feelings of confidence and pride. Postings no. 17 and no. 28 on December 30, 2002, both hail the rapid development China achieved in 2002. Jiang Lei, the general webmaster of the V-War website, wrote a long article to review the site's successful year in 2002 and to celebrate the arrival of 2003. At the beginning of the article, he reiterated China's achievements in domestic politics, economic development, national defense, and international relations and went on to denounce the dominant way of thinking before 1989 that often criticized the land-based Chinese "yellow civilization" as inferior to the sea-based Western "blue civilization."[31] As he proudly put it:

As a rising and trend-setting nation in the twenty-first century, we need to express our voice and will in a way that demonstrates our pride and self-esteem. This will not be a voice praising the superiority of blue civilization or European civilization. We need a voice truly representative of the Chinese people, a way of expression truly the representative of the will of Chinese, and a voice or a way of expression that is able to convey the rejuvenated civilization and will of this great Eastern country. V-War is a voice of this kind, and V-War is a part of the expression of this will.[32]

To have a China with a strong CNP is the ultimate wish of most V-War members, and whoever can deliver that outcome will win their support. Riding on China's rapid economic growth in the 1990s, the current Chinese "communist" rulers are in an advantageous position to win over people who share this kind of thinking. In fact, many V-War members believe that the current Chinese government has done a good job and that there is no need to change the status quo in the near future. Posting no. 27 conducted a quick survey with the title: "Do we still have confidence in the Chinese Communist Party?" It offered the following three possible answers to its question:

1. I have confidence in the CCP both today and in the future
2. I have confidence in the CCP for the time being but am not sure if I shall in the future
3. I do not have confidence in the CCP

The survey's conductor emphasized that the audience should vote based on rational thinking, rather than flinging abuse at or expressing blind support for the CCP. When I visited the page on January 2, 2003, a total of sixty-six votes had been cast. Of these, twenty-two chose the first answer and twenty-seven chose the second. Only seventeen votes, less than 26 percent, voted no confidence in the CCP.[33] This result is echoed by more sophisticated surveys conducted by political scientists.[34]

National Interests

The concept of national interest, although central to modern theories of geopolitics and international relations, has been employed in the PRC only since the early 1980s. Its pervasive use today has made Li Shenzhi, a famous Chinese liberal and one of the first to reintroduce the national interest concept into Chinese political discourse, feel uneasy. Because of the Marxist doctrine of proletarian internationalism, which denounces nationalism and sees international revolution as the ultimate goal, national interest was discarded as a bourgeois concept in the CCP's political discourse before the 1980s. Signaling a shift in the communist leadership's thinking on this issue, in the report of the Twelfth Party Congress, an independent section was devoted to discussions of China's foreign policy and its goals, replacing the old routine of discussing world revolution. Li, who helped to draft the report, explained that this was the first time that China's foreign policy had been emphasized for its own sake. It was not until 1985, however, that through subtle and sometimes undercover efforts, Li and his colleagues reintroduced the concept of national interest into Chinese academic and media circles. Thus, to today's nationalists' surprise, it was in fact Chinese liberals who played an instrumental role in reviving this key concept.[35]

As it had done with the concept of CNP, the CCP leadership, while continuing to hold nationalism to be undesirable, quickly adopted national interest as a valid concept. Deng Xiaoping asserted: "It should always be our starting point that our strategic national interests are the main concern in dealing with relations among countries."[36] Chinese intellectuals have also embraced this concept. *Strategy and Management*, a journal that focuses on strategic studies of contemporary Chinese issues and is widely read by the intelligentsia, has published a number of articles employing the concept of national interest since its inception in 1993. The third issue of 2001 included a translation of an article by Condoleeza Rice, then U.S. national security advisor, entitled "Promoting U.S. National Interests."[37] America's actions in other areas of international affairs, such as its withdrawal from the Kyoto Environmental Protocol and refusal to sign the world land-mine ban treaty, have also been mentioned on- and off-line as proofs of the United States putting its national interests first. Not surprisingly, the national interest concept was picked up by Chinese nationalists and became one of the most frequently used concepts in their arguments. The idea of national interest has thus become deeply rooted in Chinese thinking in just a decade.[38]

It is from this perspective that America's promotion of democracy, human rights, and other values is often perceived by some Chinese as a front to advance U.S. national interests. For example, postings no. 2 and no. 5 are re-postings of messages from He Xin, a well-known Chinese scholar famous after June 4, 1989, for supporting the government's crackdown on the Tiananmen movement. No. 10 is the transcript of a talk He gave to Beijing University students in June 1990 in which he defended his position and accused Western countries of using democracy and human rights as fronts for the strategic purpose of destabilizing China and preventing it from achieving modernization, thus preventing China from becoming their rival in the future.[39] Posting no. 5 is a recent newspaper interview with He Xin in which he claims that the United States is seeking to dominate the world with its own political and economic system. In order to achieve its ultimate goal, the United States will solve "world problems" one by one, with Afghanistan, Iraq, North Korea, China, and Russia first on its list; after this, even "unstable" allies, such as Germany, France, and Japan will become possible American targets. In the new world order dominated by the United States, according to He Xin, Western elites are interested in letting only 20 percent of world population enjoy a high standard of living by monopolizing the world resources and keeping the remaining 80 percent of a "rogue" world population at the level of subsistence.[40]

Numerous V-War postings have focused on what kind of strategies China should adopt to enhance its national interest and revitalize itself in the near future. These postings are often written by people with a good knowledge of international affairs and are often quite provocative in tone. Posting no. 4 is such an article, exploring China's best strategies for revival from a geopolitical perspective. Assuming that the ultimate goal of China's modernization is to seek world hegemony, either by itself or through teaming up with the United States, the author presents a detailed analysis of China's neighboring countries and discusses whether their roles will be either detrimental or beneficial to China's rise. According to this "strategist," China faces no direct threat from the north, namely, Russia, and may indeed seek potential allies in the Korean peninsula, and thus neutralize Japan, especially if China can successfully reunite with Taiwan. To the west, China should support Pakistan to contain India. Most important, China should aim at strong influence in Southeast Asia, because this is an area that is rich in resources pivotal to China's continuous economic expansion, many countries of which share in China's Confucian culture. To achieve the overall goal, the author opposes the two different approaches often mentioned in contemporary China: either seeking direct confrontation with the United States in its effort to contain China or acknowledging the superpower status of the United States and avoiding any conflict in the near future. According to the author, the best strategy is to understand China's strategic purpose, its short- and long-term goals, and subsequently to strive to achieve these goals according to the strategies that best fit the Chinese national interest.[41]

The Rules of the Game

Compared to the CNP and national interest, the concept of the rules of the game is relatively new, and it has gained popularity during China's lengthy negotiations to join the General Agreement on Tariffs and Trade (GATT) and then the World Trade Organization (WTO), which jointly set the rules governing international trade. Gaining membership requires China to conduct international trade according to these rules in exchange for benefiting from the rights to which it is entitled as a member. With its economy becoming increasingly connected to the world economy, joining the WTO has been a key goal of the Chinese government, but the challenge has been the question of under what conditions China should join. Negotiations were much dominated by a dispute between China and the United States, which invited China to join the WTO as a developed country, based on its assessment of China's economic power using "purchasing power parity" (PPP), thus requiring China to lower its tariffs in a shorter time period and giving less protection to its vulnerable economic sectors. Many Chinese saw this dispute as an example of America's promotion of its national interest to obtain a bigger market share after China's entry into the WTO in the name of upholding the "rules."

Adoption of the "rules of the game" concept, which conceives of political, economic, and strategic interactions among the different world players as game playing, marks the total de-ideologization of the Chinese perception of world affairs. The concept's rapid gain in popularity, both in elite and mass discourse, also reflects the shifting perception of the Chinese of their position in the world and, correspondingly, of how to act within it. If China's "opening-up" reflected the urgent need to redress Mao's isolationism, increasing reference to the "rules of the game" reflects a more confident China that is not satisfied only with opening its door to the rest of the world but also eager to be an active player in world affairs.

While Westerners have emphasized "rules" in dealing with Chinese, however, Chinese have focused on the aspect of "game playing." More important, Chinese use of the "rules of the game" concept does not imply that they will obey the extant rules passively; rather, they are aware of the unfairness of the extant rules to latecomers to the world political and economic system. Playing a game involves players, referees, and rule setters, and China has found itself rather in the pitiful position of applying for admission to the game, and certainly not in the capacity of referee and rule setter. The wide acceptance of this concept reflects the mainstream opinion in recent years that China has no choice but to accept the existing world system and play according to the rules, but that it can increase its status (along with its CNP), try to revise the rules (because of their innate inequity), and even become one of the rule setters (for the purpose of pursuing national interest).

The concept of national interest has been more widely contested. To the Chinese government, China's internal stability is one of the most important national interests. Clearly, the government's main purpose since the Tiananmen crackdown in 1989 has been to hold on to its monopoly on power, and the disintegration of the Soviet Union has provided it with a convenient and convincing object lesson. The economic crises Russia has subsequently endured have severely dampened the belief that political liberalization will bring economic and social progress, as often argued by Chinese elite intellectuals in the pre-Tiananmen era. The appeal of political reforms has thus been largely muted by the government's appeal for stability, on the one hand, and its delivery of high-speed economic development, on the other. Stability and development have thus become the two pillars of government policy, which national interests are often invoked to legitimize. Deng Xiaoping's famous slogan "Development makes absolute sense" is a reflection of this thinking, and it has been well received by mainstream Chinese.

Since the United States is perceived to be a real obstacle to China's reunification and a threat to China's ascension as a major power, the ideologies it represents and promotes, such as democracy and human rights, have lost their appeal for many Chinese, at least at face value. Though democracy remains an ultimate goal to many Chinese, a concern for immediate national interests such as reuniting with Taiwan outweighs everything else. Given the dominance of a de-ideologized discourse of national interests, the democracy advocate He Jiadong's claim that "democracy is the most important national interest" seems to have attracted few new followers, especially among Chinese youth.[42] In fact, as shown by posting no. 6 on the list of December 30, 2002, sometimes V-War members take the initiative to ask webmasters to enhance their censorship ef-

forts to kick out postings by overseas Chinese political dissidents, popu-
larly known as "democracy advocates." According to the message poster
named "Walking in Clouds," the real purpose of the "democracy advocates" in criticizing China's current political system and existing problems is to help their (Western) masters' vicious plot to lead China into
chaos, thus preventing China from being a threat to their ambition of
dominating the world, as well as to their national interests. Claiming that
propaganda and attacks by "democracy advocates" cannot solve the
thorny problems China is facing, "Walking in Clouds" appeals to the
webmasters to take decisive action against these "national traitors" to
prevent any possible loss of control of V-War as a space to promote patriotism online. Most responses to the posting support the position
"Walking in Clouds" holds. To avoid misunderstanding, "Walking in
Clouds" stresses that he/she speaks as an individual and has no official
status at all.[43]

In a community such as V-War, many members are very skeptical of
the information conveyed by the Western media. Posting no. 30 further
claims that the United States, Japan, and Taiwan have hired a group of
online hatchet men to post all kinds of attacking messages on Chinese
BBS as part of a coordinated propaganda campaign against China. These
postings concentrate on demoralizing Chinese patriots, disparaging China's recent achievements, exaggerating Chinese problems, spreading rumors, provoking ethnic conflicts, and promoting human rights over sovereignty. The author cites the historical precedents of the CIA's use of
defectors to conduct subversive propaganda campaigns during the Cold
War.[44] Another member posted a short message describing feelings after
"accidentally" listening to a Radio Free Asia broadcast. According to
him, a program on the Chinese democracy movement was comical, because the tone the Americans adopted to praise Chinese "democracy advocates" made it seem as if they were praising their sons.[45] Treating Radio Free Asia as a laughingstock may be an extreme response from this
particular listener, but this case shows the limits of the effect of "free information" on the majority of V-War members' interpretion of information in terms of their newly acquired paradigm.

Conclusion

The major aspects of the V-War web site give us a clearer picture of its
patrons. Generally speaking, they adopt online military personae and en-

gage in different activities in a militarized virtual community. They are well informed and can access vast amounts of information online. Many of them are enthusiastic fans of modern weaponry but also concerned with the broad political and strategic issues that will affect China's future. Their discussions on BBS forums cover topics over a wide spectrum, in which ultranationalistic postings may sit alongside ones marked by political dissent. The main themes are clear and constant: conflicts and even wars are inevitable in a world in which all countries are fighting for their national interests, and China has to triumph over its enemies to complete its rise to the status of a global power. In the era of opening up and increased information availability, the key factor in shaping their nationalist thinking is neither the communist ideology nor government propaganda but rather a new de-ideologized paradigm that they use to interpret national policies and international relations today.

In general, there are three key concepts in a new Chinese paradigm of the world. The concept of CNP gives Chinese a much-sought emotional and psychological boost and a quantitative criterion with which to express their pride in China being a rising country in the world. The concept of national interest has been emphasized as the ultimate goal of all national and international undertakings, and it legitimizes the new paradigm by giving it the basis of "rational thinking." The third concept, the rules of the game, is a practical strategy, aiming to promote Chinese interests by joining "international games" and further modifying the existing rules to China's advantage. The formation of this paradigm is the result of the convergence of reflections of old paradigms and observations of current international situations by different sections of Chinese society, with conceptual help from the West. Compared to the old paradigms, this interest-driven, game-playing paradigm is less emotionally charged, less ideologically biased, and more rationally driven. Because of these characteristics, it has become rooted in everyday Chinese thinking and has gained lasting, comprehensive power in forming a Chinese cognitive framework of the world.

In fact, from the perspective of modern Chinese history, most V-War members are very well informed nationalists compared to the Boxers in the late Qing era or the radical Red Guards under Mao, because they are well educated and can access the Internet. An informed public is less receptive to manipulation. The effect of the state-led patriotism campaign should not be overestimated, especially in the post–Cultural Revolution context, in which the effectiveness of such political campaigns has been severely weakened. The seeming convergence of Chinese nationalist thinking is more due to the interpretive power provided by this new paradigm than to deliberate political manipulation. As long as highly charged emotion is constantly attached to interpretation, the accessibility of Western media and information through satellite TV and the Internet may further enhance anti-foreign sentiment in China. It is thus not lack of access to information that is crucial, but rather the interpretation of the available information. In the foreseeable future, Chinese nationalism will continue to be driven by this interest-driven, game-playing paradigm.

Though nationalism is rising in China, the so-called nationalists are a very fluid and constantly changing group. Emotional outbursts are often a reaction to external stimuli, such as the U.S. bombing of the Chinese embassy in Belgrade in 1999 and the Sino-American plane collision incident in 2001, and such emotion can come and go very rapidly. Nonetheless, it is worth pointing out that "comprehensive national power," "national interest," and "rules of the game" have become concepts widely accepted not only by online nationalists but by many other Chinese, nationalists or not. This new development demands our attention if we want to understand contemporary Chinese nationalism and the increasing attractiveness of this new interpretive paradigm. The world has to be prepared to deal with a China that behaves more and more along these lines. But considering the fact that much of this new interpretative framework has Western origins, I would argue that even though extreme nationalistic thinking is an integral part of this paradigm, compared to the previous conceptual frameworks that led to waves of nationalism in modern China, this one is more elastic, rational, and engaged and has the possibility of being understood, handled, and played in accordance with "rules of the game" that are acceptable to both China and the world.

Conclusion

A S   W E   H A V E   S E E N, social and political contexts have largely shaped the effects of new information technologies in China. Public circular telegrams were highly influential in the last years of the Qing dynasty, and the impact of the Internet in contemporary China has been profound. Information technology does not in itself open up public space in society, however; people using the technology do. Technologies such as telegraphy and the Internet are thus neither inherently oppressive nor automatically emancipatory. Different parties can use them for very different ends. Those who make the facile assumption that a certain kind of information technology (i.e., the Internet) will change China in a certain direction (i.e., democracy) are victims of the fallacy of technological determinism, and many of the early enthusiasts of the Internet have abandoned their rosy expectations now that the reality has turned out to be more complex.

The main aim of this study has been to tackle the complex relationships between technology and society, between the applicability of new information technologies and their political outcomes in concrete Chinese historical contexts. The discussions of the previous chapters have shown that not only Chinese attitudes toward adopting telegraphy and the Internet but also foreign pressures on the Chinese to accept these technologies were historically conditioned, and the two cases are thus very different. Moreover, the historical context has also shaped the particular paradigm in terms of which many of us view information technology. In the late nineteenth century, few attempted to relate China's adaptation of telegraphy to political reform of the Qing empire. Today, however, many take for granted that the Internet plays a clear-cut political role in the PRC, unconscious of the value-laden implications of this sweeping assumption. I hope that by historicizing and contextualizing the adoption of telegraphy and the Internet in China, I have presented a more nuanced picture that will serve as a basis for further discussion.

This volume is largely concerned with how telegraphy and the Internet have helped to make Chinese politics more public, but its focus is not on the technologies per se but on the contexts within which they have influenced politics. No one denies that new means of political participation have been made technologically available by these new information technologies, but the actual realization of their potential has depended more on what I call the "receiving context" of the technology's introduction. This receiving context is the multilayered, constantly changing historical environment in which the technology is perceived, adopted, controlled, and applied. Clearly, the late Qing court faced a very different receiving context from the government of the PRC. Whereas the late Qing court resisted telegraphy for twenty years, fearing both loss of control to foreigners and damage to its interests, the current Chinese regime has actively promoted the adoption and development of Internet technology, hoping to take advantage of it to modernize the country. Different internal and international conditions explain these different attitudes. Whereas the weakened Qing dynasty sought to ward off foreign control, the more confident PRC regime has adopted a more proactive policy.

The receiving context not only affects how the technology is used but also how the information it conveys is interpreted. Social conditions lead to the technology being used in a certain way, and a hospitable receiving context then reinforces its wide usage. In the thirty-year history of telegraphy under the late Qing dynasty, it was not until the traumatic national crisis of China's defeat in the Sino-Japanese War in 1894 that the circular telegram appeared. Even though the technology had been available for more than a decade, the concerned Chinese elite only finally adopted the circular telegram as a form of political participation when telegraphy and modern newspapers were harnessed in tandem.

The subsequent national crises from 1895 to 1911 provided numerous opportunities for the Chinese elite to express their political opinions through circular telegrams, and the proliferation of newspapers resulting from weakened Qing control made public telegrams more widely circulated and influential, encouraging their use on an even larger scale. With the adoption of the circular telegram, late Qing politics was forced to become public to an unprecedented degree in the history of Chinese dynastic rule. After the turn of the twentieth century, when more and more organizations representing rising political forces in China became adept users of the circular telegram, the authority of this new genre of political text reached new heights. The status and power of their senders, their solemn textual style, and their vast reach when reprinted in newspapers were all factors that made the circular telegram acceptable to many Chinese.

It cannot be overemphasized that, among all the factors that made the circular telegram so popular, the most important one was the rise of modern Chinese nationalism. The rise of nationalism prompted the Chinese elite to recognize that the Qing empire was falling apart and even to believe that China and the Chinese "race" were facing the danger of extinction. With the advent of the New Policies, the Chinese elite was allowed more room to participate in discussions of national politics. This was the period in which public telegrams were sent in great numbers by various parties. The nationalist pursuit became the legitimate reason behind political participation and mobilization, and nationalist sentiment became the main appeal of public telegrams, enhancing the status of those who sent them and leading to their favorable reception. The desire to save China became a dominant sentiment, culminating in the Chinese elite's attempt to pursue constitutionalism, which became the most important topic of public politics in the first years of the twentieth century. The sending of public telegrams and the drawing up of public petitions were the two most popular forms of political action. It was in this context that the public telegram found a highly receptive receiving context in the early twentieth century.

The circular telegram was only one factor that made the politics more public and transparent in the last decade of the Qing dynasty. Successive national crises, weakened dynastic rule, policy disagreements among the Qing rulers, expanded room for political participation, the rise of new social classes and organizations, the proliferation of modern newspapers, and innumerable salvific ideas and strategies all contributed to making the circular telegram not only possible but also an important and popular instrument of political participation and mobilization. In summary, it was the historical context of the late Qing that made the circular telegram an effective means of political participation. It was not the circulation of the circular telegram that propelled China to adopt constitutionalism, but vice versa—it was the need to publicize and broaden the reach of the idea of constitutionalism that made sending circular telegrams an imperative political practice. In retrospect, the convergence between rising Chinese nationalism and the emerging consensus of constitutionalism was only an outcome of the working of various historical forces in Chinese politics and cannot be seen as inevitable, as demonstrated by the fact that the appeal of constitutionalism was soon replaced by zeal for revolution in 1911.

We can certainly learn from history—though when we examine the case of the Internet, we have to be careful not to overread its history. The fact that the telegraph provided a new means of political participation and eventually played an important role in political mobilization does not imply that the Internet would follow the same path, although there is considerable continuity between these two technologies. As we have seen, in less than a decade the development of the Internet enabled many Chinese to express their opinions online. This new technology seems to have more political potential than telegraphy, and the government has tried very hard to deal with it. Facing this uncharted water, the Chinese state has had to open up some online space to newly emerged netizens, while employing online tools to confront those who might use it for political purposes that go against its interests. In the meantime, Chinese intellectuals, marginalized *minjian* writers, and niche Internet surfers like the military fan groups have all made efforts to expand political participation, in which they have succeeded to a certain degree, especially in their own web sites and BBS forums. Yet so far, the Internet has not been as influential and effective in shaping the public sphere as the circular telegram was a century ago.

The reasons for this are complex and to be found in the receiving context that the Internet faces. At the state level, the Internet is facing a Chinese regime more confident and competent than the late Qing court, and the government has adopted a proactive policy attempting to take advantage of the technology, while avoiding its potential threat. Even after twenty years of reforms, the state still has an effective grasp on media and the press and does not tolerate organized political dissent, thus limiting the scope of political participation. Besides, the factors that enhanced the effectiveness and influences of the circular telegram, discussed at length in Chapter 5, hardly exist today. In terms of textual power, while public telegram texts were associated with the traditional genre of *xiwen*, many articles and messages put on the web sites and BBS forums are written impromptu and are often perceived as inferior to their print equivalents.

Worse still, the unprecedented freedom to express individual opinion online has not necessarily led individuals to engage "in rational and critical public discussions that formed the basis for a 'public opinion,'" which Habermas describes as the essence of the public sphere. As some scholars have pointed out, many messages on BBS sites in China are the online equivalent of the "big character posters" of the Cultural Revolution.[1] The abundance of "junk" messages decreases the authority and credibility of a web site or a BBS forum, often discouraging people from participating in discussions there again.

The authority and credibility of public telegrams was enhanced by the fact that their senders were often not only of high status but both resourceful and influential, especially those newly emergent organizations. Anyone with access to a computer equipped with a modem can send out messages to anyone online anywhere, however, so the authority and credibility of online discussion varies greatly and is generally hard to predict. So far, almost all online political discussions have been conducted by individual participants. Even though by the end of 2001, there were more than 230,000 registered *minjian* (unofficial or private) organizations in China, few political discussions were carried out in the name of particular organizations.[2] While a lot of hope has been invested in the power for change supposedly possessed by the rising new classes in Chinese society, like entrepreneurs and white-collar workers, these groups and their representative organizations have been very quiet and generally shun national politics, in sharp contrast to the role played by chambers of commerce in the political mobilization of the late Qing era. This shows that the PRC has firmer control of societal forces than the Qing court did, and the lack of collective and organizational participation severely limits public online texts' authority and credibility in times of political mobilization.

Perhaps the popular genre of the online open letter most closely resembles the public telegrams of the late Qing era. As its name indicates, the open letter is a public text aimed at the largest possible audience, and this genre of text has traditionally been used in China to appeal for justice or make one's position known to the public. Strictly speaking, many circular telegrams can be seen as open letters sent by telegraph. As summarized by Wang Yi, Chinese intellectuals have a long tradition of using open letters to express political opinions in modern China, best exemplified by the petition led by Kang Youwei and Liang Qichao in 1895. This genre was adopted in the 1980s by the dissident Fang Lizhi to write to

Deng Xiaoping asking for the release of all political prisoners. During the Tiananmen movement in 1989, intellectuals organized a number of mobilizations to sign public statements on the precarious situation. But owing to political pressure by the regime, the writing of open letters has not been practiced widely since 1989.

"The rapid development of the Internet, especially the online forums, has finally changed the situation [of not being able to issue open letters]," Wang Yi asserts. When the Strengthening-China Forum tightened its monitoring practices in 2000, open letters were sent to the SCF to register protest.[3] The year 2001 witnessed two waves of collective signing and circulation of open letters on the Internet. The first was from conservatives within the Communist Party who signed open letters to question Jiang Zemin's speech on July 1 proclaiming that the party would recruit private entrepreneurs as members. The subsequent investigation of these open letters led to the closing down of a number of BBS forums, as well as of a couple of conservative-leaning magazines. The other was an open letter to President Bush initiated by twenty-three Chinese intellectuals and subsequently signed by another 200, in which they expressed sympathy with the American people after the September 11 attacks. The letter ended with the sentence "tonight, we are Americans," and its signers were subsequently ridiculed as "one-night Americans" by nationalist-leaning Chinese, resulting in heated exchanges. The direct consequences of these two rounds of open letters were the breaching of the old limits and expanding the room for political expression in cyberspace.[4]

Moving on to 2002, the open letter began to be used more frequently. Wang Yi lists five waves of public signing of open letters, including an open letter to oppose the overstrictly stipulated "Software Regulations," open letters calling for reassessment of the Tiananmen crackdown, open letters to protest the issuance of "Provisional Regulations on Publication on the Internet," an open letter appealing for a fair trial for a Tibetan lama, and finally open letters protesting the arrest of Liu Di, known in cyberspace as "Stainless Steel Mouse."[5] Another example of the collective online signing of open letters by Chinese intellectuals is the "Statement by Chinese of Various Circles" in February 2003 opposing the U.S. government's plans for war against Iraq, initiated by Han Deqiang and other left-leaning scholars and signed by 400 Chinese worldwide. The statement was also made available to and broadcast on the Arabic-language Al Jazeera television network, which provoked another wave of heated debates between liberal and left-leaning intellectuals in China.[6]

A more recent development in employing the Internet to participate in national politics is the worldwide collective online signing of Chinese against Japan's efforts to gain a permanent seat on the United Nations Security Council, and the subsequent use of the Internet to organize anti-Japanese demonstrations in a dozen Chinese cities in spring 2005, which has attracted attention from Western media as well as China observers. The catalyst for anti-Japan sentiment is a newly approved textbook in Japan that distorts atrocities committed by the Japanese against the Chinese during the World War II. It is said that a total of 22 million signatures were collected in the worldwide online drive. During the process, newly available technologies, such as e-mail, BBS, Internet blog, text messages and instant online messaging, served as an organizing tool for protesters. In a significant development, some unofficial (*minjian*) anti-Japanese organizations became the main initiators of demonstration-organizing messages online and on the mobile phone.[7]

These developments certainly signal that Chinese are continually employing the Internet to expand their room for political expression, and it seems that the Internet is functioning rather like late Qing telegraphy. Nonetheless, one must be wary of overstretching the analogies between the technologies in order to show the similarity. As I cautioned before, the deciding factor is not the technology per se but the receiving context in which its potential is exploited. The receiving context of the Internet is very different from that of late Qing telegraphy in terms of the degree of state control, the authority and authenticity of texts, and the power and influence of their issuers.[8] Not even the appearance of collectively signed online open letters has substantially changed this. Most of the public letters circulating online are signed by either political dissidents or marginalized intellectuals. The influence of these open letters is also very limited, because they are usually either circulated in limited circles, such as small numbers of nonconformist intellectuals, or are unable to attract a large following from the general public, as is the case with letters issued by "democracy advocates" or overseas Chinese dissident organizations.[9]

Why are the online open letters advocating democracy and freedom of the press not as well received as might be expected? Don't the Chinese desire freedom of expression, and isn't the Internet the right technology to enable them to obtain it? A better way to answer these questions is to pause and first look at the multiple points in the processes through which the technologies (telegraphy and the Internet) convey information. These processes consist of two parts: information issuance and information receiving. The first part involves the technology, whose existence is the precondition for information transfer, and the issuers, who often have to overcome political obstacles to transfer the desired information freely. The second part consists of the receivers of the information and their social context. Internet utopians often have too much confidence in the technology and the information it conveys, believing that these are likely to have a great impact on the receivers. This assumption is not necessarily wrong, but when it is viewed as only a one-way process, it becomes problematic. In fact, history shows that information receivers do not just receive information passively; they have always played an active role in selectively receiving and actively reinterpreting it, based on the general social context.

Reader-response criticism, a major school of twentieth-century literary theory, may be of some help here. Contrary to the long-held opinion that the value of a literary work is determined by its textual composition, reader-response criticism emphasizes the role readers play in deciding how a text is received and the value attached to it. And different readers may have different responses to the same text, depending on tastes and literary connoisseurship, which are conditioned by various factors at the time. The text alone cannot dictate the responses it will get from readers.[10] From this perspective, those who believe that the availability of information can in itself change China in a certain way are overconfident about the power the information possesses. Just like the old conviction that a "good text" will make readers think it is a "good" text, these Internet enthusiasts believe that "free" information will make a society freer because the information receivers are believed to have no alternative but to be receptive to the "free" information.

Without taking account of the concrete receiving context the information faces, the above assumption is problematic for two reasons. First, it assumes that if certain kinds of information are made accessible to people, they will be influenced, affected, and changed in the precise way the information promotes. In today's political context, the catchwords are "democracy" and "free market," though it may have been something very different a hundred years ago. In fact, the criteria used to define "free" information (most of them of Western origin) are also ideologically specific and change as time passes. As demonstrated by Michael Adas, the West has adopted a number of different criteria to make the "Other" (races and civilizations) "inferior" by judging them by their mastery or otherwise of Western science and technologies.[11] Even though those criteria were often taken for granted and enjoyed hegemonic status, they have not withstood the test of history and are now discarded as erroneous and racist. The dominant contemporary discourse of liberal democracy and the free market seems to have enjoyed a similar hegemonic status, yet it is too early to believe that this is the "end of history." The superiority of "free" information thus needs to be scrutinized historically.

Secondly, the available information can be reinterpreted in a radically different way from the expectations of "free" information advocates. As discussed in the last chapter, the position of Chinese nationalists online is not explained by theorizing that they have been misled by the Chinese state and consequently do not "get it right." Rather, they are in fact well informed through the Internet and other media, but are responding in ways that are not congruent with the expected changes the information is supposed to exert upon its receivers, that is, by becoming pro-democratic opponents of the current regime. The reason is that the Chinese have adopted a new system of interpretation that examines "free" information through the "interest-driven, game-playing" paradigm that has de-ideologized much of Chinese thinking in contemporary China. Under this paradigm, the tensions and discrepancy between what information issuers claim to be "true" and "objective" information and "real" and "positioned" information does not remain unnoticed by the information receivers. It would be a big mistake if attention were only paid to how information gets through, on the assumption that the available information will automatically and inevitably influence Chinese in the desired way.

There is no doubt that because of the Internet and the availability of other media, many Chinese are able to access an unprecedented amount of information today compared to a century ago. Yet this new development may not necessarily make the Internet a more effective means than the telegraph of making politics public. At least, this has not so far been the case. I argue that, though technologies provide opportunities for the making of a public sphere in China, this sphere's actual realization depends more on human actions and strategies by both the state and societal players. Misuse and abuse of technology on both sides could impede the emergence of an embryonic public sphere that otherwise holds great promise for the future.

It is thus important to keep in mind that the ideal public sphere described by Habermas does not exist in China. What I call a public e-sphere is still in the process of being created, and, when realized, it may bear unique Chinese characteristics and differ from other public spheres. Both the state and the societal players on the Internet are exploring various ways to push the newly opened public space in the direction they want it to go. The ideal scenario for the formation of a public e-sphere is no government control, free participation by self-disciplined discussants, and the formation of sites with well-established authority and credibility. Under the current political situation however, this scenario is far from the present realities of China, and it may never exist.

The influx of Western ideas, the rise of nationalism, and the adherence of the Chinese elite to constitutionalism in the last years of the late Qing era were results of complex interactions between domestic and international politics. Public telegrams met the needs of a dramatically changing society because the receiving context was extremely receptive to telegraphic texts. That historical context is gone and cannot be revived, however, and only political fortune-tellers can claim that the Internet will function to promote democracy the way public telegrams served to promote constitutionalism. The Internet will certainly continue to be used by Chinese to expand the space for political participation, but what kind of politics will be their central focus in the coming years, whether it is liberal democracy, nationalism, or something else, only history will be able to tell.

Notes

Notes

Introduction

1. China Internet Network Information Center (CNNIC), Semiannual Survey Report on the Development of China's Internet (1997–2004), www.cnnic.net.cn/en/index/oO/o2/index.htm (accessed March 15, 2005).

2. For example, a listserv (an automated email discussion list) for scholars interested in studying the Internet in China (chineseinternetresearch@yahoogroups.com) was set up in November 2000. It had nearly 200 subscribers in May 2004. Personal communication from Randy Kluver, May 24, 2004.

3. See www.cnn.com/2000/ASIANOW/east/10/02/china.Internet.reut/index.html (accessed Oct. 12, 2000); www.newsmax.com/showinside.shtml?a=2002/11/30/120649 (accessed Dec. 18, 2002).

4. See Nina Hachigian, "The Internet and Power in One-Party East Asian States," *Washington Quarterly* 25, 3 (Summer 2002): 41–58; Shanthi Kalathil and Taylor C. Boas, *Open Networks, Closed Regimes: The Impact of the Internet on Authoritarian Rule* (Washington, D.C.: Carnegie Endowment for International Peace, 2003).

5. Michael Adas, *Machines as the Measure of Men: Science, Technology, and Ideologies of Western Dominance* (Ithaca, N.Y.: Cornell University Press, 1989).

6. James W. Carey, *Communication as Culture: Essays on Media and Society* (New York: Routledge, 1992), esp. chap. 8, "Telegraphy and Ideology: The Case of the Telegraph," 201–30.

7. For details, see Zhou Yongming, *Anti-Drug Crusades in Twentieth-Century China: Nationalism, History, and State Building* (Lanham, Md.: Rowman & Littlefield, 1999), esp. chaps. 3 and 4.

8. Shi Tianjian, *Political Participation in Beijing* (Cambridge, Mass.: Harvard University Press, 1997), 5.

9. Mary B. Rankin, *Elite Activism and Political Transformation in China: Zhejiang Province, 1865–1911* (Stanford: Stanford University Press, 1986). Mayfair Mei-hui Yang, "Between State and Society: The Construction of Corporate-

ness in a Chinese Factory," *Australian Journal of Chinese Affairs* 22 (July 1989): 31–60.

10. See, e.g., Guobin Yang, "The Co-Evolution of the Internet and Civil Society in China," *Asian Survey* 43 (2003): 405–22.

11. In fact, anthropologist Katherine Verdery has noticed the complexity of civil society issues even within the European context. She points out that the talk of "civil society" in post-socialist states, such as Romania, has encountered numerous "situational constraints." Civil society "must mean first of all something national . . . only secondarily can it mean the forms and practices of a pluralist politics." See *What Was Socialism, and What Comes Next?* (Princeton, N.J.: Princeton University Press, 1996), 129. Verdery's observation is very pertinent to the phenomena that the enlargement of political participation in China often coincides with the rise of nationalism, as we shall see in the following chapters.

12. Benedict Anderson, *Imagined Communities: Reflections on the Origin and Spread of Nationalism*, rev. ed. (New York: Verso, 1991).

13. Jürgen Habermas, "The Public Sphere," in *Rethinking Popular Culture: Contemporary Perspectives in Cultural Studies*, ed. Chandra Mukerji and Michael Schudson (Berkeley: University of California Press, 1991), 398.

14. The issue of comparability between telegraphy and the Internet is often raised by those who view my study as merely comparative, based on the argument that the Internet is more widely accessible by the public than the telegraph was in the late Qing era. Even though my study is intended to be historical, I do not, however, regard a comparative study of the two technologies as impossible. At the time this study was conceived in 1997, fewer than a million Chinese could access the Internet, and getting online was very expensive, as indeed telegraph services were in the late Qing. We have to keep in mind that even with nearly 80 million Internet users by the end of 2003, that number still represents only 6 percent of the whole Chinese population.

15. For a detailed and insightful reflection on how to conduct ethnographic study online, see Nicole Constable, *Romance on a Global Stage: Pen Pals, Virtual Ethnography, and "Mail Order" Marriages* (Berkeley: University of California Press, 2003), 31–62.

16. Raymond Williams, *Keywords: A Vocabulary of Culture and Society* (New York: Oxford University Press, 1985), 75.

17. Clifford Geertz, *The Interpretation of Cultures* (New York: Basic Books, 1973), 453, quoted in *Doing Internet Research: Critical Issues and Methods for Examining the Net*, ed. Steve Jones (Thousand Oaks, Calif.: SAGE Publications, 1999), 17.

18. Lori Kendall, "Recontextualizing 'Cyberspace': Methodological Considerations for On-Line Research," in *Doing Internet Research: Critical Issues and Methods for Examining the Net*, ed. Steve Jones (Thousand Oaks, Calif.: SAGE Publications, 1999), 57.

1. Telegraphy, Culture, and Policymaking

1. Li Hongzhang to the Zongli Yamen, July 24, 1865. In Institute of Modern History, Academia Sinica, ed., *Haifang Dang* (Taipei: Institute of Modern His-

tory, Academia Sinica, 1957), 4, pt. 1: 17–20. Similar incidents had happened in Fuzhou a year before and would occur again in the 1870s. For a detailed account, see Erik Baark, *Lightning Wires: The Telegraph and China's Technological Modernization, 1860–1890* (Westport, Conn.: Greenwood Press, 1997), 74–77.

2. Brian Winston, *Media Technology and Society: A History: From the Telegraph to the Internet* (New York: Routledge, 1998), 19–29.

3. Jin Shixuan and Xu Wenshu, *Zhongguo Tielu Fazhan Shi, 1876–1949* (History of Chinese Railway Development) (Beijing: Zhongguo tiedao chubanshe, 1986), 7.

4. Robert Luther Thompson, *Wiring a Continent: The History of the Telegraph Industry in the United States, 1832–1866* (New York: Arno Press, 1972), 241–42.

5. Laszlo Solymar, *Getting the Message: A History of Communications* (New York: Oxford University Press. 1999), 48.

6. Ibid., fig. 4.6 (a) and (b), 59.

7. Huang Jiamo, "Zhongguo dianxian de chuangjian" (The Establishment of Telegraphy in China), *Dalu Zazhi* (Mainland Magazine) 36, nos. 6–7 (1968): 171.

8. *Haifang Dang*, 4, pt. 1: 1.

9. Ibid., 49.

10. For details of the provincial officials' responses, see ibid., 5–16. For Li Hongzhang's response, see ibid., 8–9.

11. Ibid., 82.

12. Baark, *Lightning Wires,* 58–59.

13. Huang, "Zhongguo dianxian de chuangjian," 174. The following description on the Fuzhou-Xiamen line is mostly based on Huang's article. For a more detailed description, see Baark, *Lightning Wires,* 107–56.

14. Richard G. Fox, *Lions of the Panjab: Culture in the Making* (Berkeley: University of California Press, 1985), 188 and 197. For his detailed critique of the culture concept in American anthropology, see chaps. 10 and 11, 185–211.

15. For details, see Xia Dongyuan, *Yangwu yundong shi* (History of the Western Affairs Movement) (Shanghai: Huadong shifan daxue chubanshe, 1992), 67–145; 299–303.

16. Baark, *Lightning Wires,* 71.

17. Yen-p'ing Hao and Erh-min Wang, "Changing Chinese Views of Western Relations, 1840–95," in *The Cambridge History of China,* vol. 11, pt 2, ed John K. Fairbank and Kwang-Ching Liu, 190–91 (Cambridge: Cambridge University Press, 1980). Their reading of *liquan* focuses on Chinese concern about foreign economic encroachment.

18. Li Hongzhang to Zongli Yamen, Mar. 14, 1865, *Haifang Dang*, 4, pt. 1: 8–9.

19. *Haifang Dang*, 4, pt. 1: 48.

20. Shen Baozhen to the Zongli Yamen, Mar. 29, 1865, *Haifang Dang*, 4, pt. 1: 10.

21. *Haifang Dang*, 4, pt. 1: 95.

22. Huang, "Zhongguo dianxian de chuangjian," 172; 180.

23. Xia, *Yangwu yundong shi,* 182.

24. Ibid., 182–83.

25. Ibid., 183.

26. *Haifang Dang,* 4, pt. 1: 263.

27. Youdianshi Bianjishi, *Zhongguo jindai youdian shi* (History of the Post and Telecommunications in Modern China) (Beijing: Renmin youdian chubanshe, 1984), 65.

28. Based on ibid. and Baark, *Lightning Wire.*

29. Youdianshi Bianjishi, *Zhongguo jindai youdian shi,* 67–68.

30. Ibid., 58.

31. Xia, *Yangwu yundong shi,* 232–33; Youdianshi Bianjishi, *Zhongguo jindai youdian shi,* 58–59.

32. Youdianshi Bianjishi, *Zhongguo jindai youdian shi,* 65–67.

33. Xia, *Yangwu yundong shi,* 182.

34. There was a historical precedent. In 1863, the Qing court actually decided to build a modern navy to help fight the Taiping Uprising. Compared to other major "Western Affairs" initiatives, this was an early and ambitious step. The plan was eventually abandoned, however, because the Qing court could not accept the conditions that the fleet would not be under total Chinese control, as proposed by Horatio Nelson Lay and Captain Sherard Osborn. This episode shows that the Qing court did not want to compromise on the issue of control, even at the expense of delaying the modernization of China's navy. For details, see Xia, *Yangwu yundong shi,* 299–303; Kwang-Ching Liu, "The Ch'ing Restoration," in *The Cambridge History of China,* 10, pt. 1, ed. John K. Fairbank, 429–31 (Cambridge: Cambridge University Press, 1978).

2. Telegraphy, Newspapers, and Public Opinion

1. *Haifang Dang,* vol. 4, pt. 1: 10.

2. Fang Hanqi, *Zhongguo jindai baokan shi* (History of Newspapers and Periodicals in Modern China) (Taiyuan: Shanxi jiaoyu chubanshe, 1981), 18.

3. Ibid., 10.

4. Chen Gaowen, a Chinese historian of journalism, put the number at 100 or 200 in his study of early newspapers in Shanghai. See *Shanghai xinwen shi, 1850–1949* (History of Shanghai Journalism, 1850–1949), ed. Ma Guangren, 10, 14 (Shanghai: Fudan daxue chubanshe, 1996).

5. Ibid., 40.

6. Ibid., 32–42.

7. *Shanghai Xinbao,* July 31, 1869.

8. *Shanghai Xinbao,* Aug. 3, 1869.

9. *Shanghai Xinbao,* Oct. 5, 1869.

10. *Shanghai Xinbao,* Oct. 9, 1869. The original date on the newspaper was Oct. 7, obviously mistaken.

11. *Shanghai Xinbao,* Nov. 6, 1869.

12. *Shanghai Xinbao,* May 2, 1871. The list of market information did not last long, for unknown reasons.

13. *Shanghai Xinbao,* Aug. 10, 1870.

14. *Shanghai Xinbao*, Jan. 12, 1871.

15. For details, see Guan Shishen and Ding Junhui, *Zhongguo xinwen shihua* (History of Chinese Journalism) (Shenyang: Liaoning daxue chubanshe,1987), 1–8; Fang, *Zhongguo jindai baokan shi*, 1–3.

16. Fang, *Zhongguo jindai baokan shi*, 3–4.

17. Youdianshi Bianjishi, *Zhongguo jindai youdian shi*, 62–63.

18. Xia, *Yangwu yundong shi*, 35.

19. Youdianshi Bianjishi, *Zhongguo jindai youdian shi*, 70.

20. Ma, *Shanghai xinwen shi*, 86.

21. Ibid., 25, 27.

22. Fang, *Zhongguo jindai baokan shi*, 52.

23. For an example, see *Shen Bao*'s reports on Li Hongzhang on July 30 and Aug. 4, 1883.

24. Fang, *Zhongguo jindai baokan shi*, 52.

25. Song Jun, *Shenbao de xingshuai* (*Shenbao*'s Ups and Downs) (Shanghai: Shanghai shehui kexue chubanshe, 1996), 40.

26. *Shen Bao*, Feb. 6, 1884.

27. Fang, *Zhongguo jindai baokan shi*, 52.

28. Youdianshi Bianjishi, *Zhongguo jindai youdian shi*, 64.

29. Fang, *Zhongguo jindai baokan shi*, 52–53.

30. For a detailed discussion, see John R. Zaller, *The Nature and Origins of Mass Opinion* (Cambridge: Cambridge University Press, 1992).

31. Commentaries and reports on this issue ran for several years. For details, see *Shen Bao* issues for May 22, 23, 25, 1872; Feb. 4, 7, 8, 10, 12, Mar. 3, 6, 20, 1873; July 1, 4, Nov. 9, 12, 30, 1874; Mar. 4, 5, June 30, 1875; June 16, 1877; Mar. 17, June 19, 1881; and Apr. 19, 1883.

32. Song, *Shenbao de xingshuai*, 31–32; Ma, *Shanghai xinwen shi*, 65.

33. Ma, *Shanghai xinwen shi*, 65–66; 74–79.

34. Song, *Shenbao de xingshuai*, 25–30. The story has attracted the attention of Chinese ever since the late Qing, and films and dramas based on it appeared in the ensuing years.

35. Based on statistics in Song, *Shenbao de xingshuai*, 29.

36. *Shen Bao*, Oct. 29, 1874.

37. *Shen Bao*, Jan. 17, 1876.

38. Another example was that in 1882, *Shen Bao* featured an editorial criticizing the handling of the civil service exams in Jiangsu by the supervising official. The enraged official put a public notice on its office door side, prohibiting people from reading the newspaper. *Shen Bao* not only did not back down but also further angered the official by printing his notice in the newspaper and continuing to criticize him. *Shen Bao* was accused of fabricating facts and misleading public opinion, and the dispute was made known to the Qing court with a petition to shut it down by a member of the Censorate (Ducha Yuan). The emperor instructed Zuo Zongtang, then governor-general of Liangjiang, to deal with the delicate issue in order to "eradicate the bad habits [of the newspaper] for ever." Zuo obviously did not subsequently take any action against this British-owned newspaper. *Shen Bao* not only printed edicts and memorials on the issue but also

abridged the content of *Jing Bao* related to the dispute. Ma, *Shanghai xinwen shi,* 86 and 102–3n32.

39. Even though imperial edicts were also conveyed by telegrams and published by newspapers, the definition used in the discussion here excludes most of them, except when the edict was aimed at an audience larger than the group of concerned officials.

40. *Shen Bao,* May 25, 1895.

41. *Shen Bao,* June 3, 1895.

42. Ma, *Shanghai xinwen shi,* 96.

43. Fang, *Zhongguo jindai baokan shi,* 83.

44. Ibid., 86–87; Ma, *Shanghai xinwen shi,* 128.

45. Ma, *Shanghai xinwen shi,* 185.

3. Telegraphy, Political Participation, and State Control

1. Jing Yuanshan, *Ju yi chu ji* (Macao, 1901), 1: 1.

2. Ibid., 2: 47–48.

3. This event is called Jihai jianchu in Chinese. It has been pointed out that Empress Cixi became more hostile to foreigners because of their alleged interference in her attempt to replace Emperor Guangxu, a factor that contributed to her decision to use the Boxers to expel all foreigners. It also helps explain why Zaiqi, father of Fujun, was the most outspoken promoter of the Boxers in the Manchu ruling elite, because he felt the foreigners had prevented him from becoming the father of China's next emperor.

4. Fang, *Zhongguo jindai baokan shi,* 185–86.

5. Jing, *Ju yi chu ji,* 2: 31.

6. Ibid., 1: 41–44.

7. See ibid., 49–54. Zhong's ten propositions were: (1) setting up the fund-raising organization; (2) letting local gentry be in charge of fund-raising; (3) selecting able generals; (4) raising military funds; (5) recruiting an army; (6) building warships; (7) making machinery and ammunition; (8) conducting relief for war victims; (9) hiring the talented; and (10) allowing public discussions on policy issues.

8. Ibid., 55.

9. Ibid., 2: 29–36.

10. See ibid., 24–27. Among newspapers subscribed to by the clubs were the *Wanguo Gongbao* (International Gazette), *Rongxue Bao* (Agricultural Science), *Dongya Shibao* (East Asian Times), *Xinwen Bao,* and *Zhongwai Ribao;* the noticeable exception was *Shen Bao,* which under the editorship of Huang Xiexun at the time was very conservative.

11. Jing Yuanshan's contacts with Kang started in 1895 when he was asked by Zhang Zhidong to support Kang's effort to organize the "Qiangxue Hui" and served as a director on the board of the organization. But he resigned shortly afterward because of a "slight opinion difference" with Kang (ibid., 2: 64) From his correspondence with Kang, he was critical of Kang's "lack of experience," "eagerness for fame," and "lack of modesty, forgiveness, and prudence" (ibid., 4–5). Jing thought China was like a person too sick to undergo major operations such

as the reforms proposed by Kang; he preferred the more gradual approach of pre-scribing mild medicine to help to restore China's physical condition first, such as through his own establishment of the women's school and managing a modern business (ibid., 65).

12. Ibid., 2: 17, 64–65.

13. Ibid., 41.

14. In 1890, Zhang Zhidong invited Jing Yuanshan to Hubei to help estab-lish a textile administration. Jing thought this was an ideal opportunity to get back *liquan* from foreign textile companies and wrote a detailed business plan to Zhang, but he declined further involvement after finding out that Zhang was in-terested only in protecting the *li* of Hubei and that he was seeking talent based on official rank. What frightened Jing most was that "the bureaucratic atmosphere in Hubei is even denser than in Shanghai, [and this] is the most ominous obstacle to business" (ibid., 39–40).

15. Jing Yuanshan supported Zhong's allowing public discussion of national policies and commented that the fundamental purpose of advocating public in-volvement in the fund-raising was to enhance people's consciousness of civil rights. Only after this consciousness was deeply rooted in people's minds would it be time for China to set up a parliament. Jing thought establishing a parliament would facilitate exchanges of ideas between the emperor and his people and en-able wider participation in making vital national policies (ibid., 1: 53–55).

16. The full text was published in *Thien Nan Shin Pao*, Feb. 10, 1900.

17. *Penang Sin Poe*, Feb. 19, 1900; *Thien Nan Shin Pao*, Feb. 13 and Mar. 5, 1900.

18. *Penang Sin Poe*, Feb. 19, 1900.

19. *Thien Nan Shin Pao*, Feb. 9 and Mar. 8, 1900.

20. *Thien Nan Shin Pao*, Mar. 5 and 10, 1900. For the telegraph from Burma, see *Thien Nan Shin Pao*, Mar. 8 and Apr. 23, 1900.

21. *Penang Sin Poe*, Oct. 10, 1899. Liang Qichao pointed out the danger of dethronement in *Qingyi Bao* from the very beginning of its publication.

22. *Penang Sin Poe*, Oct. 10, 1899.

23. *Thien Nan Shin Pao*, Nov. 15, 1899. The full text and the names of the first twenty-five signatories were printed in the newspaper the next day.

24. *Thien Nan Shin Pao*, Dec. 6, 1899.

25. *Qingyi Bao*, no. 90 (Aug. 15, 1901): 13–14.

26. These figures included Ye Han and Wang Kangnian (*Zhongwai Ribao*), Zhang Tongdian, Zhang Binlin, and Tang Caichang (*Yadong Shibao*), Wang Yin-ian, Ma Yuzhao, Shen Shisun, and Shen Zhaowei (*Wuzhou Shishi Huibao*), and Wang Jilie and Chen Fan (*Su Bao*). See Ma, *Shanghai xinwen shi*, 188–95, 206.

27. When Wu Woyao, the editor of *Caifeng Bao*, received news that Empress Cixi had put off the dethronement for the time being, he not only wrote an arti-cle to celebrate the good news but also solicited essays in honor of Guangxu's birthday. See Ma, *Shanghai xinwen shi*, 206.

28. See reports in *Shen Bao*, Feb. 4 and Mar. 8, 1900.

29. *Qingyi Bao*, no. 36 (Feb. 20, 1900): 9–14.

30. Ma, *Shanghai xinwen shi*, 184–85, 194–95.

31. Youdianshi Bianjishi, *Zhongguo jindai youdian shi*, 68–69.
32. Ibid., 64.
33. *Shanghai Xinbao*, Apr. 22 and May 23, 1871.
34. *Shen Bao*, July 19, 1896.
35. *Thien Nan Shin Pao*, Mar. 8, 1900.
36. *Thien Nan Shin Pao*, Feb. 10 and 13, 1900.
37. There was an illustrative case. In 1911, Zhao Erfeng was appointed governor-general of Sichuan. Faced with a provincewide upheaval against the nationalization of the Sichuan-Hankou railroad, he wanted to discuss the worsening situation with Duanfang, the imperial commissioner of railroad construction, by telegraph. Since he had no secret code book on hand, his subordinate, Financial Commissioner Yingliang, presented his personal "family secret codes" for him to use. Later, when the relationship between Zhao and Duanfang became strained, Zhao suspected that Yingliang had played a role. He then ordered the provincial telegraph administration to hand over copies of telegrams sent to Duanfang by Yingliang. Using Yingliang's "family secret codes" to read these telegraph texts, Zhao found out that his suspicions were well founded. See Zhou Shanpei, *Xinhai sichuan zheng lu qinli ji* (A Personal Account of the Sichuan Railway Rights Movement in 1911) (Chongqing: Chongqing renmin chubanshe, 1957), 49–50.
38. In 1894, prices were changed to a new scale, in which users were charged five cents a character for telegrams sent to receivers in the same prefecture, ten cents for those sent within the same province, with an additional two cents added for every province they had to traverse. See Wang Kaijie, Xiu Yu, and Qian Qizong, eds., *Jindai tielu, dianxin qishiwu zhounian jinian kan* (Volume in Memory of the Seventy-fifth Anniversary of the Railway and Telecommunications), in Zhongguo shiliao congshu xuji, ed. Shen Yunlong, 924: 31.
39. Jing, *Ju yi chu ji*, 2: 47–50.
40. Paul Cohen, *History in Three Keys: The Boxers as Event, Experience, and Myth* (New York: Columbia University Press, 1997), 48–50.
41. These three memorials are reprinted in Sheng Xuanhuai, *Yu zai chun gao*, vol. 20, in Jindai zhongguo shiliao congshu xuji [series], ed. Shen Yunlong, 122: 558–60.
42. Ibid., vol. 35, in Jindai Zhongguo shiliao congshu xuji, 123: 834.
43. The five provinces were Jiangsu, Anhui, Jiangxi, Hunan, and Hubei. Because the telegraph lines connecting Beijing to the outside world had been cut, the memorial was telegraphed to Blagoveshchensk in Russia, and then forwarded to the Lieutenant-General's Office in Shanhaiguan. To guarantee that the memorial reached the court, the office was asked to make two copies of the memorial and send one copy to the Zongli Yamen and one to Ronglu, grand councilor and a confidant of Empress Cixi. Ibid., vol. 36, in Jindai zhongguo shiliao congshu xuji, 123: 842–43.
44. Ibid., 843–45.
45. See Sheng's telegraph to Liu Kunyi on June 20, 1900, and Liu's reply on the same day. Ibid., vol. 35, in Jindai zhongguo shiliao congshu xuji, 123: 837.
46. Ibid., vol. 36, in Jindai zhongguo shiliao congshu xuji, 123: 844–45.

47. Ibid., 845.
48. Ibid., biography, in Jindai zhongguo shiliao congshu xuji, 122: 24.
49. Ibid., vol. 36, in Jindai zhongguo shiliao congshu xuji, 123: 844–45.
50. Ibid., 848.
51. Ibid., 851, 853.
52. Ibid., 869–70.
53. Ibid., vol. 8, in Jindai zhongguo shiliao congshu xuji, 122: 247–48, and
vol. 12, in ibid., 325–26.

4. Public Telegrams and Nationalist Mobilizations

1. At the time, some of cities had not established chambers of commerce. The
telegram actually prompted the subsequent establishment of the Suzhou Chamber of Commerce.

2. *Shen Bao*, May 11, 1905; Xu Dingxin and Qian Xiaoming, *Shanghai
zongshanghui shi, 1902–1929* (History of Shanghai General Chamber of Commerce) (Shanghai: Shanghai shehui kexueyuan chubanshe, 1991), 71.

3. Delber L. McKee, *Chinese Exclusion versus the Open Door Policy,
1900–1906: Clashes over China Policy in the Roosevelt Era* (Detroit: Wayne
State University Press, 1977), 245n14.

4. *Shen Bao*, May 28, 1905.

5. McKee, *Chinese Exclusion*, 105.

6. Ibid., 21–22.

7. Ibid., 23.

8. Ibid., 25, 28–36.

9. Ibid., 82.

10. Ibid., 102.

11. *Shanghai Xinbao*, July 12, 1872.

12. *Shen Bao*, July 23, 1872, and June 24, 1873.

13. "On American Mistreatment of Chinese," Jan. 25; "U.S. Government
Shall Protect Chinese," Mar. 16; "Reflections on the Denial of Entrance of Chinese Merchants," Apr. 20; "On the Different Ways of Receiving Diplomats between China and the United States," May 7; and "On the Mistreatments of Chinese by France and United States," June 1.

14. *Shen Bao*, May 11, 16, and 18, 1886.

15. *Shen Bao*, Apr. 20, 1886, and June 24, 1898.

16. The fact that ordinary readers disliked *Shen Bao* was reflected in the decline in its circulation, and, as we have seen, the newspaper reading club sponsored by Jing Yuanshan did not subscribe to it. Furthermore, other newspapers in
Shanghai attacked Huang's position. In 1900, *Tongwen Hubao* issued a public
notice in ten consecutive daily issues accusing Huang of accepting a 300 yuan
bribe from conservative officials to take a pro-Cixi stance. In 1901, several
Shanghai newspapers attacked Huang and *Shen Bao* for making wrong claims
about the geography of Russia. See Ma, *Shanghai xinwen shi*, 209–12; Song,
Shenbao de xingshuai, 68.

17. An open-minded editor, Jin Jianhua, was selected as the new editor-in-
chief, and in 1906 a couple of intellectuals were appointed as editors, one of

whom was Liu Shipei, a famous scholar and a member of Guangfu Hui, an anti-Manchu revolutionary organization. See Song, *Shenbao de xingshuai*, 68; Ma, *Shanghai xinwen shi*, 261–62.

18. *Shen Bao*, Feb. 7, 1905.

19. *Shen Bao*, Feb. 8, 1905.

20. *Shen Bao*, May 5, 1905.

21. *Shen Bao*, May 10, 1905.

22. *Shen Bao*, May 13, 1905.

23. *Shen Bao*, May 16, 1905.

24. See *Shen Bao*, May 16, 26, 23, 19, and 24, 1905, respectively.

25. McKee, *Chinese Exclusion*, 108.

26. *Shen Bao*, May 22, 1905.

27. *Shen Bao*'s reports on responses to the boycott from various places were all placed in the second edition, with the exception of those on Suzhou, which were placed in the third and fourth editions on June 4, 1905. The remaining reports were: Wuhu (June 5); Changsha (June 6); Xiamen (June 20); Hangzhou (June 24); Tianjin (June 25); Zhenjiang (June 28); Yingkou (June 28); Shantou (June 29); Nanchang (July 1); Wuyang (July 1); Shashi (July 3); Yangzhou (July 3); Shaoxing (July 8); Beijing (July 9); Jiaxing (July 9); Ningbo (July 13); Nagasaki (June 6); Yokohama (June 6); Honolulu (June 17); Penang (July 1); Singapore (June 23); students in the United States (June 5).

28. Among twenty-one board members of SGCC, seventeen were from Zhejiang and Jiangsu, with eleven of them from the Ningbo area. Xu and Qian, *Shanghai zongshanghui shi*, 88–89.

29. *Shen Bao*, Aug. 11, 1905.

30. Xu and Qian, *Shanghai zongshanghui shi*, 70–71.

31. See *Shen Bao*, July 15, 17, 27, and 31 and Aug. 3, 1905. These compilations of telegrams and letters all appeared in the second edition.

32. *Shen Bao*, July 6 and 7, 1905.

33. For a detailed report on the meeting, see *Shen Bao*, July 21, 1905.

34. In the same meeting, a representative of the cigarette guild claimed that British-American Tobacco Company was now owned solely by the British and thus should be exempted from the boycott. Another attendee pulled out a pack of Pin Heads cigarettes and rebutted his claim on the spot. A further speaker who talked about the difficulty of boycotting American goods fared much worse, and was booed off the platform. See *Shen Bao*, July 21, 1905.

35. *Shen Bao*, Aug. 7, 1905.

36. *Shen Bao*, Aug. 11, 1905.

37. McKee, *Chinese Exclusion*, 128–31, 162.

38. Xu and Qian, *Shanghai zongshanghui shi*, 81.

39. According to official figures, U.S. exports to China stood at $57 million in 1905, declining to $44 million in 1906 and to $26 million in 1907, but these figures are subject to different interpretations. See McKee, *Chinese Exclusion*, 152–53.

40. Yang Yonggang, *Zhongguo jindai tielu shi* (Railway History in Modern China) (Shanghai: Shanghai shudian chubanshe, 1997), 5, 14–24.

41. Lee En-Han, *China's Quest for Railway Autonomy, 1904–1911* (Singapore: Singapore University Press, 1977), 13, table 1 note.

42. Yang, *Zhongguo jindai tielu shi,* 27–28.

43. Lee, *China's Quest for Railway Autonomy,* 14–16; Jin and Xu, *Zhongguo tielu fazhan shi,* 155–56. The other four lines that the British acquired construction rights for were Tianjin-Zhenjiang (where they were later joined by the Germans); Guangzhou-Jiulong; Pukou-Xinyang; and Zezhou-Xiangyang.

44. Yang, *Zhongguo jindai tielu shi,* 57–58.

45. Lee, *China's Quest for Railway Autonomy,* 192.

46. Jin and Xu, *Zhongguo tielu fazhan shi,* 235–36.

47. The Chinese presented a number of reasons to "legalize" the abrogation of the preliminary contract. Their key argument was that seven years had passed but the British had neither conducted a serious survey as stipulated in the contract nor asked the Chinese to sign a formal agreement on the line. An often-cited reason was that in 1903, Sheng Xuanhuai sent a notice to Byron Brenan, the British consul-general in Shanghai, who was also acting as agent of the British and Chinese Corporation, stating that unless the British carried out surveys, prepared, estimated, and concluded a final agreement within six months from the date of the letter, the preliminary contract for the Suzhou-Hangzhou-Ningbo line would be cancelled. Since by 1905 another two years had passed and nothing had been done by the British, the preliminary contract was null and void. The Chinese were unaware, however, that Sheng had not explicitly acknowledged in public that his 1903 request had been bluntly rejected by the British corporation. Sheng was ambiguous regarding this key point in his memorials to the throne and correspondence with other concerned parties. On December 11, 1907, an imperial decree ordered him to clarify whether or not the annulment of the preliminary agreement had been tacitly consented to by the British, as he claimed. See Lee, *China's Quest for Railway Autonomy,* 191–95; Sheng, *Yu zai chun gao,* vol. 14, in Jindai zhongguo shiliao congshu xuji, 122: 356; *Jiangzhe tielu fengchao* (Railway Upheavals in Jiangsu and Zhejiang), ed. Mo Bei, vol. 1 (Dec. 1907); vol. 2 (Jan. 1908), published in Shanghai, in *Zhonghua minguo shiliao congbian,* no. A17, ed. Luo Jialun (Taipei: Zhongguo Guomindang zhongyang weiyuanhui dangshi shiliao bianzuan weiyuanhui, 1968) 1: 7–8.

48. The success in reclaiming rights for the Guangzhou-Hankou line signaled the start of the Railway-Rights Recovery Movement in China from 1904 to 1911. After Americans won the concession for the Guangzhou-Hankou line, the China Development Company experienced difficulty in raising the promised amount of capital after the death of Calvin Brice, a former senator and the company's main power broker, at the end of 1898. The Belgians, followed by the French and Russians, bought two-thirds of its shares and obtained six positions on the seven-member board. This was a violation of article 17 of the contract, which clearly stipulated that the Americans could not transfer the rights outlined in these agreements to other nations or people of other nationalities. Thus, commencing in 1903, the Chinese elites in Hunan, Hubei, and Guangdong provinces appealed to the Qing to take back the construction rights for the Guangzhou-Hankou railway. The Qing court was propelled by the strong pressure from provincial elites

to negotiate a redemption deal with the Americans. The whole issue was finally settled in 1905 after China paid $6,750,000 as a "compensation fee" to buy out the contract. For a detailed account, see Lee, *China's Quest for Railway Autonomy*, 50–84.

49. Lee, *China's Quest for Railway Autonomy*, 201–3.

50. For details, see Mo, *Jiangzhe tielu fengchao*. On threats to Wang Daxie, see 1: 98–99.

51. Mo, *Jiangzhe tielu fengchao*, 1: 139.

52. *Shen Bao*, Nov. 14, 1907.

53. Ma Min and Zhu Ying, *Chuantong yu jindai de erchong bianzou: Wan Qing Suzhou shanghui gean yanjiu* (A Duet of Tradition and Modernity: A Case Study of the Suzhou Chamber of Commerce in the Late Qing) (Chengdu: Bashu shushe, 1993), 330.

54. Mo, *Jiangzhe tielu fengchao*, 2: 242.

55. The protest lingered on, however, and in the following years, the Ministry of Posts and Communications defaulted on paying the loan to the local companies. See Lee, *China's Quest for Railway Autonomy*, 210.

56. Mo, *Jiangzhe tielu fengchao*, 1: 114.

57. Ibid., 78.

58. Ibid., 74.

59. Ibid., 61.

60. Ibid., 60–61.

61. Ibid., 47.

62. Ibid., 54.

63. Ibid., 25.

64. Mo, *Jiangzhe tielu fengchao*, 2: 239–49.

65. *Shen Bao*, Nov. 14, 1907; also see Mo, *Jiangzhe tielu fengchao*, 2: 264–65.

66. Xu and Qian, *Shanghai zongshanghui shi*, 73.

67. *Shen Bao*, Nov. 14, 1907.

68. These two volumes were published in December 1907 and January 1908 respectively. The volumes also contained two other sections covering telegrams sent by railway companies and the general public opposing the loans, collectively occupying about half of each volume.

5. Telegraph Power: Textual and Historical Contexts

1. Luo Guanzhong, *Three Kingdoms: A Historical Novel*, trans. Moss Roberts (Berkeley: University of California Press; Beijing: Foreign Languages Press, 1991), 174–75.

2. Ibid., 171–75.

3. A variation of the *xiwen* that served as a secret military order will not be treated here, since our focus is on the genre's political function.

4. For example, the "Tao Wu Zhao Xi" (Denunciation of Wu Zhao), another famous Chinese *xiwen*, was written by Luo Binwang, a well-known poet, to denounce the usurpation of the empress Wu Zetian in the Tang dynasty.

5. Ma, *Shanghai xinwen shi*, 7.

6. For example, in the course of the emotion-charged movement resisting rail-

way loans, a short telegram was sent to Wang Daxie, the vice foreign minister who had negotiated the loan agreement, in the name of "Hangzhou gentry," reading: "Hangzhou is in an uproar. It is rumored that your ancestral tombs will be dug up. You should think of a way to avoid this" (Mo, *Jiangzhe tielu fengchao,* 1: 70). With its general collective signature and extremist content, a public telegram of this kind would certainly lack credibility in the eyes of the public.

7. Mo, *Jiangzhe tielu fengchao,*1: 90.

8. A term used by Silas H. L. Wu. *Communication and Imperial Control in China: Evolution of the Palace Memorial System, 1693–1735* (Cambridge, Mass.: Harvard University Press, 1970), 1.

9. The whole process faced many bureaucratic hurdles. After a memorial (or *tiben*) from a provincial official was carried into Beijing by imperial couriers, it was submitted to the Transmission Office, which would examine its content and form. The memorial would then be transferred to the Grand Secretariat for the drafting of rescripts by junior officials. Once the draft was approved by the grand secretaries, a formal draft would be written in both Manchu and Chinese and presented to the emperor for final approval. If the memorial was approved by the emperor, it would be returned to the Grand Secretariat, and draft rescripts would then be written in both Chinese and Manchu on top of and at the end of the memorial text; at the same time, the imperial endorsement was recorded. After that an appropriate board (or several boards together) responsible for executing the imperial rescripts would receive a copy. The imperial decision would be sent back to the provincial memorial presenter by post courier and the memorial would be published by *Jing Bao* and distributed to other provincial authorities. In addition, the board concerned would also send an official communication to the provincial authorities. With this last communication, the whole process was finally complete. See Wu, *Communication and Imperial Control,* 27–33.

10. The rest of the memorials were given to a small group of entrusted officials (usually grand councilors after Yongzheng's reign), who, following imperial instructions, either issued court letters and sent them back to the original senders, or issued edicts publicly through the traditional channel of the Grand Secretariat. See Wu, *Communication and Imperial Control,* 80–84, 104–5.

11. *Shen Bao,* July 19, 1905.

12. Shang Bing, *Qing mo xin zhishijie de shetuan yu huodong* (New Intellectual Organizations and Activities at the End of the Qing) (Beijing: Shenghuo, dushu, xinzhi sanlian shudian, 1995), 288.

13. Ibid., 274–76.

14. Ibid., 275. Among the 271 organizations, there were 21 educational associations, 34 anti-foot-binding societies, 25 public speech associations, 17 physical education associations, 26 student associations, 17 patriotic organizations, 18 science research associations, 16 arts and literature organizations, 16 women's organizations, 17 industry organizations, 8 health and customs reform organizations, 5 teacher training associations, and one religious organization. The rest were comprehensive organizations, touching all aspects of society. See ibid., 276, 281–84.

15. An exception was that the court prohibited the organizations of intellec-

tuals and scholars, but the court had difficulties enforcing this article in the last days of the Qing dynasty. See ibid., 288–89.

16. Ibid., 274.

17. Take the Suzhou General Chamber of Commerce as an example. The presidents and vice presidents of the Suzhou Chamber before 1912 all had high-ranking official titles, either through having passed the civil service exams or through having donated money. These titles helped them to elevate their status from merchants to social dignitaries, thus enhancing their influence in the local area. In addition, they were among the richest inhabitants of the area, involved in various businesses and also serving as landlords. See Ma and Zhu, *Chuantong yu jindai,* 59, table 1; 48–50; 25–26, table 3.

18. Theoretically, these branches were not subordinate to the general chamber and could operate independently, following government regulations aimed at preventing the general chamber from becoming the leader in business circles. In reality, however, the local branches often worked closely with the general chamber and were willing to follow the initiatives and leadership of the former, especially on issues that went beyond local concerns.

19. Ma and Zhu, *Chuantong yu jindai,* 118.

20. Another railway company that did not receive government subsidies was the Guangdong Railway Company. See Lee, *China's Quest for Railway Autonomy,* 93.

21. Tang Shouqian, the director-general of the Zhejiang Railway Company, was the former salt commissioner of Lianghuai and an active advocate of constitutionalism. Wang Qingmu, Tang's counterpart at the Jiangsu Railway Company, had been a junior vice minister at the Ministry of Commerce. His deputy, Zhang Qian, was an even more influential figure. After Zhang won the highest honor in the metropolitan civil service examination (*zhuangyuan*) in 1895, he became one of the most successful industrialists of the time.

22. The telegrams sent by the overseas Society for Protecting the Emperor were exceptions, but these organizations were viewed as anti-government and forbidden in China. Their telegrams were subject to censorship by the Imperial Telegraph Administration, and except in newspapers controlled by or sympathetic to reform advocates, it was difficult for them to be reprinted within China, thus limiting their influence.

23. For a detailed list, see Hsu, *Rise of Modern China,* 410–11.

24. Hou Yijie, *Ershi shiji chu zhongguo zhengzhi gaige fengchao: Qing mo li xian yundong shi* (A Political Reform Tempest in Early Twentieth-Century China: History of the Constitutionism Movement in the Late Qing) (Beijing: Renmin chubanshe, 1993), 27–29.

25. For a detailed description, see Ma, *Shanghai xinwen shi,* 230–38.

26. Liang Jinghe, *Qing mo guomin yishi yu canzheng yishi yanjiu* (A Study of the Consciousness of Chinese Nationals and Their Consciousness in Political Participation toward the End of the Qing) (Changsha: Hunan jiaoyu chubanshe, 1999), 1.

27. Wang Lixin, *Meiguo duihua zhengce yu zhongguo minzu zhuyi yundong, 1904–1928* (American China Policy and the Chinese Nationalist Movement,

1904–1928) (Beijing: Zhongguo shehui kexue chubanshe, 2000), 17; Lee, *China's Quest for Railway Autonomy*, 2.

28. The rest of the list included freedom, equality, independence, self-esteem, self-confidence, self-discipline, martial spirit, adventurousness, fraternity, collectivism, public morality, and nation-belonging. For a detailed description on the origin of *guomin* ideas and their subsequent elaboration at the turn of the twentieth century, see Liang, *Qing mo guomin yishi*, 9–38.

29. See Mo, *Jiangzhe tielu fengchao*, 1: 69–70, 74, 41, 60.

30. A full share of Zhejiang company was 100 yuan and a divided share was 10 yuan. A Jiangsu company share cost 5 yuan, see Mo, *Jiangzhe tielu fengchao* 1: 151.

31. Ma and Zhu, *Chuantong yu jindai*, 323–24.

32. National sovereignty and national interest would remain two key concepts in nationalistic discourse in modern Chinese history. While the former enjoyed continued popularity after 1949, the latter disappeared from official discourse in the People's Republic for about three decades because of its ostensible conflict with the communist doctrine of proletarian internationalism. However, the term has returned with a vengeance since the 1980s, and once again has become one of the key words of contemporary nationalist discourse in China, as we shall see in detail in Chapter 9. On the idea of *shangzhan*, see Wang Ermin, "Shangzhan guannian yu zhongshang sixiang" (The Idea of Commercial Warfare and the Importance Attached to Commerce), *Zhongyang yanjiuyuan jindaishi yanjiusuo jikan* 5 (1966): 1–91.

33. *Shen Bao*, June 4, July 30, and Aug. 6, 1905.

34. The assassination threat was made in a "notice to Wang Daxie." The call to dig up Wang's ancestral tomb was rejected by all the directors of the Zhejiang Railway Company and dismissed in the inaugural meeting of the Zhejiang People's Society for Resisting Railway Loans; see Mo, *Jiangzhe tielu fengchao*, 1: 98–99, 115.

35. Ibid., 121.

36. Wei Qingyuan, Gao Fang, and Liu Wenyuan, *Qing mo xianzheng shi* (History of Constitutionism in the Late Qing) (Beijing: Zhongguo renmin daxue chubanshe, 1993), 15. The idea of a Western-style parliament had caught Chinese attention in the 1840s, and a parliament had been proposed by Western Affairs Movement officials in the 1860s, but the idea of drafting a constitution came much later. See ibid., 71–76.

37. Ibid., 97–103.

38. Ibid., 147–48.

39. Nonetheless, there was another approach to building a modern Chinese nation-state, and this was to establish a republic through an anti-Manchu revolution. When discussing national political debates, one cannot avoid ongoing arguments between constitutionalists and revolutionaries in the last ten years of the Qing dynasty. While this debate has been the focus of much work on the historiography of the Chinese revolution, it is not the focus of our discussion here. There are two reasons. First, as explained in the introduction, *Shen Bao*, regardless of its political inclination, was never a "party newspaper" controlled by ei-

ther reformers or revolutionaries. It was always a mainstream newspaper, with profit as its aim. Secondly, because most of the revolutionaries were outlaws, with the exception of self-published revolutionary newspapers, the telegrams they sent would not be printed by mainstream newspapers, thus making them less visible on the public political scene.

40. *Shen Bao*, Sept. 10 and 17, 1909.

41. Hou, *Ershi shiji chu zhongguo*, 118–19.

42. Wei, Gao, and Liu, *Qing mo xianzheng shi*, 191; Hou, *Ershi shiji chu zhongguo*, 123–59.

43. Hou, *Ershi shiji chu zhongguo*, 131–33.

44. Wei, Gao, and Liu, *Qing mo xianzheng shi*, 212.

45. Liang, *Qing mo guomin yishi*, 209–10.

46. Hou, *Ershi shiji chu zhongguo*, 190–98.

47. *Shen Bao*, Aug. 29, 1908.

48. *Shen Bao*, Aug. 14, 1908.

49. Hou, *Ershi shiji chu zhongguo*, 283.

50. Wei, Gao, and Liu, *Qing mo xianzheng shi*, 293–94.

51. For example, of the 127 elected members in Sichuan, 9 were extremely wealthy, 27 had official titles, 55 had passed county exams (*xiucai*), 31 had passed provincial exams (*juren*), and 2 had passed metropolitan exams (*jingshi*). Most numbered among or had connections with the constitutionalists. Only 4 belonged to the revolutionary organization Tongmeng Hui. See ibid., 295.

52. Hou, *Ershi shiji chu zhongguo*, 292–93.

53. Ibid., 275.

54. Ibid., 308–10.

55. *Shen Bao*, Apr. 19, 1910.

56. Wei, Gao, and Liu, *Qing mo xianzheng shi*, 330–31.

57. *Shen Bao*, Nov. 10, 1910.

58. *Shen Bao*, Mar. 28, 1911.

6. China and the Internet

1. See www.nielsen-netratings.com/pr/pr_020422_eratings.pdf (accessed May 2, 2002).

2. *People's Daily*, Apr. 25, 2002.

3. Zhonghua renmin gongheguo youdianbu zhengce yanjiushi, ed., *Youdian fagui huibian, diyi ji* (Compilation of Laws and Regulations of Posts and Telecommunications, Volume One) (Beijing: Renmin youdian chubanshe, 1988), 452.

4. Ibid., 453.

5. Ibid., 589.

6. *People's Daily*, Jan. 9, 12, and 13, 1967.

7. *People's Daily*, Jan. 22, 1967.

8. The so-called democratic parties originated prior to the establishment of the PRC and are allowed to exist by the CCP in contemporary China, with only nominal political functions.

9. *People's Daily*, May 19, 1989.

10. *People's Daily*, May 22 and 23, 1989.

11. *People's Daily*, May 25, 1989.

12. *People's Daily*, June 7, 8, 9, 10, 11, 12 and 13, 1989.

13. Wang Shangyan. "Hulianwang zai zhongguo" (The Internet in China), *Qiye gaige yu guanli* (Enterprise Reform and Management), Feb. (1998): 31.

14. Chen Yan, *Internet gaibian zhongguo* (The Internet Changes China) (Beijing: Beijing daxue chubanshe, 1999), 30, 55.

15. Ibid., 89–114, 180; Wang, "Hulianwang zai zhongguo," 31; Qian Hualin, "Zhongguo kejiwang de fazhan" (The Development of CSTNet), *Xiandai tushu qingbao jishu* (Modern Library Information Technology) 3 (1997): 3–6. CNNIC: Zhongguo hulianwang fazhan dashi ji (Major Events of Chinese Internet Development), www.cnnic.org.cn/html/Dir/2003/09/22/0358.htm (accessed April 29, 2005).

16. Chen, *Internet gaibian zhongguo*, 94.

17. Zhou Baoxin, "Zhongguo hulianwang de xianzhuang yu weilai" (Chinese Internet: Current Conditions and Future Development), *Guangbo dianshi wangluo jishu* (Technologies of Broadcasting, Television and Networking) 8 (2001): 16.

18. Chen, *Internet gaibian zhongguo*, 80.

19. Ibid., 91.

20. Zhou, "Zhongguo hulianwang de xianzhuang," 18.

21. Talk given Apr. 20, 2003.

22. Chen, *Internet gaibian zhongguo*, 343.

23. See www.cnnic.net.cn/develst/report.shtml (accessed July 29, 2003).

24. See www.people.com.cn/GB/shehui/47/20020616/753947.html (accessed July 19, 2002).

25. Hannah Beech, "China Unplugged," July 9, 2002, www.time.com/time/asia/magazine/article/0,13673,501020715–300685,00.html (accessed July 15, 2002).

26. Ibid.

27. The real name of the "Ocean" café has been altered to protect the owner's identity. In the rest of this book, when the real names of informants or interviewees are used, it is with their consent.

28. During my fieldwork, the café was once raided by the Bureau of Industry and Commerce, on the grounds that it did not have the appropriate permit. Sixty computers in the café were taken away and the business was shut down. But to my amusement, only one week later, the owner got the computers back and resumed the business. I was told that he managed this by first finding connections to get in touch with top officials of the bureau, whom he then treated to an elaborate banquet in a local fancy restaurant. In addition, he also presented "gifts" to key figures, who finally consented to return his computers and let him resume business as usual. I was surprised to hear that the "Ocean" owner knew that the bureau had been tipped off by another Internet café owner to take action against him, out of envy that the "Ocean" was doing quite well at the time. Sure that his jealous business rival was not fully licensed either, several weeks later, my informant had the rival's café raided by the Public Security Bureau on the grounds that

it did not have a fire safety permit. Obviously pleased, the owner told me that he expected his rival would get back into business shortly just as he had, because "everybody has some connections and ultimately the money can buy you a way out, and we are kind of used to this kind of raid coming periodically."

29. http://groups.yahoo.com/group/chineseinternetresearch. The message was posted on the listserv on November 12, 2001.

30. It seems that the situation of illegal Internet café operation has not improved after periodic "rectification campaigns." A report about the situation in Guangzhou at the end of 2003 was illustrative. Out of 600 Internet cafés in the city, only 83 were fully licensed. http://news.sina.com.cn/c/2003-11-13/1243 1112767s.shtml (accessed Jan. 8, 2004).

31. See www.cnnic.org.cn/policy/5.shtml (accessed Aug. 16, 2003)..

32. The first regulation issued in February 1996 can be found at www.mii. gov.cn/mii/zcfg/xzfg/law20101.htm (accessed April 12, 2005); the remainder can be found at www.cnnic.org.cn/index/oF/index.htm (accessed April 27, 2005).

33. Julie Moffett, "China: Government Makes Vain Attempts to Control Internet," www.rferl.org/nca/features/1998/01/F.RU.980106133925.html (accessed April 2, 2001).

34. Ethan Gutmann, "Who Lost China's Internet?" *Weekly Standard,* Feb. 25, 2002, www.weeklystandard.com/Utilities/printer_preview.asp?idArticle=922 (accessed Feb 8, 2003).

35. The reality is more complicated than the author had hoped. Perhaps the ultimate demonstration of U.S. commitment to its belief that the Internet will change China is the announcement in August 2001 that the International Broadcasting Bureau, the parent agency of the Voice of America, will actively fund Websafe, a U.S.-based secure proxy company, to establish a network of dedicated proxy servers to help Chinese gain access to politically sensitive information. As the *New York Times* commented, this is a "significant expansion of the long-running information war" between the the United States and China. (Jennifer Lee, "U.S. May Help Chinese Evade Net Censorship," Aug. 30, 2001). In the meantime, SafeWeb had also received contracts from the venture capital arm of the CIA, In-Q-Tel to develop "Internet privacy technology" (www.safewebinc.com/pr_inqtel.html, accessed July 12, 2003). On November 20, 2001, Reuters reported that the week before, SafeWeb had "quietly shut down its service which allowed people to surf the Web anonymously for free, and is unlikely to restart it. . . . The service, which had allowed users to be practically invisible on the Internet, was the second of its kind to close in as many months" ("SafeWeb Shuts Free Anonymous Web Service," www.techtv.com/news/Internet/story/0%2C24195%2C3361 767%2C00.html, accessed June 12, 2003). Besides financial concerns, there appears to be a shifting mood in the United States that favors national security over protection of privacy. As lamented by the Electronic Frontier Foundation (EFF), a San Francisco-based organization aimed at "defending freedom in the digital world," the concern of "national security" has taken a toll on freedom of expression. The EFF puts out a list that includes web sites shut down by both the U.S. government and other governments, as well as a list of media professionals

terminated or suspended after September 11, 2001. For details, see "Chilling Effects of Anti-Terrorism," www.eff.org/Censorship/ Terrorism_militias/antiterrorism_chill.html (accessed Sept. 12, 2003).

36. Overseas Chinese dissidents were among the first to use the Internet to promote their political views, but that is beyond the scope of this book. See "Lin Hai dianyou dianfu an panjue shu" (Sentence of Lin Hai's Subversive E-mail Case) www.democracy.org.hk/chinese/moon_new/99/jan/29_1_99b.htm (accessed June 23, 2003).

37. See www.dfn.org/focus/china/netattack.htm (accessed Sept. 1, 2003).

38. For details, see Junhua Zhang, "A Critical Review of the Development of Chinese e-Government," *Perspectives*, 3, no, 7 (2002), www.oycf.org/Perspectives/19_123102/eGovernment.htm (accessed Oct.10, 2003).

39. Xie Haiguang, *Hulianwang yu sixiang zhengzhi gongzuo anli* (Cases of the Internet and Political Thought Work) (Shanghai: Fudan daxue chubanshe, 2002).

40. Min Dahong, "On Electronic Forums by Chief Editors of People's Daily Online and Zaobao Online," www.peopledaily.com.cn/wsrmlt/1stannual/mtp1/2.html (accessed Jan. 6, 2003).

41. Ibid.

42. See www.people.com.CN/GB/it/306/2209/3057/20021231/8999352.html (accessed Jan. 27, 2003).

43. Min Dahong, "On Electronic Forums by Chief Editors of People's Daily Online and Zaobao Online," www.peopledaily.com.cn/wsrmlt/1stannual/mtp1/2.html (accessed Jan. 6, 2003).

44. http://bbs.people.com.cn/gltl.htm (accessed Nov.13, 2001).

45. See www.chinese-military.com/cgi-bin/mychinacounter.p1?number=2420 (accessed Oct. 8, 2001).

46. See www.chinese-military.com/cgi-bin/mychinacounter.p1?number=2421 (accessed Oct 8, 2001).

47. Statistical data collected in fieldwork.

48. See www.people.com.cn/GB/guoji/22/86/20030129/916576.htm (accessed Feb. 4, 2003).

49. People's Daily Online often adopts and reprints such kinds of reports from other sources. A good example is the continuing attraction of any reported extramarital affairs involving Bill Clinton. The latest one appeared on June 25, 2003. See www.people.com.cn/GB/yule/1082/1933927.html (accessed June 28, 2003).

50. See www.peopledaily.com.cn/wsrmlt/1stannual/mtpl/1.html (accessed July 12, 2000).

51. Du Ping, "Zhongguo de 'wangshang tequ' " http://www.qglt.com/wsrmlt/1stannual/mtpl/8.html (accessed May 30, 2003).

52. The message boards have rules of discussion that put much more emphasis on copyrights and other legal issues. Nonetheless, as the regulations stipulate, "washingtonpost.com may monitor the discussion forums as it chooses and reserves the right to remove, edit or otherwise alter content that it deems inappro-

priate for any reason whatever without consent. We further reserve the right, in our sole discretion, to remove a user's privilege to post content in our discussion forums" (www.washingtonpost.com/wp-srv/liveonline/delphi/delphirules.htm, accessed May 4, 2002). Washingtonpost.com message boards often invite special guests to talk on specific topics online. For example, on July 3, 2003, Interior Secretary Gale Norton was invited to go online to talk about the current state of the National Park Service and take questions. When the transcript was put online, there was an "Editor's Note" reading: "Washingtonpost.com moderators retain editorial control over Live Online discussions and choose the most relevant questions for guests and hosts; guests and hosts can decline to answer questions (www.washingtonpost.com/wp-dyn/articles/a570-2003Jul2.html, accessed July 4, 2003). Inviting "special guests" to go on SCF has become an important part of forum operation. Finally, in terms of initiating talk topics, Washingtonpost.com is even less flexible than the SCF. While participants can basically talk on whatever topic they like in SCF, at washingtonpost.com, it is the privilege of the webmaster to initiate a discussion topic and others can only follow the lead. For example, at 11:56 P.M., the webmaster, Lindsay Howerton (could be a collective online persona), sent a message to "ALL" that included: "President Bush yesterday delivered a colloquial taunt to militants who have been attacking U.S. troops in Iraq, saying 'bring 'em on' and asserting that the forces in Iraq are 'plenty tough' to deal with the threat." Then the webmaster put the topic title "Bush Utters Taunt About Militants: 'Bring 'Em On'" followed by "Your comments?" Underneath is the "REMINDER" in black capital letters and the hypertext link to the washingtonpost.com rules of discussion, http://forums.washingtopnpost.com/wpforums/messages/?msg=765 (accessed July 4, 2003).

53. See www.people.com.cn/GB/it/306/2209/3057/20021231/899352.html (accessed Jan. 11, 2003).

7. Negotiating Power Online

1. To be more precise, the owner had only obtained the right to use this piece of land for seventy years, since China has not yet formally legalized the private ownership of land.

2. Zhongguo xinwen yanjiu zhongxin, "2002–2003 zhongguo baoye faxing xianzhuang yu qushi" (The Current Status and Future Trends of Newspaper Circulation in China, 2002–2003), www.cddc.net/shownews.asp?newsid=4813 (accessed Oct. 27, 2003).

3. Li Yonggang, "Wei wancheng de renwu: xie zai sixiang de jingjie guan zhan zhihou" (Unfinished Task: Reflections after the Closing Down of the Realm of Ideas). *Ershiyi Shiji* (Twenty-First Century) 2 (2001): 115–21. Also online at www.cuhk.edu.hk/ics/21c/issue/article/001217.htm (accessed May 13, 2002).

4. I interviewed Cui Weiping in summer 2001 at the Beijing Film Academy, where she holds a professorship.

5. In the 1990s, most of these old leftists were communist ideologues who had once held high-ranking positions in the propaganda department of the CCP's Central Committee. One of their spiritual leaders is Deng Liqun, who at one time was head of the department and a member of the Secretariat of the Politburo, the

policy-making organ of the party. Though Deng and his dwindling followers had become marginalized within the communist leadership by the late 1990s, they still had a certain degree of influence and resources at their disposal. The most ostensible symbol of this was that they were able to publish a number of leftist (or conservative) journals that continued to advocate their opinions. For whatever reasons, their activities were generally tolerated by Jiang Zemin until 2001. When these old leftists openly opposed Jiang's call to allow newly emergent capitalists to join the party in his speech commemorating the eightieth anniversary of the CCP, Jiang finally shut down *Pursuit of Truth (Zhenli de zhuiqiu)* and *Midstream (Zhongliu)*, the two most important journals of the group.

6. As pointed out by Zhu Xueqin, a major figure in the liberal camp, it is perhaps surprising that many members of the new leftist school are Chinese intellectuals who have returned from study abroad. See "Shijimo sixiang lunzhan: Xinzhuopai he zhiyou zhuyi zai zheng shenmo?" (Debates at the End of the Century: What Are the Differences between the New Leftists and the Liberals?), http://wyg.sunchina.net/sixiang/001107/39.htm (accessed Dec. 19, 2002). Obviously, the new leftist arguments have been influenced by critical theories of contemporary capitalism by Western Marxists and the world systems theory of Immanuel Wallerstein.

7. To the liberals, individual freedom is the paramount priority. They advocate revising the current Chinese Constitution to add articles protecting private property, believing this to be the basis for guaranteeing individual freedom in society. They want to limit government power so as to decrease its ability to interfere in individual life. While they believe in the self-rectifying power of a true market economy based on rule of law within a democratic political system, the new leftists are more skeptical of the Chinese liberals' embrace of the principles of neoliberalism, accusing them of decontextualizing these principles in a uniquely Chinese reality. The new leftists focus more on concrete social injustices and attribute their emergence to the ongoing process of marketization. They think that the liberals' appeal for individual freedom without acknowledging rampant social injustices is tantamount to their being apologists for vested interests. It is thus, they claim, necessary to advocate broader political participation by the masses to ensure that the government is committed to addressing social injustices, thus enabling more individuals to enjoy the benefits of economic development. For details of the arguments of each side, see Xu Youyu, "Zhiyou zhuyi yu dangdai zhongguo" (Liberalism and Contemporary China), http://wyg.sunchina. net/sixiang/000731/xyy.html (accessed Dec. 18, 2002); Han Yuhai, "Zai 'zhiyou zhuyi' zitai de beihou" (Behind the Gesture of 'Liberalism'), http://wyg.sunchina. net/sixiang/991114/9911142.htm (accessed Dec.20, 2002).

8. Best known is Li Ka-shing's donation of HK$60 million in 1998 to set up the Cheung Kong Young Scholars Program, which has created science research positions at major universities to attract promising researchers from both inside China and overseas.

9. David Harvey, *The Condition of Postmodernity: An Enquiry into the Origins of Cultural Change* (New York: Blackwell, 1989).

10. Wang Hui, "Dangdai zhongguo de sixiang zhuangkuang yu xiandaixing

wenti" (Current Chinese Thoughts and the Issue of Modernity), *Tianya* 5 (1997): 133–50.

11. Online at www.pen123.net.cn/readcontent.asp?WDLSH=44543, www. pen123.net.cn/readcontent.asp?WDLSH=4454, and www.pen123.net.cn/read-content.asp?WDLSH=4455 (accessed July 29, 2002).

12. *Southern Weekend*, a relatively new yet influential newspaper based in Guangdong province, was one of the earliest news outlets that published articles questioning the fairness of the awards.

13. The Cheung Kong–*Dushu* controversy was, in fact, the subject of the very first message posted in the newly opened Century Salon, at 18:25:50 on 2000–07–20, a re-posting by a netizen of a message written by the well-known Chinese writer Yu Hua titled "*Dushu* Is Truly Controversial," which defended Wang Hui's achievements both as a scholar and as editor of *Dushu*. Yu Hua accused Wang's opponents of being "media scholars" (*meiti xuezhe*) and concluded that "what the attackers of Wang Hui have done to *Dushu* this time has violated the rules of game. "Dushu Hai Zhenshi Shi Duo" http://forum.cc.org.cn/luntan/china/showcontent.php3?db=1&id=129&id1=93&mode=1 (accessed Nov. 22, 2001).

14. " 'Changjiang Dushu Jiang' Zhenglun De Yiyi," (The Significance of Debates on "Cheung Kong Dushu Awards"), http://forum.cc.org.cn/luntan/china/showcontent.php3?db=1&id=1296&id1=512&mode=1 (accessed Aug. 24, 2001).

15. For a detailed description of this controversy, see Geremie Barmé and Gloria Davis, "Have We Been Noticed Yet?—Intellectual Contestation and the Chinese Web," in *Chinese Intellectuals between State and Market,* ed. Edward Gu and Merle Goldman (London: RoutledgeCurzon, 2004), 75–108.

16. Jürgen Habermas, "The Public Sphere," in *Rethinking Popular Culture: Contemporary Perspectives in Cultural Studies,* ed. Chandra Mukerji and Michael Schudson (Berkeley: University of California Press, 1991), 398.

17. Li, "Wei wancheng de renwu." Though the Realm of Ideas site has ceased operation, the old web site has been preserved and can be accessed at http://www.boxun.com/sixiang/ (accessed April 28, 2005).

18. Fang became the deputy director of the Institute of Political Science of the Chinese Academy of Social Sciences shortly after I first interviewed him in July 2001.

19. Li was known for his co-authorship of the influential book *Behind the Demonization of China,* which criticized American media depictions of China in the 1990s. Han was known for his unusually sensational statements against China's accession to the World Trade Organization. In the liberal camp, Li and Han are generally viewed as second-tier opponents with less scholarly substance than Fang and Wang.

20. Song was one of the authors of *China Can Say No.*

21. As late as December 2002, if one conducted a key word search on the web site of the Strengthening-China Forum, one could still find more than 100 relevant entries on the book in the results list.

22. See www.pen123.com.cn/sb/index.html (accessed Mar. 25, 2004).

23. His claims can be easily confirmed by news clippings and pictures taken

with Chinese dignitaries such as Deng Pufang, the son of China's late paramount leader Deng Xiaoping and chairman of the Chinese Federation of Handicapped Persons.

24. Douglas Raybeck, "Getting below the Surface," in *The Naked Anthropologist: Tales from Around the World,* ed. Philip R. DeVita (Belmont, Calif.: Wadsworth, 1992), 3–16.

25. Because of the increasing popularity gained by the Formalization of Ideas site, for a period of time, clicking the URL www.pen123.net.cn would automatically lead one to the home page of Patrick Consulting Net (www.pen123.com.cn).

26. Unfortunately, Ma's initiative did not proceed according to his initial plan, and he left the Formalization of Ideas site in 2002 to become the webmaster of another intellectual web site, partly for financial reasons. The Formalization of Ideas site went defunct in 2003.

27. Editorial note by the webmaster on Mar. 16, 2001; see www.cc.org.cn/zhenggao/index.htm (accessed May 22, 2001).

28. Shuxie ershiyi shiji de shidai zhuti (Writing the Time Theme of the Twenty-First Century), *People's Daily,* overseas edition, Aug. 16, 2000 (www.people.com.cn/GB/paper39/1237/188562.html, accessed April 2, 2001).

29. There are, however, always dangers involved. A notable example is Frontier Forum (*Tianya Luntan*), another well-known intellectual web site, which was shut down by the authorities after it published articles that opposed the speech given by Jiang Zemin on the eightieth anniversary of the CCP on July 1, 2001, in which Jiang called for private entrepreneurs to be allowed to join the party.

30. "Ben banzhu diyihao gonggao" (No. 1 Public Notice by the Webmaster), http://forum.cc.org.cn/luntan/china/showcontent.php3?db=1&id=1935&id1=748&mode=1 (accessed Dec. 28, 2002).

31. Wang was once the chief of the Shanghai party propaganda department and is a liberal; Jin is vice president of CUHK; Wu is best known as an economic advisor to Chinese Premier Zhu Rongji (www.people.com.cn/GB/paper39/1237/188562.html, accessed Nov. 12, 2001).

32. This tolerance is further shown by the fact that Li Yonggang, the editor of the Realm of Ideas site, did not suffer direct disciplinary action from Nanjing University and was subsequently granted permission to go to the Chinese University of Hong Kong as a visiting scholar in early 2001.

33. For example, Mr. Qiufeng, a well known liberal figure online, set up a site called Liberalism Review online at about the same time that the Realm of Ideas was active. Not long after this, he was summoned for interrogation to the Public Security Bureau. The authorities' inquiries focused on finding out whether or not Qiufeng and his web site were connected with overseas organizations. After Qiufeng told them there was no relationship between him and overseas Chinese democracy advocates, the authorities let him go and have left the ultraliberal web site alone since then.

34. Mayfair Meihui Yang, "Mass Media and Transnational Subjectivity in Shanghai: Notes on (Re)Cosmopolitanism in a Chinese Metropolis," in *The Anthropology of Globalization: A Reader,* ed. Jonathan Xavier Inda and Renato Rosaldo, 333 (Malden, Mass.: Blackwell, 2002).

8. Living on the Cyber Border

1. "Lu Jiaping zhi zi Hu Dalin Hunan Shaoyang zhuo fang ji" (An Account of the Arrest and Release of Hu Dalin, Lu Jiaping's Son, in Shaoyan, Hunan Province), http://211.218.37.23/alljiapin/shiwu20020607.htm (accessed Mar. 14, 2005).

2. Erik Eckholm, "A Father's Cranky Essays on Web Site Put Son in Jail in China." *New York Times*, May 24, 2001.

3. "Zhongguo de zhanlue shiwu yu meiguo de gaoming jihua" (China's Strategic Mistakes and America's Superior Plan), http://211.218.37.23/alljiapin/shiwu/1-2.htm (accessed Mar. 15, 2005).

4. This information is formatted as an abbreviated resume, which includes his name, place of birth, age, veteran status, academic affiliation (he was a member of the Chinese Association for the Study of World War II History), publications, address, telephone number, email address, and personal web sites. It was through this information that I was able to contact him and arrange interviews.

5. "Gongchandang yidang zhizheng tizhi de youlai" (Origins of the Dictatorship of the Communist Party), http://www.usc.cuhk.edu.hk/wk_wzdetails.asp?id=327 (accessed Mar. 14, 2005).

6. "Fanfu, 'liusi' yu wenge" (Anti-Corruption, "June Fourth," and the Cultural Revolution), http://211.218.37.23/alljiapin/223.htm (accessed Mar. 13, 2005).

7. "Zhongmei zhuangji shijian—Shijie 'xinlengzhan' shiqi de shifa dian" (The Sino-American Plane Collision Incident—The Starting Point of a "New Cold War" in the World), http://www.confuse2000.com/confuse16/49.htm (accessed Aug. 11, 2005); "Zhongguo haiyao xiang hechu tui?" (Where Can China Retreat Further?), http://military.china.com/zh_cn/critical3/27/20010429/171868.html (accessed Aug. 11, 2005).

8. "Guanfang baozhi shang zhongyu you le butong de shengyin" (Finally There Are Different Voices in Official Newspapers), http://211.218.37.23/alljiapin/514.htm (accessed Mar. 20, 2005); "Wei guojia minzu shuo zhenhua shihua, women quanjia yao zaonan" (Our Family Have to Suffer Because I Speak the Truth for the Sake of Our Country and Nation), http://211.218.37.23/alljiapin/20010521.htm (accessed Mar. 22, 2005).

9. From the latest information, I would guess that Ji An most likely resides in Canada. Ji An's gender identity is only a supposition on my part. It is easy to have multiple identities in cyberspace, and one should not take Ji An's maleness for granted, even though Ji An claims to be a man in his writings. I refer Ji An as "he" here to respect the writer's own claims and also to avoid the awkwardness of continually using "he/she."

10. This is a modified version of "Yige zhongguo zhuyi zhe" (A Believer in Zhongguoism), an article Ji An wrote on February 13, 2000, which was first put online the next day at the Voice of Internet Friends (Wangyou zhisheng) forum of People's Daily Online, www.people.com.cn/item/wysy/2000/02/14/021418.html (accessed July 27, 2002). Ji An published a slightly different version in March 2002; see "Zhongguo zhuyi," www.network54.com/Hide/Forum/message?forumid=115965&messageid=993967967 (accessed Nov. 10, 2002).

11. Ji An evidently did not know that the term "Chinaism" had been used by others much earlier. A 1996 article by Xue-Qui Chiang, published on the web site of the *Yale Herald,* entitled "Why Would China Want Hong Kong?" asserts that China's efforts to "to earn superpower status through a Greater Chinaism" are the answer. See www.yaleherald.com/archive/xxii/9.27.96/opinion/hongkong. html (accessed Dec. 3, 2003). And the term "greater Chinaism" has also been used to refer to the notional economic and political dominance of a "greater China" (including the mainland, Taiwan, Hong Kong, and Macao) in Asia and even throughout the world.

12. "Ji An zhitan minzhu" (An Intellectual Discussion of Democracy by Ji An), www.network54.com/Hide/Forum/message?forumid=115965&messageid= 994392314 (accessed Nov. 29, 2002).

13. See www.network54.com/Hide/Forum/message?forumid=115965&messageid=994201765 (accessed Nov. 27, 2002).

14. See www.network54.com/Hide/Forum/message?forumid=115965&messageid=994578276 (accessed Nov. 26, 2002).

15. "Zhongguo de minzu zhuyi reihan dingyi" (The Content and Definition of Chinese Nationalism), www.network54.com/Hide/Forum/message?forumid= 115965&messageid=994251054 (accessed Nov. 30, 2002).

16. "Taiwan tongyi wenti tigang" (Outline of Taiwan Unification), www.network54.com/Hide/Forum/message?forumid=115965&messageid=995327010 (accessed Nov. 19, 2002).

17. "Ji An yuce Chen Shuibian shangtai hou taidu zai taiwan fazhan de daqushi," (A Prediction by Ji An on the Trend of Taiwan Independence after Chen Shui-bian Takes over Power), www.network54.com/Hide/Forum/ message?forumid=115965&messageid=995327100 (accessed Nov. 15, 2002).

18. I remember vividly spending a whole night in my office (owing to the time difference between the United States and China) following reactions to the Taiwan election on a couple of mainland BBS forums, especially the Strengthening-China Forum, and I encountered numerous similarly emotionally charged messages.

19. "Gongsu pantu maiguozei Wang Daohan gongsushu" (Bill of Indictment of Traitor Wang Daohan), www.network54.com/Hide/ Forum/message?forumid=115965&messageid=994251184 (accessed Nov. 19, 2002).

20. "Zhonghua renmin gongheguo tongyi xuangao" (Proclamation of Unification of the People's Republic of China), www.network54.com/Hide/Forum/ message?forumid=115965&messageid=993974283 (accessed Nov. 21, 2002).

21. "Guchui WTO de ren, zhengzai guyi huo yin youzhi fan xia de cuowu" (Those Advocating the WTO Are Intentionally or Naïvely Making a Mistake), www.network54.com/Hide/Forum/message?forumid=115965&messageid=994 251245 (accessed Dec. 3, 2002).

22. "Jiu WTO da 'Yexingzhe'" (A Reply to Yexingzhe Concerning the WTO), www.network54.com/Hide/Forum/message?forumid=115965&message id= 994470616 (accessed Nov. 27, 2002).

23. "Sanpei zhongli" ("Three Accompanying" Prime Minister), www.network54.com/Hide/Forum/message?forumid=115965&messageid=994659641.

The term *sanpei* (three-accompanying) refers to young females who implicitly agree to provide sexual services by accompanying guests in drinking, singing karaoke, and dancing at entertainment establishments. This began in the mid 1980s and became popular during Zhu's term in the late 1990s.

24. Anti estimated that the *Ershiyi shiji huanqiu baodao* had a circulation of 200,000 nationwide. The newspaper was shut down in March 2003.

25. "Wo xin jidujiao de xiangxi guocheng" (A Detailed History of How I Became a Christian), www.xici.net/board/doc.asp?id=2096933&sub=9&doc_old=1 (accessed Jan. 29, 2003).

26. One of the first things Anti did was to solicit articles jointly with the Realm of Ideas, which was also located in Nanjing and was at the peak of its popularity. However, only one month later, the Realm of Ideas site was forced to close down. Anti lamented that his friend Li Yonggang's web site was like "an early blossoming flower" that had withered. Anti praised Li for creating a space that let Chinese intellectuals breathe the fresh air of freedom of thought. Appealing to Li Yonggang's disappointed online followers to be patient and understanding, Anti believed that more mature platforms for the exchange of ideas would appear in mainland China, aided by collective effort and rich material and technical resources. "Guozao chuxian de huaduo biran bu shi pinghe de—Tan 'Sixiang de Jingjie' de guanbi" (An Early Blossoming Flower Is Not an Ordinary One—Reflecting on the Shutting Down of the Realm of Ideas), www.xici.net/board/doc.asp?id=2061906&sub=10&doc_old=1 (accessed Feb. 1, 2003).

27. See www.xici.net/board/doc.asp?id=5038188&sub=37&doc_old=1 (accessed Jan. 29, 2003).

28. "Yetan xinwen gongzhuozhe de zhiyehua" (On the Professionalizaton of Journalists), www.xici.net/board/doc.asp?id=8383426&sub=8&doc_old=1 (accessed Feb. 5, 2003).

29. "Xin xinwenren zixue shouce" (Self-Study Manual for the New Journalist), www.xici.net/main.asp?board=158363 (accessed Feb. 8, 2003).

30. Ibid.

31. "Chunxia zhijiao de meilijian dali: zhongmei zhuangji shijian zhong de yuyan, falu, zhengzhi wenti" (A Big American Gift at the Turn of Spring and Summer: Language, Legal and Political Issues in the Sino-American Plane Collision Incident), www.xici.net/board/doc.asp?id=4713446&sub=24&doc_old=1 (accessed Jan. 28, 2003).

32. Ibid.

33. "Qing gewei qiexi de zhongguo bailei shouqi nimen exin de zuilian" (To Those Who Feel Happy [about 9/11], Please Cover Up Your Disgusting Faces), www.xici.net/board/doc.asp?id=8413431&sub=16&doc_old=1 (accessed Feb. 1, 2003).

34. "Gao Ruisi quanti aiguo renshi shu" (A Letter to All Patriots in the Re-See Forum), www.xici.net/board/doc.asp?id=8465862&sub=50&doc_old=1 (accessed Feb. 2, 2003).

35. "Yanzhong jinggao Xici di shuiping de wangluo kuaizishou men" (A Stern Warning to Those Lowly Internet Butchers at the Xici), www.xici.net/board/doc.asp?id=9758651&sub=34&doc_old=1 (accessed Jan. 29, 2003).

36. "Wo shizhong baochi banfu xueliang—Ruisi gaiban shengming" (I Shall Always Hold My Shining Axe), www.xici.net/board/doc.asp?id=10008775& sub=48&doc_old=1 (accessed Feb. 3, 2003).

37. "Shenme shi Ruisi shantie de yuanze" (What Are the Principles of Deleting Postings by the Re-See Forum), www.xici.net/board/doc.asp?id=1572278& sub=18&doc_old=1 (accessed Feb. 6, 2003).

38. "Wangluo de xin huayu baquan" (The New Discourse Hegemony on the Internet), www.xici.net/board/doc.asp?id=21602597&sub=5&doc_old=0 (accessed Jan. 30, 2003).

39. "Dangdai dushi li de bianyuan zhishiren" (Marginalized Intellectuals in Contemporary Urban Centers), www.booker.com.cn/gb/paper18/35/class0018 00001/hwz187130.htm (accessed Mar. 3, 2003).

40. The URL of this webzine has changed several times. Unfortunately, by November 2002, the main web site, http://zhongguoism.home.chinaren.com/ was no longer functional, but online readers can still access many parts of *ZGZY* magazine at the URL www.network54.com/Hide/Forum/115965 (accessed May 2, 2005).

41. Lu Jiaping was also listed as a *ZGZY* editor, but he complained to me that Ji An had put his name on the list without his consent.

42. "Yetan 'minjian kexue aihaozhe'" (On "Amateur Scientists"), www.grass-land.com/cgi-bin/bbs.exe?id=qqc&msg=4883 (accessed Feb. 22, 2003).

43. "Wangluo yeyu sikaozhe de ganga" (The Predicament of Amateur Online Thinkers), www.xici.net/board/doc.asp?id=1508580&sub=26&doc_old=1 (accessed Mar. 3, 2003).

44. "Zhi Anti xiansheng lun wangluo wenhua jianshe" (A Letter to Anti on the Construction of Internet Culture), www.xici.net/board/doc.asp?id=1762685 &sub=2&doc_old=1 (accessed Feb 19, 2003).

45. See www.xici.net/board/doc.asp?id=4199445&sub=13&doc_old=1 (accessed Feb, 12, 2003).

46. See www.wangxiaobo.com/jinian/5th/1.htm (accessed April 27, 2003).

47. "Wo zai 'Shiji Luntan' de gongkai shengming" (My Public Statement at "Century Forum"), www.xici.net/board/doc.asp?id=11732553&sub=17&doc_old=1 (accessed Feb. 27, 2003).

48. See www.xici.net/board/doc.asp?id=2667293&sub=22&doc_old=1 (accessed Feb. 15, 2003).

49. Xiao, "Dangdai dushi li de bianyuan zhishiren" (Marginalized Intellectuals in Contemporary Urban Centers), www.booker.com.cn/gb/paper18/35/class 001800001/hwz187130.htm (accessed Mar. 3, 2003).

9. Informed Nationalism

1. Nicholas D. Kristof, "The Chip on China's Shoulder," *New York Times*, Jan. 18, 2002.

2. James Kynge, Edward Cheng, and Chris Bowie, "China Says Bugs Found on President's Plane." First published at FT.com, Jan. 18, 2002, 21: 41.

3. James Kynge, "Chinese Presidential Jet Bugged," *Financial Times*, Jan. 19, 2002; John Pomfret, "China Finds Bugs on Jet Equipped in U.S.," *Washington*

Post, Jan. 19, 2002. In addition, CNN.com posted the news as the default front page of its web site, and the television network ABC also did a report on the event. The plane-bugging incident was therefore covered by both traditional and new media.

4. CNN, "China Downplays Jiang's Jet Bugging," www.cnn.com/2002/WORLD/asiapcf/east/01/22/china.bugs/index.html (accessed Jan. 22, 2002).

5. The message was posted at 2002-01-20 13: 10: 43 (Beijing time). Since the SCF keeps an archive on its server, it is easier to find the old message by tracing back its original posting time, as long as the message is not deleted by the forum monitors.

6. Posted 2002-01-19 21: 30: 17 on SCF.

7. Posted 2002-01-19 21: 44: 51 and 2002-01-19 21: 35: 47 on SCF.

8. Posted 2002-01-20 11: 32: 44; 2002-01-19 21: 40: 33; 2002-01-19 21: 37: 49.

9. "Jiangzong zhuanji bei anfang qietingqi-geng xiangxi de shuofa," www.v-war.net/cgi-bin/bbs/bbs.cgi?menu=show&id=200109192313&slttitle=2002011 91. Posted 2002-01-19 15: 25: 47.

10. See www.v-war.net/cgi-bin/bbs/bbs.cgi?menu=show&id=200109192313 &slttitle=200201201, posted 2002-01-20 13: 22: 18.

11. "Kan CNN wulai jiaobian: it's common!!!" (Look at the Sophistry of the CNN: It Is Common), www.v-war.net/cgi-bin/bbs/bbs.cgi?menu= show&id= 200108092357&slttitle=200201201, posted 2002-01-20 18: 45: 15.

12. This was not the first time that strong anti-U.S. sentiment in Chinese cyberspace had been noticed by Western media, as shown by the title of a Cox News Service report by Christine Xiaoting Xu, "Chinese Chat Rooms Are Teeming with Anti-Yankee Venom," following the collision between a Chinese jet fighter and a U.S. reconnaissance plane off Hainan island on April 1, 2001. *Wisconsin State Journal,* Apr. 4, 2001.

13. See Edward Friedman, "Chinese Nationalism, Taiwan Autonomy and the Prospects of a Larger War," *Journal of Contemporary China* 6 (4) (2000): 5–32; Alan Liu, "A Convenient Crisis: Looking behind Beijing's Threats against Taiwan," *Issues & Studies,* Sept.–Oct. (2000), 83–121; Suisheng Zhao, "Chinese Nationalism and Its International Orientations," *Political Science Quarterly* 1 (2000): 1–33.

14. See Suisheng Zhao, "A State-Led Nationalism: The Patriotic Education Campaign in Post-Tiananmen China," *Communist and Post-Communist Studies* 31(1998): 287–302; Xuedong Zhang, "Intellectual Politics in Post-Tiananmen China," *Social Text* 16 (1998): 1–8.

15. See Yu Huang and Chin-Chuan Lee, "Peddling Party Ideology for a Profit: Media and the Rise of Chinese Nationalism in the 1990s." In *Political Communication in Greater China: The Construction and Reflections of Reality,* eds. Gary Rawnsley and Ming-yeh Rawnsley (London: RoutledgeCurzon, 2003), 41–61. Other works on contemporary Chinese nationalism include Suisheng Zhao, "Chinese Intellectuals' Quest for National Greatness and Nationalistic Writing in the 1990s," *China Quarterly* 152 (1997): 725–45, and Yongnian

Zheng, *Discovering Chinese Nationalism in China: Modernization, Identity and International Relations* (Cambridge: Cambridge University Press, 1999).

16. See Christopher R. Hughes, "Nationalism in Chinese Cyberspace," *Cambridge Review of International Affairs* 2 (2000): 195–209; Kim-An Lieberman, "Virtually Vietnamese: Nationalism on the Internet," in *AsianAmerican. Net: Ethnicity, Nationalism, and Cyberspace,* ed. Rachel C. Lee and Sau-ling Wong (New York: Routledge, 2003): 71–97; Ravi Sundaram, "Beyond the Nationalist Panopticon: The Experience of Cyberpublics in India," in *Electronic Media and Technoculture*, ed. John T. Caldwell (New Brunswick, N.J.: Rutgers University Press, 2000): 270–94.

17. Initially, these web sites did not attract too much attention from the authorities, until a posting revealing details concerning China's development of the J-10 new generation jet fighter was circulated on several military web sites in 1999, resulting in the arrest of a young engineer who had tried to show off to his peers in cyberspace. After the incident, popular military web sites started to feel pressure from the authorities and increased their self-censorship efforts accordingly. For details, see "Jianshi xiemi an zhen po ji" (How the Case of Leaking Secrets of J-10 Was Solved), http://chinaha.myrice.com/military/commentary/2001/019/comment–3810.htm (accessed Aug. 17, 2002).

18. Though it would be ideal to include other military web sites in my analysis here, it is simply beyond the scope of this chapter. Since many widely read online articles are often circulated on different military web sites, and a significant number of online postings at the V-War web site are "transferred" from other sites, the postings chosen from this web site are fairly representative of the general picture of Chinese military web sites today.

19. There is a shortcoming in this quantitative criteria system because some members constantly post large amounts of "garbage" messages just for the sake of accumulating enough postings to be promoted to higher ranks. It is usually the webmasters' job to discourage such behavior. If repeated warnings are not effective, the webmasters can decrease one's accumulated points for each "garbage" posting one has posted and eventually resort to the ultimate punishment of banishing the offender by blocking the individual's IP address and not allowing him or her to log onto the V-War site again.

20. See www.tiexue.net/bbs/dispbbs.asp?boardID=42&RootID=899390&ID=899390 and www.tiexue.net/bbs/dispbbs.asp?boardID=42&RootID=909862&ID=909862 (accessed Sept. 3, 2003).

21. In addition, since its inception at the end of 2000, V-War has made military fiction publication one of the focus points of the web site, devoting about two-thirds of the space on its home page to a column on "military literature" by early 2003. Online military fiction quickly came to enjoy a great degree of popularity in Chinese cyberspace. The large collection of Chinese online military fiction has certainly become an attractive feature of V-War to many Chinese military fans surfing the Internet. Unfortunately, it is beyond the scope of this chapter to discuss this new genre in detail.

22. See www.tiexue.net/bbs/dispbbs.asp?boardID=12&RootID=937749&ID=937749 (accessed Aug. 17, 2003).

23. See   www.tiexue.net/bbs/dispbbs.asp?boardID=12&RootID=775965& ID=775965 (accessed Aug 20, 2003).

24. See   www.tiexue.net/bbs/dispbbs.asp?boardID=12&RootID=576207& ID=576207 (accessed Sept. 9, 2003)

25. See   www.tiexue.net/bbs/dispbbs.asp?boardID=12&RootID=888203& ID=888203 (accessed Aug. 29, 2003).

26. See   www.tiexue.net/bbs/dispbbs.asp?boardID=20&RootID=542733& ID=542733 (accessed Sept. 11, 2003).

27. See   www.tiexue.net/bbs/dispbbs.asp?boardID=42&RootID=933542& ID=933542 (accessed Aug. 19, 2003).

28. Ray S. Cline, *World Power Trends and U.S. Foreign Policy for the 1980's* (Boulder, Colo.: Westview Press, 1980); and Joseph S. Nye, Jr., *Bound to Lead: The Changing Nature of American Power* (New York: Basic Books, 1990). Obviously, Joseph Nye's concepts of "soft power" and "hard power" influenced Huang's thinking.

29. Huang Shuofeng, *Zonghe guoli lun* (On Comprehensive National Power) (Beijing: Zhongguo shehui kexie chubanshe, 1992).

30. Huang Shuofeng, *Zonghe guoli xinlun* (New Reflections on Comprehensive National Power) (Beijing: Zhongguo shehui kexie chubanshe, 1999), 5.

31. The terms "yellow" and "blue" civilizations were popularized by the then influential television documentary *He Shang* (River Elegy).

32. See www.tiexue.net/bbs/dispbbs.asp?boardID=42&RootID=1019950& ID=1019950 (accessed July 30, 2003).

33. See www.tiexue.net/bbs/dispbbs.asp?boardID=12&RootID=1005331& ID=1005331 (accessed August 4, 2003).

34. Jie Chen, *Popular Political Support in Urban China* (Stanford: Stanford University Press; Washington, D.C.: Woodrow Wilson Center Press, 2004).

35. Interview with Li Shenzhi on August 20, 2001, by the author. Li mentioned the introduction of the concept of "national interest" in an article published under the pen name Zhizhi in *Wanxiang* (Panorama Monthly) the same year; see "Shiji zhijiao de zhanqian guhou (Reflections at the Turn of the Century), *Wanxiang* 6 (2001): 105–6. Li Shenzhi passed away in April 2003.

36. Deng Xiaoping, *Selective Works of Deng Xiaoping* (Beijing: Renmin chubanshe, 1993), 330.

37. See *Strategy and Management* 3 (2001), 53–60.

38. For a detailed discussion, see Yong Deng, "Chinese Conception of National Interests in International Relations," *China Quarterly* 154 (June 1998): 308–29.

39. See   www.tiexue.net/bbs/dispbbs.asp?boardID=12&RootID=831660& ID=831660 (accessed Aug. 11, 2003).

40. See   www.tiexue.net/bbs/dispbbs.asp?boardID=12&RootID=561028& ID=561028 (accessed Aug. 29, 2003).

41. See   www.tiexue.net/bbs/dispbbs.asp?boardID=12&RootID=538589& ID=538589 (accessed Sept. 1, 2003).

42. Interview with He Jiadong by the author, Aug. 19, 2001.

43. See   www.tiexue.net/bbs/dispbbs.asp?boardID=20&RootID=956344& ID=956344 (accessed Aug. 22, 2003).

44. See www.tiexue.net/bbs/ dispbbs.asp?boardID=12&RootID= 1010943& ID=1010943 (accessed Aug. 28, 2003).

45. See www.tiexue.net/bbs/dispbbs.asp?boardID=20&RootID=993081& ID=993081 (accessed August 20, 2003).

Conclusion

1. Chen, *Internet gaibian zhongguo*, 59–61.

2. It is estimated that the number should be much higher, because many organizations are either unregistered or not properly registered. See "Shi da yinsu zhengzai yingxiang zhongguo jin zhong qi de fazhan," *Liao Wang* (Outlook Weekly), posted on People Net on July 16, 2003, See www.people.com.cn/GB /jingji/1045/1970100.html (accessed Oct. 10, 2004).

3. See the previous notes on Kangaroo and South Sea Monk, www.chinese-military.com/cgi-bin/mychinacounter.pl?number=2421 and www.chinese-military.com/cgi-bin/mychinacounter.pl?number=2422 (accessed Oct. 8, 2001).

4. Wang Yi, "Zhishi fengzi de xingdong juezhi—2002 nian de wangluo gong-kaixin yu qianming lanchao" (The Choice Made by Intellectuals—Online Public Letters and Petition Waves in 2002), *Beijing zhichun* (Beijing Spring) 2 (2003): 22–26.

5. Ibid.

6. Relevant reports can be found at www.people.com.cn/GB/guandian/26/ 20030219/926391.html and www.people.com.cn/GB/junshi/62/20030303/ 935108.html (accessed Mar. 9, 2003).

7. For details, see Edward Cody "New Anti-Japanese Protests Erupt in China," http://www.washingtonpost.com/wp-dyn/articles/A58567-2005Apr16. html (accessed May 3, 2005); Richard McGregor, "China Web Opposition to Japan's UN Hopes Targets Beijing," http://news.ft.com/cms/s/2403c06a-a4a6-11d9-9778-00000e2511c8.html (accessed May 2, 2005); Jim Yardley, "A Hundred Cellphones Bloom, and Chinese Take to the Streets: E-mail and Text Messaging Served as Organizing Tools for Anti-Japanese Protests," http://www.nytimes.com/ 2005/04/25/international/asia/25china.html (accessed May 1, 2005).

8. Text messaging on the mobile phone played a major role in spreading early news of the planned anti-Japanese demonstrations, but it was also later used by the authorities to warn people to stay away from unauthorized demonstrations when the public security bureau ordered mobile phone service providers to send out notices this effect. See Jane Macartney, "Message to the Mob: China Texts Protest Ban" http://www.timesonline.co.uk/article/0,3-1594030,00.html (accessed May 4, 2005).

9. The state seems not to have been bothered very much by the open letter as a genre for making public appeals. In fact, People Net recently published an open letter online. Understandably, it did not address political reforms but rather complaints by a disgruntled customer appealing to Northwest Airlines to improve its lousy service on flights between China and the United States. This open letter would most likely be read by more people than most intellectual-signed open letters online. See "Renmin rexian: Meiguo xibei hangkong ruci duidai chengke" (People Net Hot Line: How Can American Northwest Airlines Treat Customers

in Such a Rude Way), posted on July 16, 2003, www.people.com.cn/GB/shehui/
1062/1969188.html (accessed July 17, 2003).

   10.   For a more detailed discussion, see *Reader-Response Criticism: From Formalism to Post-Structuralism,* ed. Jane P. Tompkins (Baltimore: Johns Hopkins
University Press, 1980).

   11.   Adas, *Machines as the Measure of Men.*

Bibliography

Adas, Michael. *Machines as the Measure of Men: Science, Technology, and Ideologies of Western Dominance.* Ithaca, N.Y.: Cornell University Press, 1989.

Anderson, Benedict. *Imagined Communities: Reflections on the Origin and Spread of Nationalism.* Rev. ed. New York: Verso, 1991.

Baark, Erik. *Lightning Wires: The Telegraph and China's Technological Modernization. 1860–1890.* Westport, Conn.: Greenwood Press, 1997.

Barmé, Geremie R., and Gloria Davis. "Have We Been Noticed Yet? Intellectual Contestation and the Chinese Web." In *Chinese Intellectuals between State and Market,* ed. Edward Gu and Merle Goldman, 75–108. London: RoutledgeCurzon, 2004.

Caldwell, John T., ed. *Electronic Media and Technoculture.* New Brunswick, N.J.: Rutgers University Press, 2000.

Carey, James W. *Communication as Culture: Essays on Media and Society.* New York: Routledge, 1992.

Chen, Jie. *Popular Political Support in Urban China.* Stanford: Stanford University Press; Washington, D.C.: Woodrow Wilson Center Press, 2004.

Chen Yan. *Internet gaibian zhongguo* (The Internet Changes China). Beijing: Beijing daxue chubanshe, 1999.

China Internet Network Information Center (CNNIC). Semiannual Survey Report on the Development of China's Internet (1997–2004), www.cnnic.net.cn/en/index/oO/o2/index.htm.

Cline, Ray S. *World Power Trends and U.S. Foreign Policy for the 1980's.* Boulder, Colo.: Westview Press, 1980.

Cohen, Paul A. *History in Three Keys: The Boxers as Event, Experience, and Myth.* New York: Columbia University Press, 1997.

Constable, Nicole. *Romance on a Global Stage: Pen Pals, Virtual Ethnography, and "Mail Order" Marriages.* Berkeley: University of California Press, 2003.

Deng Xiaoping. *Selective Works of Deng Xiaoping.* Beijing: Renmin chubanshe, 1993.

Deng, Yong. "Chinese Conception of National Interests in International Relations." *China Quarterly* 154 (June 1998): 308–29.

Eckholm, Erik. "A Father's Cranky Essays on Web Site Put Son in Jail in China." *New York Times*, May 24, 2001.

Fang Hanqi. *Zhongguo jindai baokan shi* (History of Newspapers and Periodicals in Modern China). Taiyuan: Shanxi jiaoyu chubanshe, 1981.

Fang Ning, Wang Xiaodong, and Song Qiang. *Quanqiuhua yinying xia de zhongguo zhi lu* (China's Pathway under the Shadow of Globalization). Beijing: Zhongguo shehui kexie chubanshe, 1999.

Fox, Richard G. *Lions of the Panjab: Culture in the Making*. Berkeley: University of California Press, 1985.

Friedman, Edward. "Chinese Nationalism, Taiwan Autonomy and the Prospects of a Larger War." *Journal of Contemporary China* 6 (4) (2000): 5–32.

Geertz, Clifford. *The Interpretation of Cultures*. New York: Basic Books, 1973.

Gu, Edward, and Merle Goldman, eds. *Chinese Intellectuals between State and Market*. London: RoutledgeCurzon, 2004.

Guan Shishen and Ding Junhui. *Zhongguo xinwen shihua* (History of Chinese Journalism). Shenyang: Liaoning daxue chubanshe, 1987.

Habermas, Jürgen. "The Public Sphere." In *Rethinking Popular Culture: Contemporary Perspectives in Cultural Studies*, ed. Chandra Mukerji and Michael Schudson, 398–404. Berkeley: University of California Press, 1991.

———. *The Structural Transformation of the Public Sphere: An Inquiry into a Category of Bourgeois Society*. Cambridge, Mass.: MIT Press, 1989.

Hachigian, Nina. "The Internet and Power in One-Party East Asian States." *Washington Quarterly* 25, 3 (Summer 2002): 41–58.

Han Yuhai. "Zai 'zhiyou zhuyi' zitai de beihou." (Behind the Gesture of 'Liberalism'). http://wyg.sunchina.net/sixiang/991114/9911142.htm.

Hao Yen-p'ing and Erh-min Wang. "Changing Chinese Views of Western Relations, 1840–95." In *The Cambridge History of China*, vol. 11: *Late Ch'ing, 1800–1911, Part 2*, ed. John K. Fairbank and Kwang-Ching Liu, 142–201. Cambridge: Cambridge University Press, 1980.

Harvey, David. *The Condition of Postmodernity: An Enquiry into the Origins of Cultural Change*. New York: Blackwell, 1989.

Hou Yijie. *Ershi shiji chu zhongguo zhengzhi gaige fengchao: Qing mo li xian yundong shi* (A Political Reform Tempest in Early Twentieth-Century China: History of the Constitutionism Movement in the Late Qing). Beijing: Renmin chubanshe, 1993.

Hsu, Immanuel C. Y. *The Rise of Modern China*. 6th ed. New York: Oxford University Press, 2000.

Huang Jiamo. "Zhongguo dianxian de chuangjian" (The Establishment of Telegraphy in China). *Dalu Zazhi* (Mainland Magazine) 36, Nos. 6–7 (1968): 171–87.

Huang Shuofeng. *Zonghe guoli xinlun* (New Reflections on Comprehensive National Power). Beijing: Zhongguo shehui kexie chubanshe, 1999.

———. *Zonghe guoli lun*. (On Comprehensive National Power). Beijing: Zhongguo shehui kexie chubanshe, 1992.

Huang, Yu and Chin-Chuan Lee. "Peddling Party Ideology for a Profit: Media and the Rise of Chinese Nationalism in the 1990s." In *Political Communication in Greater China: The Construction and Reflections of Reality,* ed. Gary Rawnsley and Ming-yeh Rawnsley, 41–61. London: RoutledgeCurzon, 2003.

Hughes, Christopher R. "Nationalism in Chinese Cyberspace." *Cambridge Review of International Affairs* 2 (2000): 195–209.

Institute of Modern History, Academia Sinica, ed. *Haifang Dang* (Archives of Naval Defense). Taipei: Institute of Modern History, Academia Sinica, 1957.

Jin Shixuan and Xu Wenshu. *Zhongguo tielu fazhan shi, 1876–1949* (History of Chinese Railway Development). Beijing: Zhongguo tiedao chubanshe, 1986.

Jing Yuanshan. *Ju yi chu ji.* Vols. 1 and 2, Macao, 1901.

Jones, Steve, ed. *Doing Internet Research: Critical Issues and Methods for Examining the Net.* Thousand Oaks, Calif.: SAGE Publications, 1999.

Kalathil, Shanthi, and Taylor C. Boas. *Open Networks, Closed Regimes: The Impact of the Internet on Authoritarian Rule.* Washington, D.C.: Carnegie Endowment for International Peace, 2003.

Kendall, Lori. "Recontextualizing 'Cyberspace': Methodological Considerations for On-Line Research." In *Doing Internet Research: Critical Issues and Methods for Examining the Net,* ed. Steve Jones, 57–74. Thousand Oaks, Calif.: SAGE Publications, 1999.

Kristof, Nicholas D. "The Chip on China's Shoulder." *New York Times,* Jan. 18, 2002.

Kynge, James. "Chinese Presidential Jet Bugged." *Financial Times,* Jan. 19, 2002.

Lee, En-Han. *China's Quest for Railway Autonomy, 1904–1911.* Singapore: Singapore University Press, 1977.

Lee, Rachel C., and Sau-ling Wong, eds. *AsianAmerican.Net: Ethnicity, Nationalism, and Cyberspace.* New York: Routledge, 2003.

Li Yonggang. "Wei wancheng de renwu: xie zai sixiang de jingjie guan zhan zhihou" (Unfinished Task: Reflections after the Closing Down of the Realm of Ideas). *Ershiyi Shiji* (Twenty-First Century) 2 (2001): 115–21. www.cuhk.edu. hk/ics/21c/issue/article/001217.htm.

Liang Jinghe. *Qing mo guomin yishi yu canzheng yishi yanjiu* (A Study of the Consciousness of Chinese Nationals and Their Consciousness in Political Participation toward the End of the Qing). Changsha: Hunan jiaoyu chubanshe, 1999.

Lieberman, Kim-An. "Virtually Vietnamese: Nationalism on the Internet." In *AsianAmerican.Net: Ethnicity, Nationalism, and Cyberspace,* ed. Rachel C. Lee and Sau-ling Wong, 71–97. New York: Routledge, 2003.

Liu, Alan. "A Convenient Crisis: Looking behind Beijing's Threats against Taiwan." *Issues & Studies,* Sept.–Oct. (2000), 83–121.

Liu, Kwang-Ching. "The Ch'ing Restoration." In *The Cambridge History of China,* ed. John K. Fairbank, 10, pt. 1: 409–90. Cambridge: Cambridge University Press, 1978.

Luo Guanzhong. *Three Kingdoms: A Historical Novel.* Translated by Moss Roberts. Berkeley: University of California Press; Beijing: Foreign Languages Press, 1991.

Ma Guangren, ed. *Shanghai xinwen shi, 1850–1949* (History of Shanghai Journalism, 1850–1949). Shanghai: Fudan daxue chubanshe, 1996.

Ma Min and Zhu Ying. *Chuantong yu jindai de erchong bianzou: Wan Qing Suzhou shanghui gean yanjiu* (A Duet of Tradition and Modernity: A Case Study of the Suzhou Chamber of Commerce in the Late Qing). Chengdu: Bashu shushe, 1993.

McKee, Delber L. *Chinese Exclusion versus the Open Door Policy, 1900–1906: Clashes over China Policy in the Roosevelt Era.* Detroit: Wayne State University Press, 1977.

Mo Bei, ed. *Jiangzhe tielu fengchao* (Railway Upheavals in Jiangsu and Zhejiang). Vol. 1 (Dec. 1907); vol. 2 (Jan. 1908). Published in Shanghai. In *Zhonghua minguo shiliao congbian*, no. A17, ed. Luo Jialun. Taipei: Zhongguo guomindang zhongyang weiyuanhui dangshi shiliao bianzuan weiyuanhui, 1968.

Mukerji, Chandra, and Michael Schudson, eds. *Rethinking Popular Culture: Contemporary Perspectives in Cultural Studies.* Berkeley: University of California Press, 1991.

Nye, Joseph S. Jr. *Bound to Lead: The Changing Nature of American Power.* New York: Basic Books, 1990.

Pomfret, John. "China Finds Bugs on Jet Equipped in U.S." *Washington Post,* Jan. 19, 2002.

Qian Hualin. "Zhongguo kejiwang de fazhan" (The Development of CSTNet). *Xiandai tushu qingbao jishu* (Modern Library Information Technology) 3 (1997): 3–6.

Rankin, Mary B. *Elite Activism and Political Transformation in China: Zhejiang Province, 1865–1911.* Stanford: Stanford University Press, 1986.

Rawnsley, Gary, and Ming-yeh Rawnsley, eds. *Political Communication in Greater China: The Construction and Reflections of Reality.* London: RoutledgeCurzon, 2003.

Raybeck, Douglas. "Getting below the Surface." In *The Naked Anthropologist: Tales from Around the World,* ed. Philip R. DeVita, 3–16. Belmont, Calif.: Wadsworth, 1992.

Shang Bing. *Qing mo xin zhishijie de shetuan yu huodong* (New Intellectual Organizations and Activities at the End of the Qing). Beijing: Shenghuo, dushu, xinzhi sanlian shudian, 1995.

Sheng Xuanhuai. *Yu zai chun gao.* Jindai zhongguo shiliao congshu xuji [series], ed. Shen Yunlong, vols. 122–25. Taipei: Wenhai chubanshe, 1974.

Shi, Tianjian. *Political Participation in Beijing.* Cambridge, Mass.: Harvard University Press, 1997.

Solymar, Laszlo. *Getting the Message: A History of Communications.* New York: Oxford University Press, 1999.

Song Jun. *Shenbao de xingshuai* (*Shenbao*'s Ups and Downs). Shanghai: Shanghai shehui kexue chubanshe, 1996.

Sundaram, Ravi. "Beyond the Nationalist Panopticon: The Experience of Cyberpublics in India." In *Electronic Media and Technoculture,* ed. John T. Caldwell, 270–94. New Brunswick, N.J.: Rutgers University Press, 2000.

Thompson, Robert Luther. *Wiring a Continent: The History of the Telegraph Industry in the United States, 1832–1866.* New York: Arno Press, 1972.

Tompkins, Jane P., ed. *Reader-Response Criticism: From Formalism to Post-Structuralism*. Baltimore: Johns Hopkins University Press, 1980.

Verdery, Katherine. *What Was Socialism, and What Comes Next?* Princeton, N.J.: Princeton University Press, 1996.

Wang Ermin, "Shangzhan guannian yu zhongshang sixiang" (The Idea of Commercial Warfare and the Importance Attached to Commerce) *Zhongyang yanjiuyuan jindaishi yanjiusuo jikan* 5 (1966): 1–91.

Wang Hui. "Dangdai zhongguo de sixiang zhuangkuang yu xiandaixing wenti" (Current Chinese Thoughts and the Issue of Modernity). *Tianya* 5 (1997): 133–50.

Wang Kaijie, Xiu Yu, and Qian Qizong, eds. *Jindai tielu, dianxin qishiwu zhounian jinian kan* (Volume in Memory of the Seventy-fifth Anniversary of the Railway and Telecommunications). Zhongguo shiliao congshu xuji [series], ed. Shen Yunlong, vol. 924. Taipei: Wenhai chubanshe, 1982.

Wang Lixin. *Meiguo duihua zhengce yu zhongguo minzu zhuyi yundong, 1904–1928* (American China Policy and the Chinese Nationalist Movement, 1904–1928). Beijing: Zhongguo shehui kexue chubanshe, 2000.

Wang Shangyan. "Hulianwang zai zhongguo" (The Internet in China). *Qiye gaige yu guanli* (Enterprise Reform and Management), Feb. 1998, 31–34.

Wang Yi. "Zhishi fengzi de xingdong juezhi—2002 nian de wangluo gongkaixin yu qianming lanchao" (The Choice Made by Intellectuals—Online Public Letters and Petition Waves in 2002). *Beijing zhichun* (Beijing Spring) 2 (2003): 22–26.

Wei Qingyuan, Gao Fang, and Liu Wenyuan. *Qing mo xianzheng shi* (History of Constitutionism in the Late Qing). Beijing: Zhongguo renmin daxue chubanshe, 1993.

Williams, Raymond. *Keywords: A Vocabulary of Culture and Society*. New York: Oxford University Press, 1985.

Winston, Brian. *Media Technology and Society: A History: From the Telegraph to the Internet*. New York: Routledge, 1998.

Wu, Silas H. L. *Communication and Imperial Control in China: Evolution of the Palace Memorial System, 1693–1735*. Cambridge, Mass.: Harvard University Press, 1970.

Xia Dongyuan. *Yangwu yundong shi* (History of the Western Affairs Movement). Shanghai: Huadong shifan daxue chubanshe, 1992.

Xiao Gongqin. "Dangdai dushi li de bianyuan zhishiren" (Marginalized Intellectuals in Contemporary Urban Centers). www.booker.com.cn/gb/paper18/35/class001800001/hwz187130.htm.

Xie Haiguang. *Hulianwang yu sixiang zhengzhi gongzuo anli* (Cases of the Internet and Political Thought Work). Shanghai: Fudan daxue chubanshe, 2002.

Xu Dingxin and Qian Xiaoming. *Shanghai zongshanghui shi, 1902–1929* (History of Shanghai General Chamber of Commerce). Shanghai: Shanghai shehui kexueyuan chubanshe, 1991.

Xu, Christine Xiaoting. "Chinese Chat Rooms Are Teeming with Anti-Yankee Venom." *Wisconsin State Journal*, Apr. 4, 2001.

Xu Youyu. "Zhiyou zhuyi yu dangdai zhongguo" (Liberalism and Contemporary China). http://wyg.sunchina.net/sixiang/000731/xyy.html.

————. "'Changjiang Dushu jiang' zhenglun de yiyi" (The Significance of Debates on "Cheung Kong Dushu Awards"). http://forum.cc.org.cn/luntan/china/showcontent.php3?db=1&id=1296&id1=512&mode=1.

Yang, Guobin. "The Co-Evolution of the Internet and Civil Society in China." *Asian Survey* 43 (2003): 405–22.

Yang, Mayfair Mei-hui. "Between State and Society: The Construction of Corporateness in a Chinese Factory." *Australian Journal of Chinese Affairs* 22 (July 1989): 31–60.

————. "Mass Media and Transnational Subjectivity in Shanghai: Notes on (Re)Cosmopolitanism in a Chinese Metropolis." In *The Anthropology of Globalization: A Reader,* ed. Jonathan Xavier Inda and Renato Rosaldo, 325–49. Malden, Mass.: Blackwell, 2002.

Yang Yonggang. *Zhongguo jindai tielu shi* (Railway History in Modern China). Shanghai: Shanghai shudian chubanshe, 1997.

Youdianshi Bianjishi. *Zhongguo jindai youdian shi* (History of the Post and Telecommunications in Modern China). Beijing: Renmin youdian chubanshe, 1984.

Zaller, John R. *The Nature and Origins of Mass Opinion.* Cambridge: Cambridge University Press, 1992.

Zhang, Junhua. "A Critical Review of the Development of Chinese e-Government." *Perspectives* 3, no. 7 (2002). www.oycf.org/Perspectives/19_123102/eGovernment.htm.

Zhang, Xuedong. "Intellectual Politics in Post-Tiananmen China." *Social Text* 16 (1998): 1–8.

Zhao, Suisheng. "Chinese Nationalism and Its International Orientations." *Political Science Quarterly* 1 (2000): 1–33.

————. "A State-Led Nationalism: The Patriotic Education Campaign in Post-Tiananmen China." *Communist and Post-Communist Studies* 31 (1998): 287–302.

————. "Chinese Intellectuals' Quest for National Greatness and Nationalistic Writing in the 1990s." *China Quarterly* 152 (1997): 725–45.

Zheng, Yongnian. *Discovering Chinese Nationalism in China: Modernization, Identity and International Relations.* Cambridge: Cambridge University Press, 1999.

Zhizhi (Li Shenzhi). "Shiji zhijiao de zhanqian guhou" (Reflections at the Turn of the Century). *Wanxiang* (Panorama Monthly) 6 (2001): 102–19.

Zhongguo xinwen yanjiu zhongxin. "2002–2003 zhongguo baoye faxing xianzhuang yu qushi" (The Current Status and Future Trends of Newspaper Circulation in China, 2002–2003). www.cddc.net/shownews.asp?newsid= 4813.

Zhonghua renmin gongheguo youdianbu zhengce yanjiushi, ed. *Youdian fagui huibian, diyi ji* (Compilation of Laws and Regulations on Posts and Telecommunication, Volume One). Beijing: Renmin youdian chubanshe, 1988.

Zhou Baoxin. "Zhongguo hulianwang de xianzhuang yu weilai" (Chinese Internet: Current Conditions and Future Development). *Guangbo dianshi wangluo jishu* (Technologies of Broadcasting, Television and Networking) 8 (2001): 16–18.

Zhou Shanpei. *Xinhai sichuan zheng lu qinli ji* (A Personal Account of the Sichuan Railway Rights Movement in 1911). Chongqing: Chongqing renmin chubanshe, 1957.

Zhou Yongming. *Anti-Drug Crusades in Twentieth-Century China: Nationalism, History, and State Building.* Lanham, Md.: Rowman & Littlefield, 1999.

Zhu Xueqin. "Shijimo sixiang lunzhan: xinzhuopai he zhiyou zhuyi zai zheng shenmo?" (Debates at the End of the Century: What Are the Differences between the New Leftists and the Liberals). http://wyg.sunchina.net/sixiang/001107/39.htm.

Index

CPSIA information can be obtained
at www.ICGtesting.com
Printed in the USA
LVOW11s1732210817
545810LV00002B/637/P